TINY GAME HUNTING

TINY GAME HUNTING

Environmentally Healthy Ways to Trap and
Kill the Pests in Your House and Garden

HILARY DOLE KLEIN AND ADRIAN M. WENNER

NEW EDITION

Illustrations by Courtlandt Johnson

UNIVERSITY OF CALIFORNIA PRESS
Berkeley • Los Angeles • London

University of California Press
Berkeley and Los Angeles, California

University of California Press, Ltd.
London, England

Library of Congress Cataloging-in-Publication Data

Klein, Hilary Dole, 1945–
    Tiny game hunting : environmentally healthy ways
to trap and kill the pests in your house and garden / Hilary
Dole Klein and Adrian M. Wenner ; illustrations by
Courtlandt Johnson.—New ed.
        p.   cm.
    Includes bibliographical references and index.
    ISBN 0-520-22107-9 (pbk. : alk. paper)
        1. Household pests—Control.   2. Garden pests—
Control.   I. Wenner, Adrian M.   II. Title.
TX325. K58   2001
648'.7—dc21   00-064770

Printed in the United States of America
08 07 06 05 04 03 02 01
10 9 8 7 6 5 4 3 2 1

The paper used in this publication is both acid free and
totally chlorine free. It meets the minimum requirements
of ANSI/NISO Z39.48-1984 (R 1997) (*Permanence of Paper*).

Contents

Preface to the New Edition   ix

Introduction   1
    Incredible Insects • The Toxic Tide

PART 1 · TINY GAME HUNTING IN THE HOME

The Folly of Pesticides   9
    Home, Toxic Home • Home, Safe Home •
    Quitting Pesticides for Good and Disposing of Them

Common Pests   14
    Ants • Bed Bugs • Bees • Clothes Moths and Carpet Beetles •
    Cockroaches • Fleas • Flies • Houseplant Pests • Lice •
    Mosquitoes • Pantry Pests • Rats and Mice • Silverfish • Spiders •
    Termites and Wood-Boring Beetles • Ticks, Chiggers, and Mites

Occasional Invaders   108
    Asian Lady Beetles • Boxelder Bugs • Centipedes • Cluster
    Flies • Crickets • Earwigs • Moths • Scorpions

PART 2 · TINY GAME HUNTING IN THE GARDEN

The Healthy Garden 117

The Fallacy of Pesticides • Better Soil for Stronger Plants •
Compost • Earthworms • Mulch • Organic Fertilizers •
Cover Crops • Companion Planting

The Tactics of Tiny Game Hunting in the Garden 124

Handpicking • Hosing • Traps • Barriers • Soaps •
Horticultural Oils • Dusts • Biological Controls •
Botanicals • Repellents

Allies in the Air and on the Ground 141

Bats • Birds • Lizards • Snakes • Toads and Frogs

Good Bugs 149

Mail Order Mercenaries 150

Green Lacewings • Ladybugs • Mealybug Destroyers •
Parasitic Nematodes • Parasitic Wasps • Parasites of Flies •
Predatory Mites

Good Bugs Gratis 156

"True" Bugs • Beetles • A Few Good Flies

Distinguished Native Beneficials 159

Antlions • Damselflies • Dragonflies • Fireflies

Honorably Discharged 161

Praying Mantises

Garden Pests 162

Chompers 162

Cabbage Loopers and Imported Cabbageworms •
Colorado Potato Beetles • Cucumber Beetles • Cutworms •
Fall Webworms and Eastern Tent Caterpillars • Flea Beetles •

Grasshoppers • Gypsy Moths • Japanese Beetles •
Mexican Bean Beetles • Tomato Hornworms

Root Destroyers   179
June Beetles • Nematodes • Root Maggots • Wireworms

Slimers   184
Slugs and Snails

Suckers   190
Aphids • Leafhoppers • Mealybugs • Scale Insects •
Spider Mites • Thrips • "True" Bugs • Whiteflies

Tunnelers   202
Borers • Codling Moths and Apple Maggots • Corn Earworms •
Plum Curculios

Friend or Foe?   209
Centipedes and Millipedes • Earwigs • Opossums •
Sowbugs and Pillbugs • Yellow Jackets and Wasps

Critter Control   219

Diggers   219
Gophers • Moles

Foragers   226
Deer • Dogs • Rabbits • Raccoons • Skunks • Squirrels

Resources and Mail Order   235

Select Bibliography   245

Index   249

Preface to the New Edition

Since our book first appeared in 1991, the pests-versus-pesticides predicament has both improved and deteriorated. The good news is that many more products have appeared on the market for people wishing to avoid toxic chemicals. Garden centers, hardware stores, and the Internet commonly offer tiny game hunting products, from insecticidal soaps and repellent sprays to low-toxicity dusts and traps. Insectaries that breed beneficial insects are more numerous, and scientists are working on new ways to battle insects with biological controls that affect only the targeted pest. Organic food is less of a novelty, and organic farmers have proven that their yields can equal or exceed conventional yields.

The bad news, however, keeps getting worse. As our groundwater and air are increasingly tested, and as more scientific studies appear, we are beginning to get a glimpse of the devastating consequences of the flood of toxins that have been, and continue to be, poured, sprayed, squirted, and pumped over the earth. The dangerous deception that these chemicals will not harm us is becoming more and more apparent.

Yet the deluge is growing, not lessening. In the United States, an incredible 4.5 billion pounds of pesticides are used each year. In California, according to the *Los Angeles Times,* application of toxic compounds more than doubled between 1991 and 1995. Is it doing any good? American farmers are spraying two to five times more than they did thirty years ago, some say tenfold since World War II. Yet the loss of crops to insect damage has *risen* from 7 to 13 percent.

Is the government capable of protecting us? The number of "secret" inert ingredients (ones that don't have to be listed on labels) in pesticides has doubled in ten years. Inert ingredients are sometimes more toxic than the active ingredient in a pesticide. What you don't know can hurt you.

World Resources Institute issued a report warning that exposures to pesticides pose a serious public health threat by depressing the immune system. In the past few years, pesticides have also been implicated in the disruption of endocrine systems and hormone function. Scientists have noted the feminization of animals, from alligators in Florida to polar bears in the Arctic. Human sperm counts have declined between 33 and 42 percent in the past fifty years, according to some European studies.

The EPA has identified as potential human carcinogens ninety-six pesticides currently in use. Rates of certain cancers, such as testicular and prostate cancer, have increased alarmingly. In 1960, one in twenty women found themselves with breast cancer; now it is one in eight. Last year, Parkinson's was added to the list of diseases attributed to pesticide exposure. And pesticides are now known to interfere with neurological development in children.

Humans are not, of course, the only victims. Researchers at Cornell have estimated that more than 67 million birds are killed each year by pesticides applied legally to U.S. farmland. Fish also die by the millions, as do bees necessary for pollination.

But we humans can take action. As consumers, we play an important role in our profit-driven society, and we can help turn the tide. So take the time to learn about the pests that plague you and choose the safest way to manage them.

We give you the tactics; we trust in your success.

INTRODUCTION

They creep, they crawl, they fly, they slime. They chew, suck, nibble, and devour . . . and they never give up.

We plant our gardens lovingly and laboriously, anticipating the pleasure and payoff in flowers and fresh vegetables. Then one day we go outside and the garden looks as if Sherman's troops had marched through it. Armies of bugs have chewed the little green poppy plants, the lovely lettuce is wilted, and the rosebuds are obscured by a teeming mass of frothy white trespassers. It's war.

We go into the kitchen early in the morning to start making breakfast. It takes a few minutes before we suddenly realize that we are sharing our home with hundreds—no, thousands!—of brazen ants, who are behaving as if our honey jar were their gift from the gods. It's war.

The dog does nothing but itch and scratch. He has lost most of the hair off the top of his rear, and the last time we dusted him with flea powder, he seemed to be having some kind of a fit. It's war.

Our second grader has been sent home from school with lice for the third time this year. Now we have to treat everyone in the family, vacuum like crazy, and do twenty-four loads of laundry. It's war.

Trying to protect our territory from persistent alien invaders can't help but stir up the primal juices. It's the good guys against the bad and we know which we are. We have the moral righteousness of the attacked on our side, while those tiny trespassers deserve all the fury we can heap on them.

Off we go to any number of home improvement centers, nurseries, or hardware stores. We walk up and down the aisles and study the vast array of poisons available to us. Notice the slightly sickening, noxious smell that emanates from the shelves. (Can this be good for the employees?) We squint at the labels with their chemical mumbo jumbo and their warnings. Remember that article we just read about the "end of nature." Wish we knew of a better way to take care of this.

INCREDIBLE INSECTS

Insects have been on this planet since before the first cockroach appeared 300 million years ago. Not only did they precede us by more than 200 million years, but termites had air-conditioning before we had houses, and wasps could paralyze their prey before we had anesthesia. Lowly, small, primitive, thoughtless, and short-lived though they may be, insects are nevertheless the most successful creatures on earth.

There may be as many as 10 million different species, of which perhaps a million have been described. To add to the amazing variety and complexity of life forms they present, most of these insects change their shape during development, from egg to larva to pupa to adult. "The earth has spawned such a diversity of remarkable creatures that I sometimes wonder why we do not all live in a state of perpetual awe and astonishment," Howard Ensign Evans once wrote.

We do not, however, hold bugs in awe. Even though they can outwork us, outlift us, outjump us, and outfly us, we despise more than respect them. They seem to us to live only to reproduce and to eat or be eaten. They are so utterly different from us, they seem aliens in our world. Insects have no lungs, yet they must have oxygen to live. Some have no ears, although their sensitivity to vibrations is acute. Others have no noses but can smell incredibly well. They may have ears below their knees, gills under their abdomens, or breathing tubes on their sides. They learn nothing from their parents but are born knowing everything they need to know. They carry their skeleton on the outside of their body, their blood is seldom red, and they walk on myriad legs. Is it any wonder that we have problems with insects? We regard them alternately with loathing and fear, fascination and disgust. We are woefully ignorant about them and most often end up killing the ones we need, while failing to control the pestiferous ones.

Insects exist even in the Antarctic, where temperatures drop to 85° below zero. Collections made from airplanes reveal that a column of air one mile square probably contains 25,000 insects. An acre of typical English pasture may contain over a billion arthropods (insects, spiders, mites, centipedes, etc.). We make calculations about the vast incomprehensible distances of space, but right here on earth there may be a billion billion insects. Try to write out that number.

Until the middle of the seventeenth century, most people in the Western world believed that insects came into existence through spontaneous generation. They were generally thought to be "bred by corruption" or from the dew on the leaves. Humans often turned for help to the Church, which regularly excommunicated insects for their misdeeds. Yet little progress was made toward controlling pests; even the most noxious ones, such as fleas, rats, and lice, were tolerated as an inevitable part of life.

Insects have always been our prime competitors on this planet. They eat our food, our clothing, and our houses. They even feed on us and transmit terrible diseases. A state of complacency regarding them has never been in our best interests. However, once we decided to get tough on pests, we really went overboard. We picked methods that harmed us as much as them.

We embarked on an indiscriminate, all-out war against insects. "Better living through chemistry" tried to teach us that all bugs are bad bugs and that the only good bug is a dead bug. But less than 1 percent of all insects are pests. Most are extremely beneficial. Without insects, animals like fish, reptiles, birds, and certain mammals would have nothing to eat and would starve. Furthermore, as the entomologist E. O. Wilson has pointed out, without the recycling of organic matter that insects carry out, dead vegetation would pile up and dry out all over the world, killing off plants and animals.

It may seem odd to talk about how necessary insects are in a book on tiny game hunting (and trapping and killing and repelling), but part of the problem with our pest control tactics up until now has been that we tried to annihilate them so utterly that we began to take out the birds, the fish, the bees, and a lot more along with the pests. If we keep in mind what an important role some insects and spiders play, we can control them more successfully.

THE TOXIC TIDE

Before we came up with the "magic bullet" of chemical pesticides, people were much more inventive about dealing with pests. Then the idea caught on that we could take care of the whole problem with a few squirts or sprays, and we got lazy. We thought if we dusted the dog, we wouldn't have to vacuum; if we put up a no-pest strip, we wouldn't have to repair the screen door; if we had the house fumigated, we would never again have to look for termites. We opted for the neutron bomb of pesticides and thought we were winning the war.

We read that American farmers will apply 24 million tons of fertilizer and 1 billion pounds of pesticides on our land this year. How much of this will end up in our water, our air, our food, our body fat and breast milk? Indeed, the U.S. Geological Survey has reported that every sample of stream water taken from a developed watershed was found to have pesticide contaminants. And the EPA reports that pesticides are now a major threat to groundwater.

Although TV commercials make using pesticides look perfectly safe, safety is one of the great fallacies surrounding these chemicals. The EPA says that each year millions of people suffer side effects such as nausea, dizziness, and headaches from pesticides. These are just the short-term effects. More than 80 percent of the most commonly used pesticides today have been classified as carcinogenic by the National Academy of Science. At the same time, cancer rates are increasing dramatically every year (breast cancer by 2 percent, children's cancers by 1 percent). Pesticides have also been implicated in causing learning disabilities and hyper-aggression in children. What are we doing to ourselves?

Not only are we using more pesticides, we are making them more dangerous. Mixing two pesticides together greatly magnifies their toxicity.

For instance, in 1996, *Science* reported that a mixture of endosulfan and dieldrin, two organochlorides, produced an estrogenic effect 1,600 times more potent than each chemical alone. Most fruits and vegetables are sprayed with as many as five chemicals.

The blind application of pesticides amounts to an admission that insects are smarter than we are. We believe, however, that human beings are cleverer than insects. Practicing hazardous chemical warfare against pests should never take the place of the three Os of tiny game hunting: observe, outwit, and outlast.

Doing battle with pests using the tactics of tiny game hunting is actually more gratifying than spraying with toxic chemicals. You will derive great satisfaction from trapping pests without guilt, discouraging them without peril, and keeping them away by understanding their particular habits. There is only one hard-and-fast rule for the tiny game hunter: Don't use any weapon to kill pests that could possibly kill you too.

PART 1

TINY GAME HUNTING
IN THE HOME

THE FOLLY OF PESTICIDES

HOME, TOXIC HOME

How many pesticides were you exposed to today? Perhaps there was the ant poison in the yard, the houseplant spray in the living room, the fly spray on the porch, the herbicide on the lawn, the roach killer in the kitchen.

How about the long-lasting pesticides around the house? The termite treatment around the foundations, the mothball vapors in the closet, the vapor-emitting pest strip in the basement? And that's just at home. The restaurant where you lunched may have recently been sprayed. The office has a regular extermination contract. The bus you took may have just been sprayed or fumigated, as well as the bank, the doctor's office, the department store, and, of course, the park and the golf course. According to the Environmental Protection Agency, billions of pounds of pesticides are used annually. Every breath you took today may have had a little whiff of poison in it. The same goes for every bite you took. If you eat more than 1.2 pounds of broccoli, you exceed your legal dose of pesticides for the year. Same goes for a quarter of a cantaloupe. A 1999 Environmental Working Group report, "They Are What They Eat: Kids' Food Consumption and Pesticides," stated that 20 million children under the age of five eat an average of eight pesticides a day—that's 2,900 pesticide exposures per child per year from food alone—not water, not air, not skin absorption. Sounds like a lot, doesn't it? Oh, and forty suspected carcinogens now appear in U.S. drinking water. How much do you think your body can take?

Keep in mind, too, that if you use chemicals on your lawn, you have them in your carpeting. Once indoors, they could be present for up to a year. And after pesticides have been used indoors, residues have been found to remain on toys (think babies' mouths) for a least two weeks.

Most people think DDT went away when it was banned in the United States in 1972. Wrong. Its profitability lived on, and it continued to be manufactured and exported in enormous quantities to other countries. (Mexico and Brazil each used nearly 1,000 tons—that's 2 million pounds—of DDT in 1992 alone.) Today, it is one of the commonest pesticides found on food in U.S. grocery stores. It has been linked to breast cancer. Almost everyone has DDT-related compounds in his or her body.

Many houses today have become traps for even longer-lasting toxins. Before chlordane was taken off the shelves in 1987, it was used against ants and termites (as well as other pests) in more than 30 million homes. Because it was made to decompose very slowly, it could remain active indoors, protected from the elements, for twenty years. It also accumulates in body fat and is known to make people very sick. Chlordane is considered a carcinogen, as well as a hazardous substance, a hazardous waste, and a priority toxic pollutant (according to the EPA). And yet chlordane, like DDT, continued to be shipped to other countries by its manufacturer long after its ban here, and it probably returns to this country in imported food items in what is called "the circle of poison."

HOME, SAFE HOME

One control method that works for all pests is exclusion. Keeping them out of the house is the simplest and most efficient way to deal with them. Screens provide a true coat of armor for the home. One of the reasons malaria still rages in some hot countries is that many homes lack screens. Screens should also be placed over chimneys and vents. And since rats and cockroaches live in sewers, city dwellers should make sure that shower and bath drains have strainers. Houses should be thoroughly inspected for holes and cracks through which insects can enter. Any openings where utility wires and pipes enter the house should be sealed.

Because many pests require moisture, all pipes and faucets should be checked for drips. Toilet bowls should be bolted securely to the floor and have no leaks. Condensation of pipes should be prevented with wrapping. "Repair them out!" could be the battle cry of the tiny game hunter.

"Starve them out!" could be another. Always put food (and pet food) away, or store it in pest-proof containers. Counters should be kept scrupulously clean.

Regular vacuuming is a major tactical assault against pests. Also, make a point to do a thorough spring-cleaning at least once a year. Turn the whole house inside out and rout all the critters hiding in closets and behind heavy furniture.

Apartment dwellers have to protect themselves on two fronts: from pests that enter from the great outdoors and from those that wander in from the neighbors'. All the occupants of an apartment building should meet and coordinate a sound, safe method of pest control, including how garbage is to be managed and what kind of nontoxic pest treatments can be used. Having each lone apartment dweller fiercely fighting individual battles at different times just makes the pest population move around within the building.

There is no such thing as a permanent solution to our pest problems. Thinking that we can get rid of our pests permanently in one fell swoop is like believing we will be clean for the rest of our life after taking a shower.

QUITTING PESTICIDES FOR GOOD AND DISPOSING OF THEM

Giving up toxic pesticides is a little like giving up cigarettes. One day you think you can't possibly live without them, and the next you realize how much better everything is now that you no longer depend on them. Soapy water kills ants just as dead as the poison spray that used to go up your nose. The mousetrap kills just as dead as the poison, and it won't kill the dog, either.

When you give up these poisons outdoors, you may have a period of higher insect damage. Be prepared to plant more plants, handpick the bugs, and use a few repellent sprays. The natural predators may take a while to return to your garden. It may take a few years for the balance of nature to restore itself. Remember, the pests always show up before the predators, so don't panic. In the meantime, use the tactics described in this book to hunt them down. Improve your soil with lots of organic content and minerals so that the plants are strong enough to withstand insect attack. People who would prefer a garden completely devoid of insects should possibly find something else to do with their time. We have to live with insects; we just don't have to be overwhelmed by them.

The main problem in giving up house and garden insecticides is what to do with the poisons you aren't going to use anymore. Incidentally, if the label says POISON or DANGER—the highest warning given—the contents are highly toxic. WARNING or CAUTION means the contents are toxic, but not as toxic. PRECAUTION means the government doesn't know whether the contents are hazardous or not. Some people do not even call these chemicals pesticides; they call them biocides, because they kill all life.

If you want to know more about any of the pesticides, fungicides, and herbicides you have been storing at your house, you can call the EPA-funded twenty-four-hour hotline at (800) 858-7378. Or contact the National Coalition Against the Misuse of Pesticides, 530 Seventh Street SE, Washington, D.C. 20003, (202) 543-5450.

Do *not* pour any of these products down the drain, or bury them, or flush them down the toilet! Many of these pesticides are highly toxic to fish and other wildlife. Do not toss them in the garbage either. They must be disposed of according to the laws regulating toxic pollutants. Call your local waste management division or health department and ask if they have a collection program for toxic chemicals. Or look in the yellow pages under environmental groups. Many cities have established certain days and locations for people to bring in their paints, pesticides, motor oil, and other toxic materials, which are then disposed of in special toxic waste dumps to prevent their ending up in landfills and groundwater. When you realize how hard it is just to dispose of these chemicals safely, you begin to understand the problems of using them. And they won't stop being manufactured until we stop purchasing them.

Incidentally, pest control operators can't use soapy water, because it is not on their list of EPA-registered pesticides, a sort of catch-22 that, unfortunately, encourages more toxic pesticide use. If you do call an exterminator, look for one that uses the least toxic and most environmentally friendly methods. Interview the person carefully and ask a lot of questions. Look for exterminators who practice integrated pest management, or I.P.M. But make sure their interpretation of I.P.M. isn't "inject pesticides monthly." Don't automatically believe phrases like "environmentally friendly" in their ads. (A number of them have recently been sued for this kind of "greenwashing.") If you find yourself arguing over the semantics of "toxic" with an exterminator, or if one tries to tell you, "It's not how toxic they are; it's how carefully they are handled," go elsewhere. This is not a linguistic debate. Reducing the world's dependence on hazardous pesticides requires tangible, positive action, not compromise and consumer vacuousness.

You just can't make the excuse anymore that "it's just a little bit of pesticide." Pesticides are used by 1 million farms and in 70 million households in the United States. Those numbers attest to a lot of decision makers, and you are one of them. Take responsibility! In addition to not using pesticides yourself, talk your friends out of them too. Support activist organizations. And buy organic food, which is one more way to keep hazardous pesticides out of the home. When you buy organic, you are supporting a way of life—taking care of the earth—that has profound implications for the future.

COMMON PESTS

ANTS

Some people believe that the cockroach will take over the world, but we bet on the lowly ant. Breeding colonies of ants, sometimes known as superorganisms, are resistant to both radiation and industrial pollution. Colonies of some species can even survive in flooded ground. In terms of sheer biomass, ants, along with termites, are the dominant insect species on earth. They not only outnumber us; they outweigh us. When it comes to social organization and cooperation, they are in some ways more evolved than humans, acting for the survival of the colony rather than the individual. Various ant species plant crops, herd other insects for food, wage ferocious wars, take slaves, and live with elaborate caste structures. Interestingly, ant colonies are virtual female societies; males are bred only occasionally and only for procreation.

Besides being utterly impossible, it would be foolish to attempt to eliminate all your ants, because in many ways ants are our friends and allies, and we need them. In China, ants have been used for thousands of years to help control pests in orchards, making them the first insects known to be used for biological control. Ants actually help control pests that we haven't always been very successful controlling on our own. Both indoors and out, they eat the eggs and larvae of fleas, flies, spiders, bed bugs, and probably silverfish and clothes moths. They also go after cockroaches and conenose bugs. In addition, ants patrol the perimeters of our houses and keep termites, their mortal enemies, from establishing colonies in our homes. If we let them do their job, that is.

Of the more than 8,800 known species of ants worldwide, only a small number will invade homes, some arriving in search of sweets, others drawn to meat and greasy stuff. The most common ants seen inside of houses are the **Argentine ant** (very small, brown, nests outdoors, prefers sweets, eliminates almost all other species of ant in the neighborhood); the **pharaoh ant** (small, light yellow or reddish, nests inside of buildings, attracted to all kinds of foods); the **thief** or **grease ant** (resembles the pharaoh ant, prefers meaty or greasy foods, sometimes lives in the nests of other ants); the **pavement ant** (brown or black, hairy, will eat just about anything, nests under stones, around pavement, or in foundations); and the **odorous house ant** (small, brown or black, gets its name from its unpleasant coconut odor when crushed).

The worst ant to have in the house is the **carpenter ant**, which lives in wood and can be very destructive, chewing out burrows with its powerful jaws (see below).

▶ CONTROL INDOORS

Ants are one of the commonest pests in the kitchen and bathroom. Their habit of showing up in outrageous numbers, their single-minded, almost frantic scavenging, and the way they completely ignore us (at least cockroaches have the grace to flee) provide a veritable gold mine for pest control operators. Although we have no interest in encouraging ants in our homes, we do feel that a great flood of insecticides has been unnecessarily directed at these insects, for ants are fairly easy to discourage without using highly toxic poisons.

Of course, it's always a shock when your home is invaded—especially by creatures helping themselves to your food. Ants are lickers, constantly licking something—including each other. Their active salivary glands help them predigest their food, so don't eat anything the ants have swarmed on; it may be contaminated. In hospitals, ants

Ants

have even been blamed for transporting pathogens from soiled bandages and linens to clean ones.

On the other hand, try not to overreact. Using organophosphates on ants is like using nuclear weapons to stop a riot.

Ants often move after rain disturbs their nests. Conversely, during the dry season, they come into the house in search of water, so it seems that we are constantly threatened. In dry weather, put a few sources of water outside—shallow pans or bowls or a dripping hose—and they may leave you alone. Some people even provide a food source, like honey in a container with ant holes, in hopes of keeping them happily outdoors. With that added food, however, they can raise more ants.

It may be hard to second-guess ants, but your kitchen is definitely under consideration for attack when you see solitary ants wandering hither and thither. Do not ignore them. The good tidings they take back to the nest will be bad news for you. This is the time to make your kitchen less hospitable to them. Clean ferociously. Store food in sealed containers. Don't leave dirty dishes or garbage around. Rinse off sticky jars and bottles. Wipe counters down with a cloth soaked in vinegar to make the territory less appealing to the scouts.

If you do find a steady stream of them cruising determinedly inside your house, you can still take a number of simple measures without resorting to poisons that are needless overkill.

Soapy Water—The Best Defense   Many household products such as Windex, furniture polish, and spray cleaners will destroy ants. But the cheapest, easiest, and most effective method is to put a teaspoon of liquid dish soap into a spray bottle of water and zap the intruders with that. Besides killing them instantly, it destroys the scent trails they lay down that lead other ants to food. A solution of blended citrus peels and wa-

Ants on the march

ter (or citrus rind oil, which you can purchase) will also kill ants (as well as fleas and garden pests) on contact, as will mint oil.

Before you kill off the invading ants, however, trace the columns back to their point of entry. This is where you really have to stop them. Powdered charcoal, turmeric, black or cayenne pepper (the hotter the better), cinnamon, citrus oil, and powdered cleanser all make good ant barriers. The barrier doesn't have to be any wider than a quarter of an inch, but it has to be a solid line, because ants are marvelously adept at finding the tiniest pathway. A silicone caulk will terminate the point of entry permanently, but in a pinch you can also squirt undiluted dish soap into their point of entry, dab it with petroleum jelly, or fill it with glue. Before sealing the cracks, use a bulb duster (and mask and goggles) to blow in desiccating dusts like diatomaceous earth or silica aerogel.

Sometimes it seems that nothing can keep those ants out of your kitchen. The battle goes on day after day. No sooner do you set up the barricades than these wily creatures find routes into your house you never knew existed. But since you are not using toxic poisons, the death count is entirely in your favor.

Place favorite ant targets—like the honey jar and the cat food dish—in bowls of water. Adding a little soap to the water will make such ant moats even more impenetrable.

In Germany, forest ants are protected by law because of their vital role in the health of the forests. Germans keep the ants out of houses by placing lavender blossoms near the doors. Other ant repellents include cinnamon, crushed mint leaves, oil of clove, and camphor. People who go to the trouble of putting out repellents have probably removed all the attractive food sources as well. But then again, ants rely on their sense of smell in ways we can barely imagine.

Ant Baits   Baits are the best way to do the most damage to any ant colony that has selected your domain for relentless scavenging. Ants have two stomachs, one of which is the crop, a kind of communal stomach, so any food taken from your kitchen is shared with the ants back home. A good bait contains a poison that the ants find attractive enough to take back to the nest and pass along to others before it kills them. The aim is to kill the queen back at the nest.

A number of commercial baits contain highly toxic poisons. Don't buy them. If you don't buy them, manufacturers won't make them. Instead, look for baits that contain boric acid, such as Terro or Drax (see *Tactics of Tiny Game Hunting in the Garden*). We have found that the less boric acid, the more effective the bait in the long run. Remember this is a slow treatment, taking sometimes up to a week. Have patience; it works.

To make your own ant bait, dissolve a cup of sugar in two cups of boiling water. Cool. Add a tablespoon of 100 percent boric acid. Shake well. Punch holes in the tops (or sides) of small plastic containers or film cans. Place cotton balls or cut-up sponge pieces inside, then fill with bait and set the containers along problem ant trails, spilling a few drops on the trail. (Label the baits clearly as poison.) Keep in mind that you may be sacrificing ants that are benefiting your house by eliminating other pests for you.

Carpenter Ants Chewing out burrows with their powerful jaws, carpenter ants are easily mistaken for termites. Like termites, some periodically develop wings and leave in great numbers to form new colonies. Piles of broken-off wings may be a clue that you have either carpenter ants or termites. If you see the insect itself, which is up to a half-inch longer than most other ants, you can distinguish it from a termite because the ant has a pinched, wasp waist and elbowed antennae, and its two pairs of wings are different in size. The slits carpenter ants leave in wood are sometimes visible, and their frass (fecal pellets) looks like sawdust. You can sometimes hear rustling noises as they forage in the walls. Unlike termites, carpenter ants leave their nests and scavenge for food within the house. They especially like sugar, so they can be baited. Sometimes their nests can be vacuumed out of walls. Or you can call in an exterminator to drill holes around the infestation and blow in diatomaceous earth, silica aerogel, or boric acid. Household nests tend to be satellite nests, so look for trails leading to the parent nest outdoors and treat it with a pyrethrin spray or boric acid bait.

▶ *CONTROL OUTDOORS*

Millions of billions of ants go about their business in and out of nests that range from a few inches under the soil to many feet underground, covering practically the entire world. The earth may, in fact, be just one giant anthill.

Nature truly benefits from the industry of ants, who recycle dead insects and animals to make way for the living and turn and aerate the soil, even more than earthworms. They also help spread vegetation and seeds and sometimes pollinate plants. Ant nests are actually favorable to growing plants, adding nutrients to the soil, and ants protect some plants from certain pests, such as caterpillars, larvae, moths, and beetles.

That said, there are times when ants can certainly be a pest. If you're trying to have a picnic, and the ants are trying to join you, an easy way to keep them away is to set the legs of the picnic table in pans of water. And if ants are swarming over your garbage cans, and you're afraid of what the garbage collectors are going to think, you can discourage them by simply crushing the ones on the ground every time you pass by the cans. Pretty soon they'll give up and go elsewhere (although not indoors, one hopes). Planting tansy and peppermint around garbage cans is said to deter both ants and flies.

When ants cause real problems in your garden, it is because of their fondness for the honeydew excreted by aphids, mealybugs, and scale. Look for ants scurrying up and down the stalks of plants or trunks of trees. To find out if they're up to no good, check for aphids or scale on the plant or tree. Look for the silvery sheen of honeydew or the black, sooty-looking mold that grows on it. If you find it, you need to stop those ants in their tracks.

While you can get rid of aphids by hosing them off daily or spraying them with horticultural oil, you can best control these pests by eliminating the ants that protect them.

Prune the tree so that the trunk is its only contact with the soil. Then simply wrap the trunk with carpet tape or double-stick masking tape. Or, using wide masking

Ant tending to an aphid

tape, simply wrap one layer sticky side in next to a layer sticky side out. That way, if the ants try to go under the tape, they're still sure to get trapped. You can also paint the trunk of the tree with a band of sticky substance such as Stickem or Tanglefoot, or try grease-banding it with lard or petroleum jelly (use surgical gloves). Many people paint these substances right on the tree trunk, but that can damage the bark on some trees. Others first wrap the trunk with paper or cloth, then smear the barrier on that, but ants can be pretty persistent about getting through little crevices in the bark (see *Aphids*).

Other methods of discouraging ants outside include sprinkling bonemeal, powdered charcoal, powdered pyrethrum-silica gel dust, or diatomaceous earth around the base of a plant or tree, and placing boric acid ant bait along their trails.

Organic citrus growers have told us that using enough organic matter and compost to create a four-to-six-inch layer of mulch around the trees will discourage ants. And if you can keep the ants out of your trees for a few months, the beneficials will take over.

Ants may herd aphids, but we can herd the ants by spraying their nest repeatedly with water, thereby getting them to relocate to another part of the garden, where they may not be as bothersome. They are one of the few insects able to pick up and move their whole colony.

Heavy rains keep ant populations down by flooding the nests and drowning some of the ants, but in a drought, ants multiply rapidly. Try destroying an ant nest by first spraying it vigorously with water. When the ants come scurrying out with their eggs, douse them with soapy water or a solution of blended orange or lemon peels, or citrus oil, or dust them with diatomaceous earth. Boiling water poured on the nest will also kill them.

Fire Ants   The **red imported fire ant** (related to the native southern fire ant) is the worst of the stinging ants and has become one of the major insect pests in the southern states. Already it has appeared in Southern California, where it threatens to change a famous outdoor lifestyle forever. More dangerous, more aggressive, more destructive, and more prolific than any other ants in this country, the only good thing that can be said about fire ants is that they usually do not enter houses.

Their blister-raising stings are almost as painful as those of bees and sometimes cause severe allergic reactions and death. They build mounds that cause millions of dollars in damage to farm machinery, roads, and airports. And, while they eat pests such as the boll weevil, ticks, and cockroaches, they also eat everything else, including birds, lizards, mice, and other ant species, posing a real threat to biodiversity.

In spite of an expensive battle mounted against these ants, using a flood of highly toxic chlorinated hydrocarbons, they still thrive. They now produce "supercolonies" containing multiple queens that lay hundreds of eggs every hour. In fact, the insecticides caused more damage than the ants did. In Texas, where they have been called "the ant from hell," they have become something of a cultural phenomenon, with songs and even beauty contests in their honor.

Baits are tricky to use against these ants because the poison must pass through so many ant stomachs before it gets to the queen. But there are still safe ways to kill many of them and get them to move their nests.

Spiders, dragonflies, lizards, toads, and some birds will eat newly mated fire ant queens. Fortunately, progress is being made with importing the ants' natural enemies, left behind in Brazil. These include a phorid fly that injects its egg into the ant's thorax. After hatching, the maggot moves into the head of the ant, which after a few weeks literally falls off. After eating it out, the maggot then uses the head capsule for its own pupal case.

If you must use a pest control operator, find one who will broadcast a bait that contains an insect growth regulator such as abamectin. Don't let them talk you into something more toxic to the environment. Avermectin, a naturally occurring soil fungus, is also used against fire ants.

When treating individual mounds, protect yourself from the fire ants' aggressive, multiple stings by wearing protective clothing, even rubber boots smeared with a sticky substance. Pick a cool day when the sun is out, because the colony (and, most important, the queen) will have moved up near the warmer surface. Sneak up on the nest (the ants are sensitive to vibration) and slowly pour a generous amount (one to five gallons) of boiling water into it. Other drenches that will not harm the environment include insecticidal soaps, citrus oil, vinegar, pyrethrum insecticides, or ammonia and water. (A folk remedy in Texas consists of filling up on beer and urinating on the nest.) These dousings may not succeed at first, but if they are repeated, the ants will eventually move.

BED BUGS

Regardless of public opinion, we have not yet said good-bye to bed bugs. Lusting after our blood, these creatures have the nerve to come crawling into bed with us when we are mostly undressed and entirely unconscious. And yet we joke about it.

One of the worst things about this bug is that each meal lasts from ten to fifteen minutes. (No wonder we thought up vampire legends.) A bed bug's bloodsucking causes no sensation or pain whatsoever, mainly because its proboscis is amazingly fine—hundreds of times smaller than a hypodermic needle. The reaction comes later, when inflamed welts appear. (Most people, however, have no reaction.) Intense pain and itching may last for as long as a week. Often bed bug bites have a characteristic pattern—they occur in rows of three on the skin. However unpleasant and annoying, these tormentors have not been known to kill any of us or even to make us sick. Maybe that's the reason we can laugh about them.

Hundreds of years ago, the word "bug" referred to the bed bug alone. The word itself may have had its origins in the Welsh word *bwg*, meaning "ghost," thus the word "bugaboo." One famous entomologist who specialized in bed bugs long ago collected them in hotels, good and bad, across the country. He merely set his alarm for 2 A.M., leapt out of bed, turned on the lights, and collected to his heart's content.

Bed bug

Although many a parent still says to a child, "'Nighty 'night, don't let the bed bugs bite," bed bugs are no longer the frequent bedmates they once were. The vacuum cleaner may have dealt them a big blow, but they are by no means extinct.

We may think we are rid of them, like lice—until the next epidemic appears.

After a blood meal, bed bugs are engorged to a rounded plumpness. The rest of the time they have flat, reddish bodies, giving rise to such nicknames as "mahogany flats," "B flats," or "red coats." Their shape, and tiny one-quarter-inch size, allows them to hide in narrow cracks and crevices behind wallpaper and picture frames, in windowsills, plaster cracks, or baseboards, or in the tufts and seams of mattresses. From there they march out at night in quest of a meal. They can sometimes be detected by the yellowish to reddish brown excrement they leave around. It looks like specks of dirt, but it is really dried particles of undigested blood.

These wingless crawlers cannot fly, although their ancestors had wings, and they usually shun light. They also have a very distinctive, unpleasant odor—like spoiled raspberries. They will travel far for a meal and have even been known to migrate en masse from a recently vacated dwelling to riper pickings (or suckings) next door. Sometimes they are brought into houses with secondhand furniture and mattresses.

A female bed bug generates from 100 to 500 eggs in her lifetime, laying a few a day. These are coated with a sticky cement and adhere to any surface. Even after the bug has hatched, the eggshells remain cemented in place. Newly hatched bed bugs are paler versions of adults and require blood feeding before they can reach adulthood.

Like cockroaches, bed bugs are gregarious. They seem to hang out in groups, although they go on feeding expeditions as solo operators. They can last for up to a year without feeding on humans and will also take meals from other animals, such as chickens, birds, mice, rats, rabbits, and guinea pigs.

We have been nothing if not fearless and reckless when it comes to exterminating our pests, and bed bugs are no exception. The Greek philosopher Democritus advocated hanging a dead deer at the foot of the bed. Well into the 1940s, recommendations for killing "vermin" included rubbing bedframes with spirits of turpentine and kerosene oil and filling the cracks in floors and walls with hard soap. All very practical advice. But the author went on to recommend putting a quarter of a pound of brimstone (sulfur) in a dish in the middle of the room and lighting it. This treatment, he added, would also bleach the paint on the walls. At the turn of the century, an energizing tonic consisted of sorghum juice, black beans, garlic, rum, and seven freshly killed bed bugs. (The thought alone must have acted as a tonic on some.)

In his book *202 Household Pests*, Hugo Hartnack complained in the 1930s about a chemical used for bed bugs that was so caustic that it took the finish off metal beds. He also described a bed bug trap that consisted of painting a strip of special "glasslike" enamel all around the lower walls of the room, leaving one small opening. The bugs couldn't get a foothold on the glassy surface, so they came through the opening, where a metal container was set to trap them.

In the 1770s, an insect called the pentatomid bug was used against bed bugs—one of earliest examples of biological control in America. A few such bugs placed in a room would clear out all the bed bugs within a few weeks. Another insect, the assassin bug (sometimes called the "masked bed bug hunter") was also welcomed in homes for years as a bed bug annihilator, until it was discovered that it bit people when it ran out of bed bugs.

In the western United States and Latin America, a relative of the assassin bug—the conenose bug, also known as the kissing bug—also bites. It can cause severe reactions and can transmit Chagas disease, a serious illness in Latin America.

▶ CONTROL

The U.S. Department of Agriculture has stated that bed bugs may have become resistant to the more toxic pesticides (lindane and DDT) commonly used against them in the past. Dusting the area with pyrethrum will poison them without poisoning you. Diatomaceous earth or silica aerogel can also be applied in cracks with a bulb duster. Use a mask and goggles around dusts.

If the situation is desperate, an immediate remedy is to smear petroleum jelly all around the legs of the bed so that they can't crawl up and get you. Or place each bed leg in a container of water. This will only work if the bed bugs are not already in the bed. Furthermore, a number of victims have described seeing bed bugs walk up the wall, travel across the ceiling, and get into position to drop down on the bed. If you suspect bed bugs are in a bed, have the mattress steam cleaned.

As with cockroaches, getting rid of bed bugs involves eliminating all cracks and crevices in a room by caulking, replastering, or painting.

Since bed bugs can also migrate from birds or bats, eliminate all birds' nests around the house and make sure you don't have bats in the attic.

Ants, especially pharaoh ants, will also eat bed bugs or their eggs, and spiders make wonderful bed bug predators. This seems only fair, because spiders have traditionally taken the blame for many a bed bug bite. People learned long ago that they got much more sympathy for a spider bite than for a bed bug bite. One can easily tell the difference between the two, though. A spider bite is two closely spaced punctures; bed bugs usually leave three in a row.

BEES

Insects can live without people, but could people live without insects? When it comes to bees, we probably couldn't. You could grow the most beautiful peach trees in the world, but if you didn't have bees, you might never sink your teeth into their succulent peaches. In fact, without bees to pollinate plants, we would have little interesting food to eat.

Bee populations are declining around the world because of their vulnerability to herbicides and insecticides. Monoculture and habitat destruction also account for why so few feral bees, out of around 5,000 native species, are seen on our farms. In 1970, a pesticide called carbaryl (Sevin) killed off so many bees in Oregon and Washington that 2 billion of them had to be imported to pollinate the fruit trees. Today, transporting hives into certain areas (migratory beekeeping) has become a necessary and standard practice. Even that practice has become threatened by the inadvertent introduction of mite parasites of bees.

Bees have been "farmed" for their honey and "wrangled" for their pollination. No other insect has been used like bees, which may also be the most studied of all insects. At the same time, most people want to stay as far away from them as possible. About 1 percent of the population is extremely allergic to bee stings, and many others have strongly uncomfortable localized reactions. The entire human population has a healthy respect for bee venom.

As beneficial to nature as bees are, they can be a real nuisance, especially when a swarming colony gains access to a home through a hole or crack and sets up housekeeping within its walls. In certain instances, bees have been known to fill most of the spaces in the walls of a house, literally creating a house made of honey.

Away from the nest, bees will rarely sting unless they are sat on, stepped on, leaned against, or otherwise placed in threatening situations. Near the hive, however, guard bees will not hesitate to defend their home.

"Killer Bees"   All bees are usually irritable after a rain, because pollen and nectar have been washed away, but certain bee colonies are more irritable than others. Africanized honey bees, often labeled "killer bees," are quicker to anger, stay riled longer, sting faster, and pursue for far greater distances. Their venom is no stronger than the honey bee's, and they can only sting once. However, they will attack in much greater numbers. Since their accidental release in Brazil in the 1950s, they have steadily moved northward, accompanied by much media hype and some well-deserved respect. They are now successfully colonizing Texas, Arizona, and California. On the positive side, beekeepers in Brazil have adjusted to the ways of these bees and now benefit from higher yields of honey.

If you are unfortunate enough to get attacked, cover your head with clothing and run, run, run to a shelter such as a car or a house.

▶ CONTROL

One can minimize the chances of getting stung by any bee by not wearing perfume, aftershave, or bright-colored or strikingly patterned clothing. If you do get stung, do not pull out the stinger but scrape at it as soon as possible with a fingernail or credit card until you dislodge it. That keeps more poison from being pumped into the skin.

A swarm of bees can be a truly awesome sight. But with no home as yet and no young to protect, they are quite benign. If you see a swarm of bees landing in a tight cluster on a tree limb or pole on your property, look in the yellow pages and call a beekeeper, who may happily come and take the bees to a good and productive home. It is a lot easier to get rid of them at this point than later, when they have set up a hive in a wall void. If you live in an area known to have Africanized (or "killer") bees, call your county agricultural agent or the fire department. Soapy water is lethal to bees, but with a swarm, it's best to get help. Africanized bees will form colonies closer to the ground. Watch out for them in tree cavities, old tires, paint cans, water-meter boxes, and even abandoned cars.

If you spot a bee or two outside the wall of your house, flying along in little bobbles, they may well be looking for a hole or entranceway. Perhaps you neglected to screen that attic vent or close up that hole left by the cable company. Bees also favor cracks around the edges of chimneys.

If bees are entering and exiting from a hole in your house, flying out like a shot, and weaving back and forth on their return, you may already have a colony in your home. Call a beekeeper first to see if the hive can be taken out alive. If not, call around to find the person who will get rid of them with the least toxic method. We had a beekeeper who, after tearing out a good portion of a closet wall, vacuumed out the bees (wearing full beekeeping regalia). This allowed him to take out and use the honey. Afterward he spread diatomaceous earth around to kill any bees returning to the colony from the field. After eliminating a colony, the entrance has to be sealed off; otherwise the pheromones and honey can attract a new colony. We assume ants took on the job of cleaning up the rest of the honey in our walls.

If your problem is one solitary bee in the house, by all means let it out. Open one window and take off the screen. (You do have screens on all your windows, right?) Close the doors to the room and pull all the curtains shut except for those at the open window. The bee will fly toward the light and, one hopes, depart. If this method doesn't work, you can always spray with soapy water or vacuum up any bees on the windows. They won't survive long in the bag.

Bee entering a house

Since one of the tiny game hunter's standard treatments, diatomaceous earth, is lethal to bees, don't dust it on flowers or around places where bees may land in the garden. It is also not a good idea to use *any* spray when trees are flowering. Even pyrethrum is toxic to bees, although it breaks down much faster (in about six hours in temperatures over 55°). If you use pyrethrum, spray at night, after the bees have quit for the day. Ryana, another botanical pesticide, is less toxic to bees.

CLOTHES MOTHS AND CARPET BEETLES

CLOTHES MOTHS

Pests eat our food, our flowers, our houses, and our pets. They even eat us. The least they could do would be to leave us the clothes on our backs— or in our closets.

If you see a little moth flying around indoors, chances are it's either a flour moth (see *Pantry Pests*) or a male clothes moth. The female clothes moth doesn't fly much; she keeps out of sight, and anyway she's too laden down by her burden of 100 to 150 eggs to take to the air. Just barely visible to the naked eye, the eggs, laid on fabric, are not attached in any way, so wearing, shaking, or disturbing clothing is a good way to protect it. Be sure to do the shaking outdoors, however.

Actually, adult moths are innocent when it comes to ruining clothes— they don't even have functional digestive tracts—but their larvae eat fur and wool. The larvae can take anywhere from a month to four years to develop, depending on temperature and other conditions. Clean wool will not sustain them; the larvae actually need the stains on clothing, including food, sweat, hair oil, and urine, to get their vitamins and nutrition, or they can't develop properly.

Three species of moths assail clothing. They all look fairly similar to one another. The **webbing clothes moth** is the most prevalent in our homes today. This moth spins itself a "feeding tube" right on the fabric it's eating, incorporating little bits of the fabric. Besides clothing, it also feeds on carpeting, upholstered furniture, and even piano felts, which is another reason to practice the piano every day.

The **casemaking clothes moth** carries its case with it wherever it goes, like a little sleeping bag, by which it retains moisture. The **tapestry moth** attacks the coarser fabric of tapestries and carpets and can even eat horsehair and horn.

▶ *CONTROL*

Cedar has been used to repel moths for centuries. The Greeks and Romans used oil of cedarwood on the backs of parchment manuscripts to prevent insects from eating them. The incense cedar tree is itself entirely unaffected by insect pests. Squirrels are known to line their nests with cedar needles, possibly because of their insect repellent qualities. Admittedly, the odor of cedar will weaken over time. This can be remedied by rubbing the wood with oil of cedar or sandpapering it lightly.

Other moth repellents include lemon verbena, lavender, eucalyptus, coriander, whole cloves, pennyroyal, and citron. But don't think repellents can take the place of clean clothes in a clean closet.

An article on controlling moths written in the 1950s actually recommended that clothing be saturated with a liquid DDT solution. And a pamphlet from a university extension service recommended painting closets with chlordane. These treatments are no longer recommended, for obvious reasons, but we are still letting loose in our closets and homes the vapors of mothballs or flakes containing naphthalene or paradichlorobenzene (PDB). Of the two, PDB is by far the more toxic, but both can cause severe health problems in humans. Furthermore, they have to be in a closed and sealed space to work, or the vapors will not build up sufficiently to kill the larvae. Thus many people use them ineffectively and breathe them foolishly. We strongly advise against using these products.

According to the Bio-Integral Resource Center, although camphor is also poisonous to humans, it doesn't build up in fatty tissues like naphthalene and PDB. Camphor, which comes from the camphor tree, has been used in the past for medicinal purposes, and it is reputed to have both repellent and insecticidal properties. It can be used just like traditional moth crystals. Since camphor gives off a vigorous smell, clothing should be aired or cleaned after storage.

Moth traps are only good to warn you of an infestation, since they trap only the adult moth, not the damaging larvae. But since moths tend to do their damage in places that are hidden and undisturbed, traps are an excellent warning system. Traps used more than fifty years ago took advantage of the fact that clothes moths are attracted to the smell of fish oil. Impregnate a piece of rough wool with any fish oil (such as sardine oil), set it back in the closet and monitor it closely. Or put a little fish oil (or fish food) on a homemade sticky trap. A commercial trap called Clothes Moth Alert recommends that it be hung at eye level.

Since clothes moths have a definite preference for soiled, worn (handled), or sweat-stained clothing, the very best method of protecting clothing is to clean or launder it before storage. Then place it in a tightly sealed container, or cardboard that has been securely taped, or a heavy sealed plastic bag.

Sunlight is the enemy of the clothes moth. Hang clothing in the sun, and shake it, beat it, or brush it to dislodge any moth larvae hidden in the folds and seams.

Regular vacuuming will eliminate much of the lint and hair that the larvae live on. Vacuum thoroughly in corners, cracks, crevices, heating and air ducts, and, of course, closets and storage areas.

Ironing clothes will kill any eggs and larvae. They cannot survive high temperatures, and if kept at over 104°F for a week, they will die. Storage during the summer in a stifling hot attic will thus provide good protection. Placing wrapped items in the freezer for a few days can also kill the larvae.

Clothes moths are often attracted to the carcasses of dead animals. The practice of poisoning rats and mice instead of trapping them may lead to a clothes moth infestation. The moths come along and take care of the fur, then turn their attention to your clothes.

Certain predatory flies and mites are the enemies of clothes moths, as are many spiders. But the best way to deal with moths is to prevent them from getting started in the first place.

CARPET BEETLES

Like clothes moths, carpet beetles eat wool, fur, and feathers. As with clothes moths, their true role in nature is to eat the fur and skin of dead animals after the flies and vultures are finished, for which we must summon a certain gratitude.

Clothes moths get blamed for a great deal of damage actually done by carpet beetles, also known as dermestid beetles or hide beetles. When carpet beetles attack clothing or textiles, they leave small round holes instead of long jagged ones like moths.

These beetles are tiny, about one-eighth to one-quarter of an inch long, and shaped like ladybugs. They can be black with red and white or yellowish markings, and they tend to be scaly or hairy. Their larvae are hairy little worms. As with clothes moths, only the larvae do damage. The larval stage can last from nine months to three years, during which time they will eat dead insects, dust, lint, and hair. They can eat holes in carpets, upholstery, and curtains. They crawl around quite a bit and can even get into food.

The adult beetles will fly and are attracted to light. They can be found sometimes clustered at windows, clamoring to get out. Outdoors, they live on plants, and they are sometimes brought into the house on cut flowers.

▶ CONTROL

Frequent vacuuming will control carpet beetles, especially if you take the trouble to move heavy furniture and vacuum under it, as this is a favored habitat. Make sure you have no bird, bee, wasp, or rodent nests near the house—all of these can harbor beetles and moths.

An old-fashioned trap for carpet beetles consists of pieces of wool with bits of cheese placed on them. Put them in an infested room in corners or under furniture. When the beetles have crawled onto the traps, dump the bugs into soapy water. Then get out the vacuum cleaner and go to work.

COCKROACHES

The cockroach has to be the hands-down winner of the award for the most loathed insect on earth. Could this possibly be because it has a greasy, crunchy body, six hairy legs, and eighteen knees? Known as the "rat of the insect world," this sneaky, obnoxious night scavenger infiltrates our living quarters. Once it gets behind enemy lines, its numbers increase dramatically, and it is extremely difficult to rout.

Even though they don't sting like scorpions, and they haven't killed us by the millions, the way disease-transmitting fleas and mosquitoes have, cockroaches are not totally harmless. Because they sometimes enter dwellings through sewer pipes, having them prancing across your food is definitely a bad idea. Roaches have been suspected of transmitting numerous diseases, although this is unproven. They are, however, the second most common cause of allergies, after house dust mites. Their brittle discarded skins turn to fine dust and are easily inhaled, causing misery to millions of asthmatics. In large infestations, they have been known to nibble on children's eyebrows.

The Romans named this insect *lucifuga,* or "flees the light." Fossilized cockroaches indicate that the insect has existed for at least 250 million years, virtually unchanged in structure. The cockroach bid both hello and good-bye to the dinosaurs, and it is somewhat discouraging to realize what a successful organism it is. With over $1.5 billion spent annually to eliminate them, cockroaches have rightfully been called "the exterminator's bread and butter."

The most common cockroach is the ubiquitous **German cockroach**. (The Germans call it the Russian cockroach.) It's a real reputation ruiner. This species is the one you are most likely to see in bathrooms, kitchens, and restaurants. One feature that distinguishes this roach—besides the two stripes on the shield that covers its head—is the female's habit of carrying her eggs in a capsule attached to her body. She goes into a safe hiding place before they hatch—thirty to forty of them. It has been calculated that under optimum conditions, one female cockroach could produce 100,000 offspring in a year. Is it any wonder some of us feel overrun by them?

The large, dark, almost black, **oriental cockroach** frequents basements, crawl spaces, and dark, moist areas such as water-meter boxes. It also has the unfortunate predilection of traveling freely between buildings. People sometimes call it a waterbug or black beetle.

The smallest and palest household cockroach is the **brown-banded cockroach**, so called because of the brown bands across its wings. These

(From left to right) German cockroach, brown-banded cockroach, American cockroach, oriental cockroach

cockroaches hang out in warm, dry habitats, rather than moist ones, and commonly exist in other parts of the house besides the kitchen and bathroom. Thriving in temperatures around 80°F, they can often be found high up on the walls and in the top folds of curtains. They deposit their egg clusters on vertical surfaces—behind pictures, on curtains, underneath chairs and tables. They also seek out warm places in electric clocks and televisions—thus their other name, the TV roach. The results are particularly disastrous when they get into computers.

At almost two inches long, the **American cockroach** is the largest of these common pests. This reddish to blackish brown roach likes warmth and high humidity and will even walk through water, especially in sewer systems. According to the *Guinness Book of World Records*, this is the fastest-running insect, having been clocked at about three miles per hour, for a very short distance.

Closely related to the American cockroach, and almost as large, the dark brown, almost black, **smokeybrown cockroach** is found in the Gulf states and the Southeast. It lives outdoors but has been known to come in from the cold in great numbers. Like all our cockroach pests, it is not native to America.

The **Asian cockroach**, which hitchhiked into Florida from the Orient sometime in the 1980s, promises to be just as unpopular as its relatives. It resembles the German cockroach, but, unlike many other cockroaches, this one can fly well. It lives and breeds in huge populations out-of-doors. It is attracted to light, so people find their houses virtually under siege at night. These roaches even fly into malls. This is a very prolific bug and may well spread throughout the country.

Roaches like the warm, slightly humid, protected environments of our homes and the shelter of extremely narrow cracks and crevices. In fact, they prefer to have both the upper and lower portions of their bodies touching something, which is why they find stacks of newspapers and grocery bags so appealing.

Roaches are true omnivores, and their tastes are broad indeed. Besides any leftover food or garbage you carelessly leave out, they will eat toothpaste residue on toothbrushes, wallpaper paste, bookbindings, the glue in grocery bags, soap, dirty clothes, paper, bed bugs, other live and dead insects, and stale beer. Unfortunately, they can also survive for three months without any food and for thirty days without water.

Although poisons can kill a lot of cockroaches initially, such poisons have ultimately proved ineffective. Poisons are virtually useless against the sealed egg cases, unless they can persist until the eggs hatch or are administered repeatedly. Neither treatment really benefits humans, of course, and millions of gallons of cockroach poisons have been sprayed, squirted, and fogged around kitchens and bathrooms, places where people spend a great deal of time.

Despite their broad tastes in food, cockroaches always sample it first with their fine sensory hairs. Dr. Walter Ebeling, formerly at the University of California, Los Angeles, showed that cockroaches are repelled by poison and thus avoid spots where it has been placed. They are one of the few insect species noted for their learning ability. Roaches have also developed resistance to many pesticides.

▶ CONTROL

A book published in 1885 advised holding up a looking glass in front of a roach. "He will be so frightened as to leave the premises," the author promised. We feel this method would be too time-consuming: for each cockroach you see in your home, there may be hundreds lurking in the cracks and crannies.

Beleaguered chefs in roach-infested kitchens have been known to slice cucumbers and line them up around the perimeter of their work stations to keep the crawlers away. This may work, but it is the desperate action of someone under siege and out of control of his environment. Recently, cockroaches have been found to be repelled by catnip. However, the best method of cockroach control, with special emphasis on sanitation, consists of figuring out where they hang out and killing them with lethal agents that are safe for humans.

Traps   A very old cockroach trap consists of dampening a rag or cloth with beer and placing it on the floor in an out-of-the-way place. The cockroaches are attracted to the beer and will congregate under the cloth, where they can be stomped on in the morning.

A teeter-totter cockroach trap

Entomologists who maintain live roach cultures keep them in glass jars coated on the upper inside with petroleum jelly. You can make this trap by wrapping the outside of a pint jar with masking tape and smearing a good two-inch wide band of petroleum jelly on the inside of the jar below the neck. Put dog food, pieces of banana, or some flour and beer inside for bait. Place the traps along the wall, with a ramp extending from the floor to the rim of the jar. The insect will crawl up and readily drop down inside but can't get out. The trap works even better with a few trapped cockroaches inside. It won't work for the flying Asian cockroach, however.

When sticky traps came on the market in the 1960s, they were a welcome relief for many people as an alternative to poisons. These traps (Roach Motel, Roach Magnet, Mr. Sticky, etc.) can come impregnated with pheromones to make them even more attractive. By themselves, however, these traps will not eliminate all your cockroaches. Use them to reduce infestations, to figure out where they are mostly living, and to prove that you are rid of them. Be sure to place them along walls.

By mail order you can purchase electronic roach zappers, which lure the cockroaches in and electrocute them and their eggs with a low-voltage charge.

Predators   "The cockroach is always wrong when arguing with a chicken," says an old Spanish proverb. This may be the reason that people used to let chickens move freely in and out of their dwellings. Unfortunately, cockroaches have a chemical defense that makes puppies and kittens throw them up. Other animals that do eat cockroaches include scorpions, wasps, toads, hedgehogs, and birds, which probably led to the evolution of their instinct to hide out of sight.

Dusts   Boric acid is the one anti-insect substance that poisons but does not repel roaches, and they haven't developed resistance to it after decades of use. It is much more effective and less expensive than synthetic pesticides, and it will not harm people or pets unless they eat it.

Boric acid was commonly used as an eyewash and antiseptic, and you can still find the powder in drugstores. But better formulations of boric acid are now available, ones that have been electrically charged to keep it from caking. Others have been colored or bitterly flavored to keep kids from eating it.

You can get cockroaches to ingest boric acid by using it in a bait, or you can simply get them to walk through it by dusting it around their habitat with a bulb duster or a narrow-tipped bottle. It has to be dusted extremely finely over the areas where roaches may pass, not dumped in lumps, which they will simply walk around. Having walked through it, roaches will then ingest it while cleaning their feet, because they are constantly and fastidiously grooming themselves.

After using sticky traps to figure out where roaches are living, blow boric acid into cracks and crevices, between walls and under sinks, and along baseboards. Puff it around under refrigerators and stoves and other appliances. You can even add it (or Borax) to water and mop the floor and wipe down walls and counters with it.

You can also treat for roaches by dusting with diatomaceous earth or a silica gel. These dusts scratch the protective waxy outer layer of the cockroach, leading to desiccation and death. Like boric acid, they are applied in such a way that the insect ends up walking through them. Goggles and a mask should be used with all dusts, even though they are nontoxic in the usual sense. This is one treatment that, if undisturbed, does not have to be reapplied.

Baits   Baits are easy to use, there are no vapors to inhale, and the poisons are less toxic. Furthermore, back in the roach hangouts, baits continue to kill, because the nymphs eat the feces of adults.

To make your own bait, use a cup of boric acid or Borax, half a cup of flour, a quarter-cup of powdered sugar, and one-half cup of ground oats. Keep it away from children and pets. It can be used where the humidity is too high for dusting with boric acid alone. Place it inside of folded cardboard to make it even more attractive to roaches.

Commercial baits in little bait stations have the advantage of being child- and pet-proof. (They also come in gel form for out-of-the-way places.) You can find these baits containing boric acid or hydramethylon, also a stomach poison with low toxicity to mammals. Environmentally safe baits also come with insect growth regulators or extracts from a soil microorganism (avermectin). Or look for cockroach-attacking nematodes and a species of deadly (to cockroaches) fungus, which they take back to their refuge, where it spreads to others.

Baits will be most effective if placed right along the edges of walls, between hiding places and food sources.

These baits are not quick-kill and can take from one to four weeks to work. You may even see more roaches for a while, as sick ones start appearing.

▶ PREVENTION

Cockroaches come into your home looking for two items: food and water. Deprive them of both. Remember: roaches are odor-driven. Also, baits work best if the roaches are hungry.

Eliminate their food

- Keep food in tightly sealed containers.
- Never, never leave the dishes undone—especially at night.
- Wipe off counters thoroughly; sweep the kitchen floor.
- After the pet has eaten, wash out its bowl. Or place the pet dish in a bigger bowl of soapy water.
- Use a garbage can with a good, tight lid.
- Wipe up the grease that collects around stoves.
- Vacuum frequently, especially in the kitchen and areas where the family snacks. Vacuuming helps get rid of egg cases and untold future generations. Seal the vacuum cleaner bag carefully in double plastic bags when disposing of it.

Eliminate water for roaches

- Check regularly under sinks and around the house for dripping pipes and faucets. Look for pipes with condensation, dripping air conditioners, and leaky toilets. Check for moisture under refrigerators and around houseplants.

Seal cracks and crevices

- A young cockroach can fit into a crevice as small as one-sixteenth of an inch. Use caulk or steel wool to eliminate every little crack and crevice along baseboards, shelves, sinks, and utility pipes and inside cupboards. Remove or reglue loose wallpaper. Before caulking, treat with boric acid.

Check appliances

- Roaches love the warmth and dark hiding possibilities of refrigerators, stoves, water heaters, and dryers. Sometimes a house will become infested as a result of buying a used refrigerator inhabited by cockroaches. Pull appliances out from the wall when possible and vacuum thoroughly. Remember: the minute an overhead light goes on, the roaches are gone, so when you look for their harborages, do it with a flashlight. When you find evidence of cockroaches, vacuum well and then wash with a strong soap.

Further tactics

- Make sure doors and windows close tightly.
- Remove stacks of lumber and firewood near the house.
- Put a few inches of gravel in your water-meter box to reduce moisture.
- Remove stacks of newspapers, stored magazines, piles of old clothes, cardboard boxes, and used grocery bags.
- In winter try turning off the heat, opening the windows, and letting the cold drive them away.
- Roaches dislike breezes and will flee from moving air. Fans and air vents can be used to create an unfavorable climate.
- Thermal heat treatments can eliminate cockroaches (see also *Termites*).

FLEAS

With a mouth like a set of blades, a body like a machine, and an appetite for fresh blood, this pest has probably caused more misery than any other. A little armor-coated silhouette, the flea is narrow enough to pass between the hairs on its host. Its hard, chew-proof shell can withstand tremendous pressure and is covered with a series of combs and spiky spines, while its legs are all bristles and hooks. All of these enable it to latch on to its host and hang in there despite frantic scratching, licking, and biting by its victim.

People were once as plagued by fleas as dogs and cats are today. **Human fleas** were as much a part of daily life as dandruff and daydreams. When we add to this the widespread torments of bed bugs and body lice, we can only surmise that life before hot showers was full of itching and scratching.

Flea remedies were as common as the fleas themselves. The Egyptians used to smear a slave with the milk of asses and make him stand in the room as a human flea trap. In the sixteenth century, women wore fur pieces around their necks, hoping that the fleas would settle in them. In the seventeenth century, women wore decorative flea traps in their bodices. Some were fashioned with ivory and filled with blood-soaked cloth.

Better hygiene led to the widespread demise of the human flea. It was simply no match for a soapy bath, a pass of the vacuum cleaner, or a tumble through the clothes dryer.

There are around 2,000 known species of fleas, and each one has its own preferred host. In the absence of the favored host, they readily feed on other animals, including humans. The two fleas found most often in our homes are the **dog flea** and the more pervasive **cat flea**, which is found on both cats and dogs and, alas, goes after humans, too—along with rats, chickens, opossums, and raccoons, among other animals. It can cause severe allergic reactions in its victims.

Another flea, the **oriental rat flea**, caused the terrible pandemic outbreaks of bubonic plague that have periodically swept through civilization.

Flea

Fleas account for more deaths than all the wars ever fought. In the fourteenth century, nearly half of Europe's population was felled by the Black Death. But not until the late 1800s, and another outbreak of plague, which killed 6 million people in India, was the rat flea finally proved to be the vector of the plague bacillus. When this disease kills the rats carrying it, their infected fleas immediately look for another host and move on to humans.

Although plague can now be cured by antibiotics, the threat of it is still very much with us. In the United States, wild rodents such as ground squirrels and chipmunks may well carry the disease, so it is very unwise to have any contact with them; domestic animals should be kept away from them, too.

Fleas can also transmit typhus, tularemia, and tapeworm.

In the past few decades, flea remedies almost as noxious as the fleas themselves have been used. Flea collars and shampoos poison animals as well as fleas. Foggers fill the house with toxic residues, which accumulate on furniture and toys. They poison our air, our groundwater, and our children. And after all that, your pet only has to go into the neighbor's yard, bring back a few of their fleas, and the whole cycle starts all over again. Fortunately, there have been innovations in effective nontoxic controls, so the least you can do is conduct this battle without harming yourself or your pet.

FLEA METAMORPHOSIS

Understanding the life cycle of the flea will help explain why it has failed to succumb to the massive doses of insecticides used against it. Fleas spend only a small percentage of their life cycle making pets and humans miserable. The rest of time is spent away from the host, somewhere in your rugs, floor, furniture, or yard. A pair of adult fleas can produce offspring that could be in your house for as long as two years. Getting rid of fleas requires a war on four fronts: against adults, eggs, larvae, and pupae.

Under ideal conditions, fleas can lay up to 25 eggs a day—as many as 400 in a summer and 800 in a lifetime. Fleas usually lay their eggs right on the host, but they soon fall off.

When fleas suck blood, their mouths tear open the skin. They send an anticoagulant (the cause of the itch) into the wound and start pumping out the blood. They take more blood than they need, and the excess passes right through them. If you're not sure if your pet has fleas, comb the animal over damp white paper. The flea excrement, or "exhaust," which looks like ground black pepper, will turn red on the paper.

When the eggs hatch, the larvae—tiny white, hairy worms—find and feed upon the dried fecal blood of the parent fleas, which has also fallen off the host, as well as on dirt and debris. Then they spin a cocoon (the pupal stage), which is soon covered with dust and hard to see.

In a house that has been empty while the owners and pets are away, the fleas remain in waiting. No sense emerging from the cocoon if there isn't going to be a meal available. If already emerged, they also wait—a flea can survive for months without a meal.

Highly sensitive to vibration and heat, fleas rely on these clues as signals to jump for their blood meal. They also have the ability to detect currents of air and probably carbon dioxide too. So when people reenter a house that has been vacant, the famished fleas arise and attack en masse. In the South, people used to send a sheep into a vacant house ahead of them to take the edge off the flea bites.

▶ **CONTROL**

Think of flea control as a full-time job, like feeding your pet, because fleas will always come back, especially if your pet leaves the yard, or if other animals enter your yard.

Fleas thrive in warm, humid weather. A rainy summer is flea heaven. Excessive heat, dryness, and cold are fatal to fleas. Flea populations often explode in the late summer and fall. Get ready to step up your offensive during these times.

Central heating helped eliminate human fleas from homes, as did vacuuming. Consider turning on your heater during flea season to dry out the house.

Poisons that contain organophosphates and carbamates have proven to be a short-term remedy. They have only built a better flea, causing pesticide manufacturers to make ever-stronger—and more dangerous— products. In their zeal to control the problem, pet owners often overuse these chemicals. Many of them are nerve-paralyzing agents that can cause convulsions, nausea, and respiratory arrest. Yet veterinarians say that often the poisoned animals they treat *still* have fleas.

Products that contain insect growth regulators have been used with success. Lufenuron (Program) is given to the pet internally, so when the flea ingests the pet's blood, it gets a dose of birth control. Methoprene and fenoxycarb are sprayed around the house to kill flea eggs and prevent larvae from emerging. They take a while to work, but they are believed to have low toxicity to mammals. "Spot on" insecticides, such as Advantage and Frontline, also claim to have low toxicity to mammals and have proven to be both convenient and popular. Applied periodically right between the animal's shoulder blades, they spread through the sebaceous glands and result in high rates of mortality for fleas.

Clearing Fleas off Your Pet   One of the most important things you can do for flea control is comb your pet regularly with a special fine-tooth flea comb to remove its bloodthirsty guests. When pets become accustomed to this procedure, they love it, although, in flea season, long-haired dogs may need to be trimmed. A dab of petroleum jelly along the ridge of the comb immobilizes fleas. Once you snag some fleas in the comb, dip them in a glass of water to which a few drops of rubbing alcohol or liquid soap have been added. Do not crush them with your fingernails, no matter how tempting—they could be carrying diseases.

If you find you are snagging more fleas than usual, it's time for other measures. A bath will get rid of many fleas by drowning them. But it can't be a splash-splash, okay-you-win-fella type of affair. Avoid products containing organophosphates, petroleum distillates, and piperonyl butoxide, which can be absorbed through your skin as well as your pet's. We recommend a mild shampoo or lemon-scented Joy dishwashing soap. Safer's insecticidal soaps for pets will safely kill fleas.

Make use of the insect-killing properties of citrus. Buy products that contain linalool or D-limonene (which also kills ticks), both of which disrupt the moisture balance of the insects. Or make your own. Chop up three or four lemons or oranges and pour two cups of boiling water over them, skin and all. Let this stand overnight, then sponge it on your pet. A reader of *Prevention* magazine suggested scoring the skin of an orange to release the citrus oil and rubbing the fruit right onto the animal.

Pets can be dusted with dusts like diatomaceous earth. Just as with humans, take measures to keep your pet from inhaling the dust.

Products containing pyrethrum (derived from chrysanthemum flowers) are effective, but they can cause allergic reactions in some pets and are toxic to bees and fish. A friend of ours says his dog never gets fleas—he swims in the pool every day.

Getting Rid of Fleas in the House   For every flea on your pet, there may be as many as a hundred in its environment. To trap fleas inside the house, take a wide, shallow pan partly filled with soapy water. Place it on the floor and hang a low-watt light bulb above it. Or use a sturdy, well-anchored gooseneck lamp (a Tensor lamp works well). The fleas will be attracted to the heat of the bulb, jump up, and land in the pan. The soap in the water breaks the surface tension, making it impossible for them to jump back out again. This particular trap has its origins in much older versions that used candles. You can also purchase excellent versions that come with replaceable sticky trays.

To determine where the worst flea infestation is, put on a pair of white fuzzy athletic socks and walk around the house or yard. The fleas will jump on and get caught. Throw the socks into hot soapy water in the washer.

If your pet sleeps in the same place all the time, you can control a prime flea habitat by using easily removable covers, or just a towel, on the pet's bedding. Every morning, gather it up and drop it into a washing machine already filled with soapy water. Presto. Put a clean cover on the bedding before the pet's next nap.

Simple flea trap

Larval-stage fleas feed on dirt, debris, and hair that accumulates in floor cracks, in rugs, around baseboards, under cushions of chairs and couches, and especially wherever a pet lies down. Clean thoroughly to remove the sources of their food. That translates to vacuum, vacuum, vacuum. Vacuuming, of course, gets rid of flea eggs, pupae, and possibly fleas themselves. So vacuum again. Seal the vacuum cleaner bag in plastic and dispose of it carefully. Putting it in the hot sun will kill the fleas.

Vacuum cleaners with water filters are ideal for flea control. Adding soap to the water really kills them off. Steam cleaning is even better than vacuuming for killing fleas in rugs and on furniture. One pest control company in California that specializes in nontoxic pest control uses a dry steam machine that heats up to 250°F. It then sprays an insect growth regulator for the next generation. Look for exterminators that use methods like these (or liquid nitrogen to freeze fleas) and give them your business.

Certain products can be sprinkled around the house to kill fleas without harming humans, but these can be messy, and you will have to keep traffic away for the duration. Many have reported success with a form of borax, known as Rx for Fleas; sprinkle it on carpets and upholstery, then vacuum. It is available from FleaBusters, which also provides home flea control services. Dusts like horticultural diatomaceous earth and silica aerogel will shred the waxy coating of the flea, causing dehydration and death. Use a mask and goggles to avoid inhaling them. Some people have used a light dusting of noniodized salt, but don't try this if the humidity is high. Then vacuum.

If you do not have pets but have just moved into a flea-infested home, sprinkle the laundry booster Borax on the carpets and flooring. Leave it on for a couple of days and then vacuum. Do not use it around pets, especially cats, who might lick it off their paws.

Outdoors   Outdoors, especially around where your cat or dog likes to snooze, you can mix diatomaceous earth with water and sprinkle it around with a watering can or spray it with a hose-end sprayer. Using it dry is even better, but if you choose this method, be sure to wear a mask and goggles.

From pet stores, veterinarians, or nurseries, purchase parasitic nematodes (Bio-Fleas-B-Gone, Lawn Patrol, Guardian) that attack flea larvae. Safer flea soap can also be used to treat outdoor areas. The highest concentrations tend to be in areas that are shady and slightly moist. If your yard is extremely dry or extremely wet, fleas cannot survive in it.

Make sure that your yard is not harboring rodents that carry fleas.

▶ PREVENTION

This job goes on and on. Herbal extracts can be useful as repellents to keep your pet from picking up fleas in the neighborhood and bringing them home. Eucalyptus, citronella, cedarwood, pennyroyal, orange oil, peppermint, and pine are among the best. Look for them in powders, collars, shampoos, oils, and sprays. If you use essential oils, be sure to dilute them with water. You can even make your own herbal flea collar by soaking a piece of string or light rope in oil of pennyroyal or any other repellent for twenty-four hours and tying it around your pet's neck. Or string together pods from a eucalyptus tree. Apply repellents outdoors so that the fleas don't jump off inside the house.

Cedar-filled bedding for pets makes a good flea repellent.

Spread fresh eucalyptus branches around the house for a day or two to make the place inhospitable to fleas. If you can find them, black walnut leaves are an excellent repellent. Even better, plant a black walnut tree in your yard.

Pay attention to the health of your pet. Exercise is extremely important for animals. This means at least a vigorous twenty-minute walk each day. Try feeding your pet a diet of fresh foods: grains, raw and cooked greens, fresh meat and liver, and a teaspoon of safflower oil (for linoleic acid) daily.

Fleas inflict themselves on certain animals more frequently than on others, just as they do with humans, and it is suspected that the better the health and condition of your pet's skin, the more resistant it will be. Some pets get fleas because of their dry, flaky skin, not the other way around. Fleas love this kind of skin, because it's already so raw they hardly have to bite to get at the blood.

Brewer's yeast, kelp, and zinc added to the diet will cause your pet to become less acceptable to fleas. Pet stores and veterinarians carry these products formulated for pets. Or try garlic as a repellent. Use one minced clove per day for a cat and up to three cloves for a dog, depending on its size.

Take heart in your arduous battle with fleas. We humans finally wrested ourselves and our sanity from the human flea. By paying close attention to the entire life cycle of our pets' fleas, with vigilance and perseverance, we can free them, too.

FLIES

Flies have been an irritant to humans for so long, they have entered into our legends. In Western culture, flies came out of Pandora's box. In Japanese legend, a terrible one-eyed goblin that liked to eat humans was destroyed and burned, but its ashes turned into flies—and so the torment continues.

Fittingly named for what they do best, with wings that beat 165 to 200 times a minute and a built-in "gyroscope" on their backs, flies are among nature's most fantastic fliers. We have identified around 85,000 species of flies, and we're still counting. They breed so rapidly that it takes only eight hours for certain eggs to hatch, and they adapt to virtually every environment. Fortunately for us, many flies starve to death, while others are eaten by birds, fish, and other insects—another reason for using nontoxic pesticides.

House fly, eggs, and maggot

Sometimes we forget that we are at war with the fly and think if we ignore it, it'll simply go away and die soon. "Oh, what's one little fly?" we say when we see it buzzing around the kitchen. Well, one little house fly carries about 4 million bacteria. It's a walking, flying, stomping, slurping germ vector, which has been held responsible for spreading hookworm, tapeworms, pinworms, typhoid, cholera, dysentery, diarrhea, hepatitis, salmonella, and dozens of other diseases.

Common **house flies** and their close relatives **dung flies** are sometimes known as filth flies. **Blue bottle flies** and **green bottle flies** also go by the name of flesh flies. The names fit. They buzz around the world looking for garbage, drawn by the odors of decay. They lay their eggs on wet rotting material—food, excrement, or dead animals—25 to 100 at a time. The eggs hatch into pointy-headed maggots, destined to feed happily on the putrefaction.

Ironically, the age of the automobile was hailed as an end to pollution—the pollution of flies that proliferated in the manure of so many horses. Today, however, we actually have more horses in this country than before the automobile. We also have incredible amounts of dog feces, a major life-sustaining material for these insects.

Flies can walk on the ceiling, because they have little pads on the bottoms of their feet that secrete a sticky substance. This sticky stuff also picks up bacteria from everything else they land on, so when they crawl over your food (while tasting with their feet), they leave little calling cards.

And then there are their table manners. No biting, no chewing—these creatures suck and sponge up their food. To do this, they vomit or dribble saliva into it and liquefy it. Their long tongue (proboscis) then unfurls and sucks it up. Of course, they always leave some dribble, and in doing so they spew around even more bacteria. When you see fly specks, the dark ones are excrement; the light spots are regurgitated food and saliva. This information always makes a good conversation starter.

Living about a month, flies can reproduce ten to twelve generations over the summer. Most die over the winter, but, alas, some manage to hibernate as larvae or pupae and emerge in the spring.

Mosquitoes are actually types of flies, but dragonflies, butterflies, damselflies, fireflies, mayflies, and stoneflies are not. Midges, bots, warbles, and gnats are also flies.

As horrific as the house fly is when it comes to low-life tastes, bad hygiene, and prolific bacteria, many other flies are much more dreadful. A **horse fly** can bite through leather, and it takes big bites. The **stable fly** has a built-in hypodermic by which it draws blood. It bites the ankles of its victims, and socks are no deterrent. Certain **black flies** leave an itching blood blister. **Midges** crawl right into eyes, noses, and mouths. The **screwworm**, a blow fly, feeds on the raw flesh of open wounds.

The **human bot fly** lays its eggs on a mosquito or other biting fly. When the mosquito lands on a person, the egg immediately hatches and burrows under the skin, where it lives and grows for weeks. A species of black fly causes blindness in certain parts of Africa, sometimes affecting up to 30 percent of the adult men. The **tsetse fly,** armed with sleeping sickness, literally kept the Arabs from taking over Africa.

Not all flies are terrible, however. **Tachinid flies** and **hover flies** feed on the insides of pest insects while in the larval stage. As adults they live on flower nectar. One species of tachinids saved the sugarcane industry from the sugarcane borer. Others are useful against gypsy moths and Japanese beetles. As a group, certain flies are second only to bees in the cross-pollination they perform. And their use in biological control has been a tremendous boon to agriculture.

Moreover, let us not forget fruit flies' important role in the laboratories of scientists who've advanced our understanding of human biology. Their genetic codes are so similar to humans', they have been called "little people with wings," and they have been vital to our understanding of genetics. Today scientists are studying fruit flies for links between genes and behavior, hoping to gain clues about sleep disorders, memory, longevity, and much more.

▶ CONTROL

Fly-swatting has a long, honorable tradition of success. For every fly you kill, several hundred (even a thousand) will not be born. Some people say a mesh flyswatter works best. Others prefer a rolled up newspaper— easily available and conveniently disposable. In addition to 4,000-faceted eyes, flies are equipped with ultrasensitive hairs that detect fine currents of air. That's why they seem to take off before they could possibly have known you were coming. A fly takes off slightly backward, however, so aim just behind it. If you clap your hands over a fly, its takeoff pattern will land it right between your palms. Please wear gloves if you want to test this.

You can knock out a fly with a squirt of soapy water, spray starch, hair spray, or rubbing alcohol in a spray bottle, but it requires both stealth and a good aim.

If a fly is buzzing around the room, close all the doors and drapes, leaving a slit of light at one window. When you frighten the fly, it will go to that window, and you can swat it there.

Repellents   Flies are drawn into the house by going upwind toward odors, for which they have an exquisite sensitivity. Fortunately, just as we can't stand the odors (decay, offal, ammonia, etc.) that they are drawn to, they are in turn repelled by some odors we find attractive, like citronella.

Traditional fly repellents have included hanging sweet clover in net bags around the room, especially over doorways; making a potpourri of bay leaves, cloves, pennyroyal, and eucalyptus leaves; and planting sweet basil, tansy, or rue around doorways. Both camphor and chinaberry trees have been planted to keep flies away. Marigold leaves are sometimes hung in dog kennels and around stables. Mint has been a traditional repellent. People have crushed it and rubbed it on their animals to keep flies from tormenting them.

Traps   Trapping flies, like swatting them, is a reliable way to keep down their numbers. In Africa, amazing progress has been made in the eradication of the tsetse fly by using simple baited traps made from plastic bags, a few feet of cloth, and some staples. Fly traps are effective because flies are so mobile and so inquisitively hungry. A trap with flies in it will attract more flies, because they are drawn to each other.

Fly traps that range from small glass bottles with special lids that flies can get into but not out of to traps that will hold up to 25,000 flies can be purchased, along with chemical attractants, from garden centers and mail order suppliers. If everyone made an effort to acquire and maintain a few of these traps, the entire population of flies would be considerably diminished.

Fly traps: bottle trap, screen trap, flypaper

You can make a screen trap that consists of a baited dish set beneath a pair of cones made from screen sewn with wire or nylon fishing line. The inside cone has an opening at the top. Flies land on the bait, then go up—toward the light— out of the top of the inner cone and find themselves trapped by the outer cone, which is closed at the top. One person we know tossed his trap into the fire and burned the flies away when it was filled.

A similar trap can be made by cutting the top third off a large plastic water or soft drink bottle and inserting it into the bottom of the bottle. Use clothespins to set the trap above a bait station, and puncture holes in it with a needle so that it doesn't get too hot.

Make your own baits using ingredients such as beer, buttermilk, rotting fruit, or a bit of raw hamburger. Mix one part molasses to three parts water and add active dry yeast to make a fermented solution. Ammonium carbonate and yeast is another successful mixture, and a piece of meat or fish in water also works. Cornmeal and molasses ferment into a fine bait. Sometimes a mixture of meaty bait and sweet bait will draw more flies. Be sure to keep the bait moist. Experimentation is in the true spirit of tiny game hunting.

Directions for these traps always say to place them well away from the house. This is not because the baits—and the dead flies—are going to stink, but because the traps will draw flies from far away; you won't want the new arrivals coming near the house.

Traps are more effective if placed in the sun, but watch out that the bait does not dry out. If you have ants in the yard, the bait must be kept away from them, either by hanging the trap or putting it in a shallow basin of water.

To make an effective fruit fly trap, put a small amount of cut-up ripe fruit (bananas are ideal) in the bottom of a clear glass jar and insert a funnel into the top. The flies enter and can't escape. Beer or a mixture of molasses, water, and yeast is also a good bait. A slight drawback to this trap is that inside the bottle, the tiny flies proceed to eat and breed quite happily. You can end the party by pouring boiling water into the funnel, killing the flies, and starting all over.

Another way to trap fruit flies is to place a glass containing an inch of brandy or sweet liqueur near the infestation. Or use equal parts vinegar, sugar, and dish soap. By morning the flies will be floating in the liquid.

The old standard, flypaper, really works. Hang it near the ceiling for best effect. We like the one that has been decorated with little drawings of flies. You can also buy a window version that traps flies inside a decorative envelope. For use outdoors, the FlyFinder is a spool of wide white sticky tape, imprinted with random black dots as an added lure.

Electric zap traps can be useful in enclosed indoor facilities such as restaurants or barns. *Do not use these traps outdoors!* Flies do not see the ultraviolet light well during the day, and they are not active at night, so you are foolishly killing beneficial bugs with these traps.

Predators and Parasites   Flies were the first insects to develop resistance to DDT in the 1940s. This must have been quite disappointing, because DDT was touted as "the killer of killers," and people truly believed that flies were going to be eradicated within their lifetime. Parents were even told to use DDT-impregnated wallpaper in children's rooms to protect them from flies. When DDT failed, other, sometimes stronger, sprays were—and still are—used. And the flies are still around. The flush toilet did more to remove flies from our presence than DDT ever did.

Spraying pesticides for fly control results in a spectacular quick kill—at first. Then the resistant "superflies" start multiplying and take over. Unfortunately, spraying kills the beneficial fly parasites and also contaminates the air you breathe. Remember, if you can smell it, it has already passed into your lungs.

Do not use vapor-emitting fly "traps" or pest strips. If, as the directions say, they are not to be used around food preparation, babies, or old people, why should they be used around you? They have also been implicated in children's cancers.

Where biting black flies are a problem, the bacterial insecticide, *Bacillus thuringiensis israelensis,* or Bti, has been a successful means of control.

Wherever large amounts of manure are generated, flies can be successfully contained by introducing fly parasites on a regular basis. These parasites, which are not pests themselves, deposit their eggs right into fly larvae or pupae in the manure, preventing them from ever becoming adults. Since the parasites need some dry manure, do not clear all manure away at one time. See *Resources and Mail Order* for companies that sell these biological controls. Many of them will consult with clients about specific problems.

Both ants and wasps prey on flies. Ants eat a considerable number of fly larvae in your yard, which is one reason why ants should be tolerated. In one of our yards, ants climb an English walnut tree and help control the walnut husk fly maggots.

Birds, frogs, toads, snakes, and spiders also eat lots of flies. In the house, spiders are the best tiny game hunters of all, so let them do their share of the fly catching.

Years ago people actually used to hang a wasp's nest near barns or stables or even inside their houses, because the wasps were preferable to the flies, which they preyed on quite efficiently. We don't recommend this, however.

PREVENTION

Sanitation is the most important means of fly control.

- Do not leave any food uncovered in the kitchen. Wipe counters and sweep the floor after food preparation. Ripe fruit, especially overripe fruit, attracts true fruit flies as well as vinegar flies, which can sometimes enter through screens.
- Don't let your garbage be a breeding area for flies. Studies of "average" garbage cans have found them to be the source of literally thousands of maggots. Regularly wash and dry garbage cans thoroughly. Sprinkle the bottoms with powdered soap. Making sure that the lids to the cans are as tight and secure as possible amounts to a civic duty. Ideally, garbage cans should be placed on platforms to allow air to circulate under them and eliminate fly breeding places.
- Separate your wet organic garbage from the dry garbage and seal it well. The drier garbage is, the less flies will be attracted to it. Wrap it in layers of newspaper before disposing of it. If you use a closed container compost system, flies will not be a problem.

Otherwise cover the top of organic material with a layer of dirt
or black plastic as quickly as possible before flies can lay their eggs
in it.

- Rinse out all cartons, cans, and bottles before recycling them.
- Disposable diapers can be fabulous breeding places for flies. Either
  don't use them or take great care in getting rid of them.
- Flies are also crazy for animal droppings—their true medium after
  all—but they have to be moist. If the droppings are dry, flies can't
  breed in them. If you can't bury them immediately, cover them
  with sawdust. Or flush them down the toilet, or seal them in
  newspaper or plastic bags and dispose of them in the garbage.
- Don't leave out the dog or cat food. For flies this is an invitation
  to a party.
- We highly recommend screens. They work, especially if they are
  tight-fitting and don't have holes.
- Fans will also deter flies. Their acute sensitivity to air currents
  makes them uncomfortable in moving air, which is one reason
  you see overhead fans in meat markets and restaurants. You can
  now buy a device that creates a wall of moving air over a doorway
  (see *Resources and Mail Order*).

HOUSEPLANT PESTS

Houseplant pests often infiltrate our homes by hitchhiking in on new
plants. They also sneak in by hopping rides on people wandering in from
the garden, or hide on cut flowers, or blow in through screens. The pests
become a problem because none of their natural predators live inside the
house. With nothing to slow them down, the damage can be quick and
devastating.

Another reason houseplant pests get out of hand is the too-generous
watering and fertilizing that some plants get indoors. This causes a very
high nitrogen content, which plant-sucking pests such as mealybugs,
aphids, and scale thrive on.

Some people recommend throwing away plants that are infested. We
think most pests can be defeated—and without polluting the house with
pesticides. Nevertheless, the presence of pests on a plant may be a sign

that the plant is under stress; perhaps it doesn't get the light it needs or is over- or underwatered. So while you're fighting the pests, try improving the plant's environment: move it to a new location and try watering it less or more. Especially don't let it sit for long in a saucer of water!

Try a little indoor companion planting. Plant a single garlic plant right in the pot with your plant by peeling a garlic clove and placing it, pointed end up, about an inch under the soil between the plant and the edge of the pot. This should help keep pests away. You can also plant chives, which have more delicate tops.

Pests won't always be visible on newly purchased plants, so the best defense is to establish a quarantine for all new plants. Keep them in an isolated room for several weeks to make sure they are pest-free.

If you garden both indoors and out, always do the indoor gardening first. It's far better to take an indoor pest outdoors than vice versa. Sometimes the simplest solution for household plant infestations is to take the plants outdoors and let the natural enemies have at them.

THE USUAL SUSPECTS

The most common pests of houseplants are aphids, mealybugs, scale, spider mites, thrips, and whiteflies. **Aphids** cover the tips and buds of plants. **Mealybugs** look like little tufts of waxy cotton in the crevices between stalks and stems. **Scale** looks like small bumps on the plant. **Spider mites** and **thrips** are very small and may need to be identified with a hand lens. **Whiteflies** are much more visible; when the plant is disturbed, a cloud of white insects rises. **Fungus gnats** are tiny flies that rise up from the soil. Less frequent visitors (although their numbers can be great) are **ants** and **cockroaches**.

Cockroaches enjoy houseplants. They may actually be attracted to the water in the plant saucers. And while they're refreshing themselves, they may do some chewing—even quite a bit of chewing—on the leaves. Pine-oil cleaners are said to repel cockroaches. Try sprinkling diatomaceous earth in the plant saucers for a sharp and deadly demise. See *Cockroaches* for getting rid of them permanently.

Ants will sometimes set up a nest in a houseplant pot (or even in an outdoor pot), where they may disturb the roots of the plant (see *Ants*).

To get rid of ants, the Bio-Integral Resource Center in Berkeley suggests placing the potted plant in a big pan or bucket. Set a pot filled with dirt, humus, or compost next to the infested pot and make a bridge between the two pots with a piece of wood. Flood the infested plant repeatedly with water. The ants will come scurrying out, carrying their pupae, and set up lodgings in the new pot, which you can then place where they won't do any harm.

To keep a cat out of your houseplants, take a cotton ball and saturate it with lemon oil furniture polish or dampen it with ammonia. Place it on the soil at the base of the plants, and the cat will lose interest.

▶ CONTROL

Water   Plants with smooth leaves and stems can often be treated successfully by rubbing the stems and both sides of the leaves with a dampened cloth or cotton gloves to dislodge both pests and their invisible eggs. This technique works especially well for aphids and scale. Or wipe off the leaves with a solution consisting of half a teaspoon of vegetable oil to one quart of water. Not only will this kill or suffocate any insects, but the plants, being less dusty, will breathe better and look better.

Sprays   Soap sprays, homemade or commercial (see *Tactics of Tiny Game Hunting in the Garden*) can be used for almost all household pests and are often the only step you need to take.

Commercial light dormant oil is also good for killing pests on houseplants, especially thrips and whiteflies. Test it on a few leaves first. Don't use it on ferns or African violets.

Taking houseplants outside and giving them a strong squirt of water will rout many pests. If the plant is small enough, simply hold it under the faucet and give it the water treatment. Be sure to spray the bottoms of leaves. We like to set a plant in the bathtub and use the strong jet of a Water Pik to dislodge the stubborn bugs.

Dips   If a plant is seriously infested, particularly with aphids or spider mites, a soapy water swirl bath is the treatment of choice. Houseplants (with the exception of African violets, cacti, and plants with hairy leaves and stems) have a definite advantage over garden plants in that they can be unceremoniously picked up, turned upside down, and dunked into containers of water. Secure the soil in the pot by covering it with plastic, aluminum foil, crumpled newspapers, or a towel.

Use a container large enough to dip the plant into it without breaking off its stems. Fill with water and add liquid soap at a ratio of two tablespoons to one gallon of water. Turn the plant upside down and swish it around in the soapy water for several minutes, drowning, killing, or otherwise discouraging the bugs. Rinse the plant, using your fingers to rub the undersides of leaves to displace any holdouts and send them down the drain.

This is particularly effective for thrips, barely visible pests that leave little brown specks of excrement and streaked areas on the leaves. Dips also spell doom for aphids, spider mites, and some scale.

A stronger dip can be made by taking a couple of cigarettes (or pouch tobacco), breaking them up, soaking them in water for a few days, and then adding the nicotine liquid to the soapy water.

If spider mites on a houseplant are being really stubborn about departing, try a dip made by adding a tablespoon of salt to a gallon of warm water. Another dip for mites is made by mixing two cups of buttermilk into a gallon of water. Dip the plant in this solution and let it remain on the leaves overnight before rinsing it off.

Spider mites (and thrips) prefer a dry habitat, so misting plants often with a squirt bottle will create an inhospitable environment. If the plants do have mites, use a strong jet of water to dislodge them and their webs. These tiny pests spread very easily, so wash your hands before going to the next plant.

Other Tactics Mealybugs are one of the commonest houseplant pests and, if not checked, one of the most destructive. To kill them, take a pipe cleaner or paintbrush dipped in rubbing alcohol (or fingernail polish remover) and swab it onto each one, being careful not to touch the plant. Alcohol kills pests because it penetrates the outer membrane, drying them to death. You can also mix equal parts of water and rubbing alcohol in a spray bottle and spray it on the plant.

Pick off scale or mealybugs with a toothpick or pointed knife, or dislodge them with a small sponge or toothbrush.

Another noxious treatment involves putting the infested plant into a plastic bag and blowing cigarette smoke into the opening before sealing it. Victorian greenhouses used to have "smoking cabinets" for these nicotine treatments.

At the least disturbance, whiteflies take to the wing. It can be very satisfying to vacuum them out of the air. You can buy yellow sticky traps for whiteflies. Or take a piece of bright yellow plastic, such as a ruler or child's toy, coat it with a solution of two parts petroleum jelly to one part liquid soap, and stick it in the soil, or if possible hang it above the plant for an easy trap. Give the plant a little thump now and then to force the flies into the air; they will most often come back down and land on the trap.

Catch thrips and fungus gnats in these same traps by placing them flat on the soil. Thrips are also attracted to the color blue. To kill the larvae of fungus gnats, which really do the damage, use a neem insecticide or Bti drench. Don't overwater.

If you prefer that others do the dirty work, you can order predators for houseplant pests. For instance, you can get mealybug destroyers to deal with mealybugs, or ladybird beetles for aphids (see *Good Bugs*). Tent the plants in fine netting so that the predators stay in place. Use stakes to hold the netting off the plant. It only takes a few predators for an average-size plant, so the rest of those purchased can be released outdoors. When all the pests have been eaten, don't let the predators on the houseplant starve; turn them loose in the garden to carry on the good work.

LICE

Among schoolchildren, head lice spread faster than the flu. To parents, their presence can come as a painful shock. For everyone involved, getting rid of them is a formidable task. There are no shortcuts when it comes to hunting down and eradicating lice.

In the past few years, louse infestations among schoolchildren have escalated to almost epidemic proportions, vexing parents, school officials, and children alike. Some schools suffer repeated infestations, and many lice have developed a resistance to pesticidal shampoos.

Lice are universally despised—except perhaps by monkeys, who eat them. Wherever warm-blooded mammals and birds live on this earth, these tiny, bloodsucking parasites live on them. Koalas are one of the few animals who do not get lice. Interestingly, they eat a lot of eucalyptus leaves.

There are thousands of species of lice, divided into biting and sucking varieties. We humans have three kinds—head, body, and crab lice. They are all sucking lice—demeaning, demoralizing, and tormenting. Calling someone a louse is the epitome of contempt.

Believed to be descended from ancient sucking bugs that had wings, lice may have been with us right from the beginning. Certainly, they accompanied Egyptian mummies to their tombs. Clay tablets dating from 2500 B.C. document a Sumerian doctor prescribing sulfur for use on crab lice. Perhaps the sense of shame we feel about lice comes from the fact that we've battled them so long but are still losing.

Although we do very well without lice, they cannot survive without us. Away from the human body, a louse lives only a few days. They even have color adaptation to us—lice on brunettes tend to be darker, those on blonds quite pale. About one-fifth of an inch long, lice are just thin enough to pass between hairs. Their bodies consist mostly of a big abdomen. Like most insects, they are exquisitely adapted to their manner of getting nourishment. With three sharp stylets around the mouth, they drill into the skin and suck out blood. They don't gorge themselves the way fleas and mosquitoes do; rather, they feed over and over. A growing louse will feed every one to two hours, making a new puncture and causing new irritation and itching each time. Its anticoagulant saliva causes the itching and burning and, of course, scratching. Scratching in turn can cause more bleeding (which the louse feeds on) and secondary infections.

Lice do not make everyone itch, however. Perhaps evolution is favoring those forms that cause less of an allergic reaction to their saliva. Also, sometimes it takes a few weeks for a person to develop a sensitized reaction. And people who have no idea they have lice can easily spread them to others.

Climate doesn't matter to lice, because human beings are the perfect temperature for them—except when we die or get a fever. Then lice abandon us.

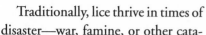

(Left) Body louse; (right) crab louse

Traditionally, lice thrive in times of disaster—war, famine, or other catastrophes, when people are forced to live in close quarters without bathing or changing clothes. Because body lice are carriers of typhus, as well as trench fever and relapsing fever, their presence during these times has amplified the prevailing misery and mortality.

Nicknamed "cooties" in World War I and "motorized" or "mechanized dandruff" in World War II, lice have always been a fact of military life. In World War II, more than three-fifths of U.S. army toilets had signs posted: "For those with crabs." When Napoleon invaded Russia in 1812, he did so with an army of 500,000 men; only 3,000 men returned. Most of the soldiers had fallen to typhus, spread by body lice. In fact, World War II was perhaps the first major war in which man succeeded in killing more people than typhus did.

Body lice and **head lice** look alike, but their behavior differentiates them. Body lice have adapted to living in clothing, and they lay their eggs in the folds and seams of clothing, thus the name "seam squirrels." Dirty, continuously worn clothing can harbor large populations of lice. But lice are vulnerable to showers and washing machines.

Head lice live on the head, using the grasping claws of all six legs to keep a firm, tenacious grasp on their host's hair. Scratching doesn't dislodge them, and neither does bathing. They actually prefer clean hair. A female louse lives only about a month, but she can lay up to 100 eggs, or nits, a day. She cements these nits securely onto the host's hair, right near the scalp. No known chemical will safely dissolve their cement. The eggs hatch after a week or so, but the empty shell remains on the hair. You can tell how long ago an egg was laid by how far up it is on the hair shaft.

Crab or **pubic lice**, an entirely different species, carry their own stigma, choosing as they do to live "down there," but they are the most innocuous of the three kinds of lice. Their viselike claws give them a resemblance to tiny crabs. Crab lice can be spread by sexual contact—in France they have been called "the butterfly of love" (*papillon d'amour*). Their victims suffer real embarrassment, but these lice have never been considered responsible for spreading any disease.

Do not use treatments that contain lindane. Crab lice can be treated fairly easily without using pesticides that are known to be harmful. Live ones can be killed by a good long soak in a hot bath. Shaving the body hair of the affected area will get rid of the nits. Special combs to remove crabs and their eggs are also available. Be sure to launder all clothing and bed linens in hot water.

▶ CONTROL

Millions of schoolchildren come home each year infested with head lice. According to the National Pediculosis Association, a nonprofit organization devoted to this scourge, the reason for the endemic state of head lice among children today is the lack of a standardized approach to prevent it. This, coupled with the widespread abuse and misuse of chemicals, and the resistance lice have developed to pesticides, has made lice a major headache for parents of schoolchildren.

Lice do not jump or fly, but they easily pass from child to child through head-to-head contact and are transmitted via hats, brushes, scarves, collars of jackets, athletic helmets, headphones, upholstered furniture, sheets, pillows, bus seats, and other louse "bridges." In vehicles and movie theaters, children's heads often come in contact with the seats, which may be another reason why so many children acquire lice.

Children bring lice home and spread them to the rest of the family. A school can be reinfested over and over again if just a few families neglect to take care of the problem at home. Admittedly, it can be a lot of work, but it can be done successfully in a nontoxic manner.

Shaving the head or treating it with kerosene used to be a common treatment. Today one of the more disastrous approaches has been to coat the head with Vaseline, which proves to be a child's worst icky nightmare. Perhaps misunderstanding the word, one woman doused her child's head in gasoline, whereupon the vapor burst into flame from a pilot light.

Nit Patrol   Given the magnitude of the lice problem, checking for nits on children should become a part of everyone's regular household routine. Since many schools are adopting a "no nits policy," this will also keep children from being sent home.

Under a strong light, closely examine the hair. A magnifying glass helps, but good eyesight often suffices. The nits, or eggs, look like pieces of oval dandruff attached at an angle, right on the hair shaft. Unlike with dandruff, passing the hair between your nails will not dislodge them. Adult lice, either pale or brown, are about the size of a sesame seed and move fast.

The National Pediculosis Association (NPA) recommends avoiding all insecticidal treatments. We agree. Strains of lice have evolved that are now resistant to these insecticides. Furthermore, it is appalling to think of a pesticide being applied to the fine skin of children's heads, especially when pores may have been opened by warm water, making its absorption into the bloodstream more possible. In their frantic zeal to get rid of lice, people have been known to exceed the recommended duration and frequency of applications. Lindane, for years commonly prescribed, is a chlorinated hydrocarbon. Its toxicity is equal to or greater than that of DDT, and it can cause convulsions, seizures, and brain damage. Although considered much safer, pyrethrum is often mixed with toxic synergists and solvents. Furthermore, when insecticides kill live lice, they don't always kill 100 percent of the eggs.

The best way to eliminate the problem is to sit the child down in a strong light and use a special louse comb to comb lice and nits out of the hair. Think of it as a chance for quality time with your child. The NPA advocates using a comb called the LiceMeister, which users say really works. After removing all tangles, systematically part the hair into small sections and run the comb through it from scalp to ends. Clean lice and nits from the comb by dipping it in water after each pass. Look carefully for live lice scurrying around the head. Some people recommend coconut oil, olive oil, or other vegetable oil to facilitate the process. It can be shampooed out afterward. Then blow dry the hair.

Soak combs and brushes in very hot water for thirty minutes.

Look daily for more nits. Repeat the combing if necessary. The aim is to eliminate them one and all.

Since lice can survive a day or two away from the head, launder all bedding and clothing that has been worn recently. Vacuum thoroughly, including blankets, upholstered furniture (don't miss the backs), pillows, mattresses, helmets, car seats, and headrests. Seal in plastic bags for at least two weeks any bedding, pillows, and toys that can't be washed or vacuumed.

Every member of the family must be checked and treated if necessary.

▶ *PREVENTION*

- Vigilance is the best defense. Be alert for frequent head scratching.
- Conduct a nit patrol on the entire family at least once a week.
- Teach children not to borrow one another's combs, hats, scarves, and headphones.
- Make sure each child has his or her own coat hook, cubby, locker, or sleeping mat at daycare or school.
- Immediately clean clothes taken out of the lost-and-found.
- Be supportive of a "no nits policy" at your child's school. It has proven to be most effective.
- Check the National Pediculosis Association Web site for updates (www.headlice.org).

Note: If reading this material has left you scratching your head uncontrollably, don't worry. *Delusory parasitosis* is a genuine condition. People who have it fervently insist that microscopic insects of some sort or other are biting them without mercy. They even develop welts, rashes, and, of course, scabs. The suffering of these people is certainly genuine, but usually no insects can be found. We seem to be as vulnerable to our feelings about insects as we are to their feedings.

MOSQUITOES

First the good news: only half the mosquito population sucks human blood. The males of the species do quite well on nectar alone. Females, however, need the protein from a good meal of blood to develop and lay their eggs. If they don't get it, the only way they can lay viable eggs is to consume their own wing muscles.

The female half of the mosquito population has been responsible for some of the most dreaded and deadly diseases known to humankind. Before the twentieth century, one of every two deaths may have been due to diseases transmitted by mosquitoes. In the Spanish-American War, for instance, 400 Americans were killed in battle, while 4,000 were killed by yellow fever—called yellow jack—carried by mosquitoes.

Although we have succeeded in freeing ourselves from the constant companionship of fleas and body lice, the battle against mosquitoes is far from over. More deadly than sharks, snakes, and grizzly bears, they cause millions of fatalities a year. In 1996, the World Health Organization declared them to be "the greatest menace" of all disease-transmitting insects. They spread malaria, yellow fever, dengue fever, and encephalitis, all of which are on the rise. Every year, 300 million cases of malaria, mostly in Africa, result in as many as 3 million deaths. Although once eradicated in this country, malaria has recently reappeared.

More than 3,400 mosquito species exist in the world. The word "mosquito" comes from the Spanish for "little fly." Delicate, slender, lightweight members of the fly order, mosquitoes weigh in at $\frac{1}{25,000}$ of an ounce. A mosquito is so adept, it can fly through a rain shower dodging individual raindrops, and so light, it can stand on water without getting wet. It can alight on your skin without arousing a tactile response.

Mosquitoes may have a light touch, but it's a cruel one. The female mosquito punctures your skin and steals blood by using a piercing sucking mouthpart (proboscis) with six stylets, four of which cut the skin, while the remaining two form a tube that draws up the blood. A duct in the tube secretes saliva as she sucks, increasing the blood flow and keeping it from clotting, thus allowing her to extract blood as quickly as possible. Her saliva causes an allergic reaction on the skin and the subsequent torments of itching. It also transmits viruses and germs from person to person.

After sucking up three or four times her weight in blood, the female goes to find water on which to lay her eggs. Different species prefer different bodies of water: tidal marshes, ponds, tree boles or holes, swamps, or irrigation ditches. For some species, any small undisturbed body of water (preferably stagnant) will do—a hoofprint with a little water in it,

Mosquito, larva, and pupa

a pothole, an empty snail shell, or an old tin can. In fact, old tires do so well that the millions of used ones piled up all over the world are major mosquito breeding grounds. Our throwaway lifestyle has been a great boon to this minuscule enemy of ours.

In the water, mosquito eggs hatch in just a few days. The mosquitoes will spend the next two stages of their metamorphosis in the water as wrigglers (larvae) and tumblers (pupae), but breathing air. That is why spreading oil on the water suffocates the young.

Of the 150 species of mosquito in North America, most painful is the bite of some of the **Aedes** species; they gave New Jersey the nickname "The Mosquito State." The *Aedes* mosquito, which can carry yellow fever, dengue fever, and dengue hemorrhagic fever, holds itself parallel to the surface on which it has landed, with its butt down.

The Asian tiger mosquito, a particularly aggressive *Aedes* mosquito, has spread to twenty-five states since its introduction in 1985, thanks to its affinity for breeding in used tires. Their black bodies with white stripes, along with their potential for transmitting dengue fever and encephalitis, have earned them the nickname tiger mosquitoes. They are fast, skittish, persistent, and annoying predators, and they attack during daylight hours without the characteristic warning whine of other mosquitoes.

The **Anopheles** mosquito transmits malaria, a debilitating and even fatal disease. It has very long legs and imbibes blood with its butt up in the air, often nearly at a 90° angle.

The **Culex**, our commonest house mosquito, transmits encephalitis, which is on the rise in this country, and dog heartworm. It rests with its body completely parallel to the surface. *Culex* mosquitoes commonly feed on birds as well as humans.

▶ CONTROL INDOORS

Almost everyone has listened with dread to the disquieting, high whine of a mosquito on the prowl in the bedroom. Like fleas, mosquitoes are sensitive to the carbon dioxide animals give off. They can also sense the moist, warm air around a potential victim and seem to be able to differentiate between chemical blood contents, showing definite preferences for one person over another.

To keep mosquitoes out of the house, make sure that every window has a screen and that every screen is in good repair. Screen doors should always open outward. Planting tansy or basil near doorways or even around outdoor patios helps create a mosquito barrier. Using a yellow "bug light" outside a doorway will, in addition to attracting fewer moths, also help keep mosquitoes from coming inside. They do best in darkness or dim light.

Remember, mosquitoes can breed anywhere. In your house they could be breeding in flower vases, houseplant saucers, even fishbowls and aquariums.

To drive mosquitoes out of a room, open a bottle of pennyroyal or oil of citronella. Camping-supply stores carry citronella candles that are very effective.

Mosquitoes also dislike blowing air, so a fan can be used to keep them away.

▶ CONTROL OUTDOORS

As with other major pests that threaten human health, mosquitoes have been the object of a tremendous onslaught of pesticides, beginning with DDT (to which they are now mostly immune). More than $100 million is spent annually to control mosquitoes in North America, often adding pernicious toxins to the environment.

Successful mosquito control means limiting their aquatic breeding areas. Getting rid of all sources of standing water amounts to a civic duty. Make a habit of looking out for all possible reservoirs of stagnant water, from tin cans and watering cans to wading pools and gutters. All it takes is a pint to nurture 500 wrigglers. Fill in holes in trees and stumps. Refill birdbaths with water every few days. Change your pet's water daily. If you have a rain barrel, make sure it is covered. Many species look for blood no farther than a couple of hundred feet from where they developed.

If you can't empty out the container, add a little soap or neem oil or oil formulated for mosquito control to the water to keep wrigglers from getting out alive.

Effective biological alternatives now exist. One of the most successful, *Bacillus thuringiensis israelensis* (Bti), kills mosquitoes without harming humans or the environment. It can provide complete killing in twenty-four hours, but since it only lasts for about three days, it needs to be reapplied periodically. Garlic oil can also be used for biocontrol— the active ingredient in garlic, allyl sulfide, kills mosquitoes. Another biological control, Laginex, contains a naturally occurring water-mold fungus and controls mosquitoes safely for three to four weeks.

Many areas of the United States have set up mosquito abatement districts, which will supply you with a mosquito-eating fish, *Gambusia*, for ponds, ornamental water gardens, and other possible breeding sites. These tiny fish are only two and a half inches long, but they are tremendous mosquito eaters and are being bred specifically for this purpose in numerous fish hatcheries. In cold climates they need to be restocked annually. You can also buy goldfish, minnows, guppies, or backswimmers (insects) for your garden and put them in a pond or rain barrel. These fish are fairly hearty and don't require any special care, except for some protection from predators, like a segment of pipe to hide in. Don't put them in bodies of water where native fish live.

You can buy excellent electrocution mosquito traps, with lights to attract, fans to suck them in, and screens to keep out bigger beneficials. Some even come with a scent that mimics cow's breath. You can use pieces of dry ice, which gives off CO_2, as an attractant. Do not buy zappers that kill all flying insects indiscriminately.

Encourage mosquito predators in your yard. Praying mantises, birds (purple martins especially), frogs, turtles, lizards, ants, spiders, and dragonflies eat mosquitoes. Bats are superb mosquito eaters. Many reports of bat attacks may really be bats swooping down to expertly pick off a mosquito zeroing in on a person. In the research station on Santa Cruz Island off Santa Barbara, California, a bat makes nightly foraging trips above the bunks of sleeping scientists.

Repellents   A backwoodsman in the 1880s wrote of his infallible mixture of pine tar, castor oil, and pennyroyal oil, claiming, "I have never known it to fail. A good safe coat of this varnish grows better the longer it is kept on."

If you are getting attacked at night, try eating a dinner prepared with garlic. Rubbing apple cider vinegar on exposed skin is said to deter mosquitoes for a short while. Some people crush fresh parsley and rub it on their skin. One of the great insect repellents is Avon's Skin-So-Soft. Some people won't travel anywhere without it.

Here is a formula that people in Alaska swear by, including one man who'd looked for a good repellent for forty years. (Alaska is where they say the mosquitoes are so big they show up at the airport for refueling.)

    1 cup Avon Skin-So-Soft bath oil
    1 cup water
    1 tablespoon eucalyptus oil

This works for ticks too. Without making any claims for the effectiveness of Skin-So-Soft bath oil as an insect repellent, Avon now markets a whole line of Skin-So-Soft insect repellents, including moisturizer and sunblock formulations.

The most successful commercial repellents contain a chemical compound known as DEET (N,N-diethyl-meta-toluamide). It is a powerful chemical. Parents are warned not to use concentrations stronger than 10 percent on children. Labels warn: "Do not let children rub eyes." Some people say it should never be put on skin, only on clothing and tents. It causes rashes, dissolves plastics, ruins zippers, melts cameras and watches, even dissolves the handles of Swiss Army knives. Does this sound safe? It isn't; it has been known to cause convulsions, seizures, and death.

Alternative repellents include peppermint, vanilla, bay, clove, sassafras, and cedar. However, products containing citronella, pennyroyal, eucalyptus, geranium oil, and neem have been given the best ratings. They have to be applied more frequently than DEET. They come in candles, lotions, sprays, and wrist bands.

Adult mosquitoes hunt at night, especially around dusk and at dawn.

If you're having an evening barbecue, try tossing citrus peels or herbs like sage and rosemary on the coals to repel the mosquitoes. Set an oscillating fan on the patio. Or light citronella candles, mosquito coils, or incense containing myrrh.

PANTRY PESTS

Nothing is quite as distressing as opening a package of food and discovering that little creatures have claimed it for their own. It is especially annoying when you lift the lid after you have cooked rice or cereal and see little wormy fragments and insect parts.

For years, many grain products were routinely fumigated with chemicals now banned from use. A widely used fumigant, methyl bromide, is known to be highly toxic. Even packaging materials have sometimes been treated with insecticides. These are all part of the invisible toxic tide our culture swims in.

Today, however, there are many options for nontoxic pest controls, including cooling, using pathogens such as *Bacillus thuringiensis* (Bt) to infect the pests with diseases, new kinds of packaging that keep insects out, and insect growth regulators that put an end to their reproductive feats. Pheromone lure traps—which use the sex attractants of the insects themselves—are available for detection and control of pests in stored food.

COMMON CULPRITS

Mediterranean and Indian Meal Moths   These two moths are fairly similar in looks and habits. If you have them in your food, you will see them flying around the kitchen at night. Not attracted to light, they are fairly small, light brown moths with a somewhat slower flight pattern than other moths. You think you can smack them between your palms, but they easily evade you. (It's the air current you create that blows them away.) The moths themselves eat hardly at all, but the females can lay 300 to 350 eggs apiece, and their hatched larvae—wormy little creatures—eat your food. They'll go for anything dried: soups, nuts, rice, flours, grains, seeds, crackers, candy, chocolate, dried fruit, red peppers, tobacco, and pet food.

If you see the moths, find their food source and get rid of it. Look for fine silk threads the larvae spin as they eat. These threads cause the food particles to clump or mat together, especially along the sides of the package. In the past, eating "weavilly" food was considered normal, but we do not recommend it.

Carpet Beetles   Carpet beetles can also be pests of stored food. See *Clothes Moths and Carpet Beetles.*

Weevils   Weevils are beetles with long snouts that get into grains and seeds. The weevil has a pair of mandibles at the tip of its snout. With these, it eats an opening into a seed and then deposits an egg, which hatches into a larva that eats out the inside of the seed, leaving the shell intact.

Grain weevil on a grain of wheat

Flour Beetles   Found even in the tombs of the pharaohs, flour beetles eat all kinds of grains, crackers, beans, peas, chocolate, spaghetti, dried fruit, and nuts. They are tiny—from one-tenth to one-half an inch long. The commonest ones are the red flour beetle and the confused flour beetle, perhaps so named because we get confused trying to distinguish it from the other beetle. Both are rust red and quite abundant.

The sad thing about them for us is that they need absolutely no water. They lay sticky eggs that become covered with flour and adhere to the sides of containers. These hatch into grubs (called bran bugs), which feed, grow, and then crawl to the surface of the food, where they form white pupae.

If you find them in your food, throw it away—they excrete a vile-smelling chemical that discolors and contaminates the food.

Mealworms   "Mealworm" is one of the names for the larvae of the flour, darkling, or false wireworm beetle. The adults are shiny black or brown, while the larvae are yellow to yellowish brown. They live in flour, grains, or cereal and do well in all kinds of conditions from very dry to moist. They are most commonly found in areas with poor sanitation where flour or grains have fallen to the floor and been ignored.

Pet stores raise mealworms as food for turtles, toads, fish, and birds. We haven't heard of anyone keeping a turtle in the kitchen to control them, however.

Drugstore Beetles Sometimes called bread beetles, these insects are colored brown or rust brown and are covered in fine hair. They have often been found in stale bread, but they were named initially because they infested the dried medicinal plants once sold in drugstores. They also ate some drugs. In the home, they feed on paprika, hot spices, dried beans, and cereals. They also get into books and leather. In fact, it has been said that these bugs will eat anything except cast iron, including aluminum foil and lead sheathing.

Cigarette Beetles These beetles are little, reddish brown, and, like the drugstore beetle, have fine hair. From the side, they appear to be humpbacked. Deprived of tobacco, they feed on just about anything, including dog food, paprika, wool, hair, cloth, books, and even some insecticides. If you have a problem with these beetles, buy your spices in glass bottles, not in metal cans.

Saw-Toothed Grain Beetles The midsection, or thorax, of this little brown beetle has sawlike projections protruding on each side. They attack all kinds of food, especially grain and grain products, dried fruit, nuts, candies, and powdered milk.

▶ CONTROL

If you are not sure what kind of pest you have, capture one and put it in a container in the freezer to kill it. Then take it to your county agricultural agent or local natural history museum for help in identifying it.

If you do have an infestation, take out all your stored food and throw away anything that looks suspicious. Don't just dump it in the kitchen garbage, because food storage pests are quite mobile and will go from the garbage back to the shelves. If you are not sure if the food is infested, put it in the freezer for a week.

Once you have examined and removed all infested food, do a thorough cleaning of the area where the food has been stored, because these pests seek out corners and crevices to lay their eggs. Some larvae also crawl away from the food to pupate elsewhere, so vacuuming is essential. Washing with a wet cloth creates paste-filled cracks—future food sources for pests.

Shelves—particularly the cracks—can then be dusted with diatomaceous earth or silica aerogel or pyrethrin to kill the insects as they crawl around in it. As always, use a mask and goggles when applying dusts.

Diatomaceous earth can also be added to stored food to kill pests. We have added it generously to a container of brown rice and left it open in the hope that they would go to it first. A quick shake of the rice in a sieve removes most of the diatomaceous earth, but it is safe to consume in any case and is fed to animals to control parasites.

The Chill Factor   When you first bring grains home, put them in the freezer for a week to kill any hitchhikers. Big grain and flour companies, such as Arrowhead Mills, which are committed to selling nonfumigated and nonpesticide-treated food, have found that if they store their grains at 40°F, they can keep pests out. Store commonly infested food, such as whole wheat flour, in the refrigerator.

People who store large bags of grains recommend using large plastic trash cans and putting down a layer of dry ice on the bottom. As the ice evaporates, they keep the lid ajar; then, when the ice has dissipated, they close it tight. The CO_2, being heavier than air, remains inside, creating an oxygen-free (and therefore pest-free) environment.

Heat Treatment   Treat infested food with heat by putting it in the oven at 135° to 140° for thirty minutes. Spread the product out on cookie sheets to distribute the heat evenly. Use a thermometer to gauge the temperature of the oven. Some ovens are hot enough with just the pilot light. With others, you may need to prop the door open with the stove set at warm to keep it from getting too hot, which destroys some of the nutrients.

Drop infested dried fruit into boiling water to kill bugs.

Traps   Pantry moths are not attracted to light, but you can find a number of effective traps in garden stores or order them through the mail. These sticky traps contain pheromone lures specifically attractive to different pests, along with sticky traps for catching them. They are most effective if hung near the ceiling.

As a general rule, try to keep as little stored food on hand as possible. Look out for the opened box that has been sitting in the back of the cupboard for months.

Insects do not like to be disturbed. An old-fashioned way of keeping weevils out of grain was to shift the grain by turning the bags upside down in the storage room. Other storage facilities make a regular habit of stirring or agitating the grain. When you rummage through your own pantry, pick up boxes or containers and give them a good thump.

The cooler and drier the storage area, the fewer the pests. You may not be able to lower the temperature, but you can buy dehumidifiers, such as silica gel, from hardware stores and keep them where you store your food.

▶ **PREVENTION**

One of the favorite methods we have come across for keeping pests out of stored food dates back to classical times. Before a storage room was filled with grain, a toad was tied by the leg to the door, where it apparently stood sentinel against encroaching bugs. We have found that when we leave the long-legged spiders in our panty alone, we have less of a problem with meal moths.

Bay leaves are a well-known repellent for pantry pests. For years people have put them around their shelves or placed a leaf right in the storage container with the flour. Fenugreek and rhizomes (roots) of turmeric have also been used in other countries. Another technique is unwrapping sticks of spearmint gum and putting them on the shelves.

Remember that repellents do not kill the bugs. We think people tend to underestimate the power of a repellent, however. They prefer to go for the big kill, when sometimes a deterrent is all it takes to keep the bugs away in the first place.

The Department of Agriculture's Stored Products Research Laboratory in Savannah, Georgia, has done studies indicating that coriander, dill, cinnamon, lemon peel, and black pepper repel or kill some insects found in stored grains. These can also be sprinkled on your shelves.

Put black pepper into foods that you would normally pepper anyway—flour you plan to use for gravy or rice, for instance. Black pepper will actually kill the pests. A USDA researcher discovered that 500 parts per million of black pepper killed 97 percent of the weevils present in wheat.

Many pests of stored food can be found in the nests of birds and rodents. Eliminate these from the vicinity of the house. If a bird builds its nest under the eaves of your house, its mites and other pests can become your pests too. Dead rodents also attract these pests, as well as clothes moths. Rather than poisoning rodents, trap them and dispose of them immediately, so that they don't die in places where beetles and moths will come after them.

Inspect all packages carefully before you bring them home from the store. Some of these pests lay their eggs under the flaps of packages, so look for loose seals. Inspect boxes for the tiny holes insects have used to gain entry to the food.

When you get food home, put it in bug-resistant containers, inspecting it as you do so. We like heavy plastic sealable freezer bags. Look for clumps that cling to the sides of the package. Some of these pests produce unpleasant odors. Since some pests can even crawl around the grooves of screw-top jars to get to the food, use glass jars with rubber seals.

Quarantine packages you're not sure about. Put them into plastic bags and keep an eye on them for a week or so. Treat them with heat or freezing.

RATS AND MICE

RATS

Rats have adapted so successfully to a lifestyle entwined with ours that we can hardly call them wild animals. Just like us, they are both intrepid travelers and house dwellers. Quintessential freeloaders, they eat our food, give us their diseases, live in our homes, and skulk about the premises. The more we try to beat them back, the more they are with us. From luxury liners to city sewers, if we build it, they move in.

Rats can reproduce at prodigious rates and endure incredible physical challenges. In a year, a rat can have between 30 and 80 offspring, depending on the species—one pair could generate 15,000 rats in their life span. Described as "more cunning than man," a rat can fall fifty feet with no injury (it flattens its body for resistance and lands on its feet), climb a pipe only an inch and a half in diameter, squeeze through a hole the size of a quarter, tread water for three days, dig four feet straight underground, and survive an atomic bomb test. Is it any wonder we can't get rid of them?

Rats and mice destroy tons of food, causing millions of dollars in damage each year. By urinating and defecating in food, they ruin vastly more than they eat, and it has been estimated that they destroy 20 percent of the world's food supply every year. Although their favorite food is grain, they survive beautifully on anything we eat and can even subsist on manure and urine. Rats are compelled to gnaw to wear down their constantly growing incisors, and they can chew through bone, wood, plaster, brick, asphalt, and metal.

Rats (and mice) chewing through the insulation in wires probably cause a majority of unexplained fires. They bite thousands of people every year, most often small children, and they spread at least thirty-five diseases, including typhus, salmonellosis, dysentery, Lassa fever, tapeworm, hookworm, rat bite fever, LCM virus (a form of meningitis), and bubonic plague. No wonder they have been called the "lapdogs of the devil."

The **Norway rat**, also called the brown rat, gray rat, wharf rat, sewer rat, or wander rat, is the most pervasive species in the United States. A large (seven to ten inches), aggressive specimen, it prefers urban areas, likes water and damp places, and lives at ground level or underground in burrows and sewers. Its tail is shorter than its body.

The **roof rat**, or black rat, also called the house rat, ship rat, and "bare-tail squirrel," is a great climber and lives in dense vegetation, trees, vines, and attics, liking coastal towns and rural areas. This agile rat infested ships, exploiting its ability to climb ropes. It uses its tail, which is longer than its body, almost as a fifth leg. Also called the plague rat, this is the nefarious rat that carried the Black Death, or "Sword of God," in the fourteenth century, killing 25 million people in Europe alone.

MICE

Our feelings about mice are so convoluted that it is not unusual to find little pet mice tenderly nurtured in cages in the kids' room, while the parents put out mousetraps in the kitchen.

The word "mouse" is said to be cognate with the Sanskrit word *musha*, which means "to steal." This clearly describes its nighttime forages among our food supplies. Despite its fragile frame, dreadful eyesight, and delicate little legs, this tiny mammal has managed to extend its habitat all over the world, finding homes in the depths of English coal mines as well as the tops of Hawaiian volcanoes. As Richard Conniff wrote: "The Bible says the meek shall inherit the Earth. The house mouse is living proof that they already have."

The reproductive capabilities of this "mammalian weed" are almost explosive, an evolutionary response to the fact that mice are a staple food for so many predators, from skunks and foxes to snakes and birds. A female starts to bear young at around six to eight weeks and thereafter can have a litter of four to six babies every four weeks.

Unlike rats, mice can and do live quite independently of humans outdoors. Among the many species of this little creature—deer mouse, meadow mouse (vole), Mickey Mouse, and harvest mouse, to name a few—the house mouse is by far the most prevalent.

The outbreak of deadly hantavirus in 1993 in the United States called attention to the danger of mice. The virus is contracted by stirring up and inhaling dust contaminated by mouse droppings, mainly those of deer mice. Mice carry numerous other diseases as well.

▶ CONTROL

Many of the methods for dealing with rats and mice are similar. Nevertheless, it is important to determine whether you have a rat or a mouse problem. It is unlikely that you have both: rats kill mice, and it has even been suggested that placing several rats in cages around the premises will prompt the departure of all mice.

Most people realize that they have a problem when they hear sounds of scampering and scraping in the ceiling or walls at night. Or they may find droppings, gnawed wood, or even dirty smudge marks along the rodents' runways. Or the cats and dogs may start acting strangely around the house. If you actually see a rodent, it may mean that the infestation is large.

You can tell if your problem is rats or mice principally by the size of their droppings, since those of mice are considerably smaller, about a quarter of an inch long (like a grain of rice), while rat droppings are from one-half to three-quarters of an inch in size. If the droppings are fresh, they will be shiny and black. Any gnawing or bites taken from fruit or butter will reveal the size of the rodents' teeth. If you are still not sure, put a fine sprinkling of odorless talc on the floor and then analyze the footprints, which may also lead you to the nest. Rats generally leave tracks that are approximately three inches across, while mice leave tracks that are half an inch wide.

Never handle a dead rat or mouse with your bare hands. Getting infected by a disease and acquiring the rodent's parasites (fleas, lice, and mites) are very real dangers. Use gloves, along with tongs or a shovel. Put dead rodents in sealed plastic bags to trap the parasites.

Poisons Rats have been fed poisons by the ton. Since the 1950s, warfarin has been the chief rodent poison used worldwide. An anticoagulant that causes internal bleeding, it has been popular because if it is ingested by humans or animals, an antidote (vitamin K) can prevent a fatality. Eventually, some rats and mice developed a genetic immunity to it; strains of "superrats" can now survive a dose 100 times stronger than what was once enough to kill one. Newer formulations of anticoagulant poisons (Quintox) or activated forms of vitamin D (Rampage) are being used with success. In small doses, these are not toxic to other mammals, and they are considered even less toxic to humans. They may take a week or longer to work.

However, besides breeding resistant rodents, many poisons and fumigants present definite drawbacks to people and other animals. They cause rats and mice to die in the walls of buildings, where they attract flies, carpet beetles, and moths. The stench can also be offensive, and the rat's parasites—fleas and mites—may move to people.

Nevertheless, poison can be an effective control. Get tamper-proof bait stations, which keep pets and kids out and give rats a cozy place to nibble, if you do decide to use poison. Patrol frequently for dead rodents. Sometimes flies will lead you to them.

Predators   Don't rely entirely on a cat to kill all the rodents, although it can be a good deterrent. Dogs have actually been the traditional rat killers—that is how rat terriers got their name. In England in the nineteenth century, these dogs were used in gruesome rat-killing contests in which bets were placed on which dog could kill the most rats in the least time. The rats that got away were used the next time. Think of them the next time you use the phrase "rat race."

Other predators that eat rodents include buzzards, ravens, snakes, skunks, and owls. In an effort to cut down on poisons (spurred on by the rats' immunity), New York City has tried building nesting boxes in its parks to attract families of barn owls, citing the fact that a family of six owls will consume from fifteen to eighteen rats per night.

Traps   After eliminating all food and water sources for rats and mice, trapping is the best way to exterminate them. It requires time, dexterity, and a certain dedication.

The search for a better mousetrap continues to inspire the imagination of inventors. Since 1838, thousands of patents for mousetraps have been registered in the United States. One of our favorites, the Ratapult, hurls the rat fifteen feet into a waiting cage or bucket—without hurting it! Another "humane" trap affixes a bell collar on a mouse, with the idea that it will scare all the other mice away. In Japan, the Ikaro Corporation has devised a system using pneumatic tubes. When a rat enters through a hole in the tube, a heat sensor closes the hole, and the rat is sucked through the tube into a freezer to a sanitary death and disposal.

Despite competition from traps that guillotine, harpoon, incinerate, and tranquilize, the standard snap trap is still holding its own. For best success with these snap traps, use a lot of them at once—twelve or more for a house and from five to ten where rodents are active. Although this costs more, it will be more effective, because once a rat springs a trap without getting caught, it will be exceedingly shy of it.

Mice are said to be eagerly inquisitive, but rats are suspicious of anything new. Outsmart them by baiting the traps for a few days without setting them so that the rats get used to feeding from them.

Set your traps where you find rodent droppings, as close to the nest as possible. Rodents follow a system of "runs" along walls, because they can't see well, and they mark the path with fairly constant urine dribbles. The urine will glow under ultraviolet light. For roof rats, the traps may need to be nailed onto tree trunks or vine-covered fence tops, where the rats are known to travel.

Traps should be set with the baited end closest to the wall. In tight spaces, a pair of traps can be set parallel to the wall, with the bait facing outward in opposite directions. Set two or three traps an inch apart for mice, and three inches for rats, so that if they leap over one, they may be caught by the next.

New traps can be left outdoors or buried to get rid of human smells, but coat the metal with vegetable oil to prevent rusting before you do this. When setting traps, use gloves to eliminate the human smell. Before reusing them, scrub the traps in soapy water, and then dip them in boiling water and rub them with a little vegetable oil.

Tiny game hunters have their own favorite baits, ranging from walnuts and peanut butter to bread and raw bacon. Gumdrops and dried fruit are said to entice mice. Norway rats like meat, such as hot dogs, whereas roof rats prefer fruit and nuts. In tribute to their dexterity, fasten the bait onto the trap with a little fine wire or thread. One person we know places new, unused traps in the toaster oven to melt the cheese in place. Sprinkle oatmeal around the trap to make it more enticing. Placing a piece of cardboard slightly bigger than the width of the trap under the bait holder will cause the trap to go off if a rat or mouse merely steps on it. Instead of food, a piece of fluffy cotton, string, or dental floss can be secured to the trap. Desiring it for nesting material, the mouse or rat will try to pull it off. Snap!

Some people bury their traps in pans of sawdust or cornmeal so that the rat doesn't even see them.

If a trap catches a rodent without killing it, use a shovel to pick it up and dump it into a bucket of soapy water (the soap kills the parasites).

Electrocution has been seen as a good means of rat control, because it is clean, fast, and humane. The Rat Zapper consists of a metal tunnel that the rat enters. When it steps on a plate, it is electrocuted. Battery-operated, and safe around children and pets, it even comes with an attachment that will dial your pager number if it catches a rat!

Glue boards are popular for rodent control, because they do not require the dexterity called for by spring traps. They work better for mice than for rats. Cruelty is not a good trade-off for convenience, however. The rodents often do not die quickly, and they may "worry" themselves to death. Don't use glue boards unless you are willing to check them very, very frequently and kill the victims yourself—by holding them under water or bashing their skulls.

Nonlethal live traps, such as Havahart traps, are readily available, simple to use, and easy on the conscience. Many of these traps (Ketch-All, Mouse Master, Tin Cat) will hold many mice. Once a curious mouse enters, others may follow to keep it company. (Mice trapped together, however, often begin eating one another.) You would need to release them several miles away (three for mice, five for rats), although this is illegal in California. Better yet, contact local wildlife organizations or pet stores, who are often in need of live food for snakes and birds.

To make your nonlethal trap, take a large stainless steel or glass bowl and smear it generously with butter. Place a little bait in the bottom and then improvise a couple of ramps leading up to the edge—small boards, books, toy tracks. The mouse will go down into the bowl for the food and be unable to escape because of the slippery sides. This is an especially good trap for pet mice, hamsters, and gerbils that have escaped from their cages.

In the past traps were made from barrels filled with water, with a layer of paper taped tightly over the top. A slit in the form of a cross was cut in the paper, right in the center, and some kind of bait was dangled above the slit. Going for the bait, the rat thinks the paper is secure, but it will fall through. *Dick's Encyclopedia of Practical Receipts and Processes* (1879) advises placing bait for several days on the paper without slitting it, "until they [the rats] begin to think they have a right to their daily rations from this source," and suggests putting a rock in the barrel, with room on it above the water for only one rat. The first rat that falls in will climb on the rock. When a second one falls in, a fight for the space on the rock will ensue, and the sound of the battle is said to be guaranteed to draw numerous other rats.

Electronic Sound Devices Most literature on the topic indicates that electronic sound devices for repelling rodents do not work well. Furthermore, they may be harmful to the ears of other animals or people. However, one person we know uses one in the basement of a Montana house that is empty for long stretches of time. He is not bothered by mice infestations, possibly because the device is used in a bare, open room and nothing obstructs the "sound" it emits. Newer devices, which emit a succession of varied sounds, may be more successful, because it has been discovered that rodents can get used to a single frequency. You need to have units or speakers in each room, however. Be sure to buy a device with a money-back guarantee.

▶ *PREVENTION*

Whenever poisons eliminate great numbers of rats, those remaining (for instance, on a neighbor's property) immediately step up their breeding and quickly restore the population. Since the limiting factor for rat populations is not death by poison but rather availability of food, water, and shelter, a rat problem is really a people problem. In fact, when food is less available, there's more competition and greater mortality among rats.

As the saying goes, "If you don't feed them, you don't breed them." This calls for good sanitation and careful control of garbage, which means changing human behavior.

Starve them out
- Indoors, all sources of food should be out of reach. Fruits and vegetables should not be left out on counters, and all stored food should be in rodent-proof metal or glass containers. When you discover you have rats or mice, keep as much food as possible in the refrigerator until they have been eliminated. Counters and floors should be clean and free of crumbs.
- Pet food and birdseed are plentiful sources of food for rodents. They should be stored at least eight inches off the floor in metal containers.
- Wash and put away pet dishes.
- Clean up below bird feeders. Install seed catchers and animal guards.
- If you have an avocado or other fruit tree, remove ripened fruit as soon as possible and clean frequently under the tree.
- Ideally, garbage should be stored in metal containers on platforms eighteen inches high. Keep dogs out of the garbage.
- Wood piles should be stored on raised platforms.

Build them out
When rodent proofing your home, remember that rats are the Houdinis of the pest world. They can jump three feet in the air and four feet across, easily traverse wires and cables, squeeze through minuscule holes, and swim up toilet traps.
- Any opening into a building, including holes for utility cables, basement windows, pipes entering the house, vents, and cracks in the foundation, should be rodent proofed with caulking, hardware cloth, steel wool, copper gauze, or metal barriers. All it takes is a quarter of an inch for mice, and half an inch for rats, to make themselves welcome.
- Make sure the bottoms of doors have metal kick plates or sweepers, and that doors close automatically.

- Screen air vents.
- Get rid of piles of newspapers and magazines, where rats or mice can make nests. Inspect storage closets, attics, and basements regularly. Storage boxes should be put on raised platforms at least twelve to eighteen inches high.
- Remove wood, debris, and weeds.
- Trim trees at least three feet away from buildings.
- Attach rat guards to the trunks of date palm trees—a favorite harborage. (These need to be replaced every year.)
- Pick up pet feces, a source of food for rodents. Get your community to enforce pooper scooper laws.
- Get rid of ivy. In Southern California, where the roof rat thrives, numerous fruit trees give it ample food to eat, and many popular ground covers provide perfect habitats. Large-leafed ivy also provides a habitat for one of their favorite foods: snails. Replace ivy with cape weed, chamomile (snails hate it too), Indian mock strawberry, carpet bugle (ajuga), gazanias, dichondra, creeping thyme, or creeping speedwell.

In an emergency, a rodent hole can be temporarily stuffed with a rag soaked in a strong mixture of cayenne and water. Rodents are also repelled by the smell of mint (especially peppermint), camphor, and pine tar. If you want to experiment with natural repellents, try baby powder or mustard powder. A product called Rat and Mouse Repellent claims to create an invisible barrier when sprinkled outside buildings. It has to be renewed every three months and will not get rid of any present tenants.

A TRIBUTE

We would be remiss if we did not acknowledge the 20 million rodents who give their lives to science each year. A recent search for "rats" on an academic database yielded the following topics: "memory," "brain function," "Parkinson's," "kidney disease," "addiction," "light perception," "glucose absorption," "breast cancer," and "spinal cord damage." This is but a minuscule portion of the research carried out on lab rats. In ways we can hardly imagine, many of us owe our very lives and health to them.

SILVERFISH

These pearly, primitive, wingless nibblers are thought to be relatives of the oldest six-legged creatures. They belong to an order named for its "fringe tails," three long filaments at the posterior end, but they get the name "silverfish" from their silvery, overlapping scales. These scales rub off easily if you touch them, giving the impression that this insect is greasy.

Silverfish move as if they were swimming. They slither and slide about, hiding between narrow cracks. Shy and retiring, they usually stay out of sight and do their scavenging at night. They arouse distaste in people, but they don't smell and they don't bite. Furthermore, they even get into ant and termite nests and eat their young.

Although they find house dust nutritious, and will even eat each other, they especially favor the starches we provide for them, particularly flour and the glue and sizing in books. They also eat wallpaper paste, postage stamp glue, and the coating on glossy paper. Because they nibble on linen, silk, cotton, and rayon, they are also sometimes called fish moths. In the days of starched collars, they could be a terrible problem.

Silverfish

Silverfish like damp basements but can get into all parts of the house. They can come in on building materials, damp wood, cardboard boxes, and used books. Contrary to popular opinion, they do not come up through the drain, but they can be found in bathtubs and basins, where they crawl in and can't get out. Very hardy, living as long as eight years, they build up in numbers close to a food source.

The firebrat, a close relative that is more gray than silver, prefers hotter temperatures and has been known to hang out around heating ducts, furnaces, hot-water pipes, summer attics, and bakeries.

▶ CONTROL

Look for these nocturnal creatures by night with a flashlight. To trap silverfish, buy or make sticky traps and bait them in the middle with oat-

Silverfish trap

meal or flour. Or take a small glass jar and wrap the outside with masking tape. Bait the jar with wheat flour and place it near stored papers or in a recessed corner. The silverfish climb up, drop inside, and can't get out.

Silverfish thrive in high humidity. Use light, cleanliness, and ventilation to eliminate them. If you find silverfish in your bookshelves, take out all the books and vacuum thoroughly. Use dehumidifiers or fans or put out bags of dehumidifying gels (available in hardware stores). Check for leaks and other causes of humidity. Infested books can be microwaved for thirty to sixty seconds or frozen for two days, sealed well in plastic to keep moisture out (these methods are not recommended for books with color photos).

Using boric acid, silica aerogel, or diatomaceous earth in cracks and crevices will kill silverfish, just as these products kill cockroaches. Stored books may benefit from being placed in a box that has been treated with one of these dusts. Take care not to inhale the dusts when using them— use a mask and goggles. Boric acid–impregnated packets made by Dekko can be conveniently spread around in out-of-the-way places.

Washing surfaces with a solution of Dr. Bronner's peppermint or eucalyptus soap may have a repellent effect. The herb santolina, sometimes called lavender cotton, can also be put among books to deter insects such as silverfish.

SPIDERS

For many people, spiders are the scariest bugs of all. In reality, they merit our greatest respect and admiration, for spiders are the finest tiny game hunters we know.

Why are we so hard on spiders? Is it a genetic warning system because, as with snakes, a few of them are potentially very dangerous? Or is it that two legs are fine, four legs okay (even lovable), six legs are odd and weird, but eight legs are simply horrific? Certainly, spiders deserve much greater respect and appreciation.

Virtually all spiders, of around 40,000 known species, are carnivores, their meat of choice being insects. Their entire lives are spent hunting and devouring bugs. They have been called the dominant predators on earth, because they kill more insects than birds do and destroy them more efficiently than insecticides. Someone estimated that the bugs spiders eat in one day outweigh the entire human population.

In China, farmers build little teepees out of straw for hibernating spiders that kill pests in their fields. Gardeners everywhere would do well to cherish the spiders that kill their own pests. What's more, household spiders also kill lurking insects. Exterminators who create a fear of spiders generate a market for their services, but spiders are the *real* exterminators. They eat flies, bed bugs, gypsy moths, cockroaches, grasshoppers, and more. Just name a bug you don't like; chances are it's eaten by a spider.

Spiders also consume beneficial insects, including bees and even other spiders; but the good they do far outweighs the bad. The worst enemies of spiders (besides other spiders) are humans, another example of how we don't always act in our own best interests. One of the reasons pesticides fail to increase crop production is that they decimate spider populations.

Spider silk is stronger than tensile steel of the same diameter and so fine that it has been used for crosshairs in optical instruments and gun sights. It has also been used as a folk remedy to clot blood in wounds. Theoretically, a spider fiber with the thickness of a pencil could stop a Boeing 747. Attempts have been made over the centuries to harness silk-spinning spiders the way we have silkworms, but these were greatly hampered by the spiders' need for live insects and lots of space—most spiders prefer to live in solitude. Scientists are now engaged in very promising experiments utilizing spider genes to create spider silk from bacteria. They are also exploring the uses of spider venom in medicine and insecticides.

The old Saxon word for spider was *attercop*, or "poison head." Almost all spiders possess venom and paralyze their victims, but few spiders can harm humans; their jaws don't have the strength to break human skin. Most bites that are blamed on spiders are really inflicted by fleas, mosquitoes, bed bugs, and other insects. Even the reputation of the dreaded tarantula is quite unfounded—its bite is no worse than a bee sting for most people.

Of the 3,000 or so species of spiders in North America, only the black widow and brown recluse spiders cause serious injury to humans. Both bite only defensively, but their venom is quite powerful, depending on how much is injected, and the very young and the very old are most vulnerable. The incidence of bites is very low, however. You stand a much greater chance of getting hit on the freeway than you do of getting bitten by one of these spiders.

If you find a spider in the house, we would recommend leaving it alone to assist in tiny game hunting. Spiders prefer a tranquil, undisturbed existence. Shy and unaggressive, they will run away or try to hide if hassled, and for the most part they just want to be left alone to hunt. Most of them can't even see very well beyond a few inches. Many of them remain in their webs and can hardly walk on flat surfaces.

Removing a spider is easy. Quickly cover it with a glass jar and slip a stiff piece of paper between the jar and the surface. Even then, you will be doing yourself a favor by releasing the spider outdoors instead of killing it.

If you are worried about the spider and would like to have it identified, put a top on the jar and place it in the freezer for a day or two. Or pour rubbing alcohol in the jar to kill it instantly. Then take it to a natural history museum or county extension agent for identification.

If a cobweb in the house is visible and dusty, it is generally no longer being used and can be vacuumed up without destroying the spider. So being tolerant of spiders doesn't mean you have to put up with dirty old webs all over the house.

One way to tell if you've been bitten by a spider is to look for two tiny, closely spaced red spots; most insect bites and stings leave only one mark. If you are bitten, try to capture the spider in a jar, don't panic, and get medical attention as soon as possible.

Black Widow Spiders   Black widow spiders have probably been responsible for the deaths of millions of innocent spiders because of their fearful reputation. Their name comes from attempts by the female to eat the male after mating. A black widow spider only bites on extreme provocation, or if her web contains an egg sac and is disturbed. She is much more likely to run away and hide than to stand and fight. Nevertheless, her bite can be extremely painful and is not to be

Black widow spider and prey

taken lightly. The neurotoxic venom of the black widow is fifteen times stronger than rattlesnake venom, but only a small percentage of bites are fatal today, because an antivenom exists.

A big, shiny black spider, with a body about the size of a large pea, "the fat lady of the spider world" can be found all over North America. Its distinguishing feature, a red (or sometimes orange) hourglass mark, is located on the underside of its abdomen. The male of the species doesn't resemble the female and is not dangerous to humans.

Black widow spiders make an irregular, untidy looking web, usually low to the ground, and hang upside down in it waiting for victims. They live in out-of-the-way, undisturbed spots, such as piles of wood, rubbish, stones, tires, stacked pots, utility boxes, corners of garages, storerooms, basement windows, and sheds. Many black widow bites have occurred in outhouses. Blame it on the flies.

Brown Recluse Spiders   A yellow tan to brown spider, the brown recluse is also called the violin spider because of the light, violin-shaped mark on the back of its head and upper body (the cephalothorax). This spider used to be almost unheard of, and the first documented bite in the United States was in 1957. It is now fairly common in the South and Southwest and seems to be spreading. A fairly small spider—three-sixteenths to five-sixteenths of an inch long—it has long slender legs. It also has only six eyes, whereas most spiders have eight.

Like the black widow, the brown recluse spins a messy web. This spider can be found indoors more frequently than the black widow spider—in basements, attics, boxes, piles of paper, closets, and clothing that has been untouched for a while, especially if left lying on the floor. And like the black widow, it only spins webs down low and in undisturbed places. Unlike the black widow, however, the brown recluse spider generally hunts away from its nest and will sometimes take temporary shelter in clothing or blankets. People are most likely to be bitten if they put on clothing or shoes that a spider has crawled into, and a good precaution is to always shake out these items before putting them on. Outdoors, the spider inhabits rock piles, rubbish, wood piles, little-used sheds, and tires.

The poison of this spider is necrotic—it destroys the tissue around the bite and can even cause gangrene. The bite becomes very unsightly (gruesome actually) and is slow to heal, although rarely fatal.

▶ CONTROL

- Using yellow bug lights, screening, and sealing to keep out insects will keep out spiders, too. The fewer insects you have in the house, the fewer spiders will be around for the feast.
- Don't allow spiders (or insects) access to boxes and other storage containers. Seal them well. Be especially careful when going through boxes and stored papers.
- Vacuum frequently around baseboards and inside closets.
- Always shake out clothing and blankets that have not been used for a while.
- Outdoors, trim plants and hedges away from the house.
- Don't let refuse build up in the yard.
- Always wear gloves and a long-sleeved shirt when cleaning out places likely to be infested with these spiders.

If you go looking for these spiders, search at night with a flashlight, since they are mostly nocturnal hunters. Any time you find a spider in an unwanted place, you can easily kill it by crushing it with a stick. A soapy water spray is just as effective as a poison, and both have to hit the spider. But if you don't want another spider to move in and take its place, change the habitat where you found it or its nest.

When you think a spider has bitten you, get to a doctor or emergency room. Take the spider with you for identification, even if you have squashed it. Far too many bites are blamed on the wrong creature.

TERMITES AND WOOD-BORING BEETLES

TERMITES

One of the strange ironies of this planet is that the supreme builders of the insect world are those who eat, ravage, and destroy our own dwellings. Every year termites cause more damage in the United States than fires, storms, and earthquakes combined. In 1990, according to the *Los Angeles Times*, termites ate the equivalent of fourteen houses in Los Angeles County. The money homeowners spend on exterminators and repairs is astronomical—over $1 billion a year in California alone. And yet, as the saying goes, there are only two types of houses, those that have termites, and those that will.

In the forest, termites recycle dead wood and timber, eliminating trees and debris that would otherwise take hundreds of years to decompose and thereby prevent vital new growth. In tropical climates, they also turn and aerate the soil. Humans have traditionally eliminated forests and trees when they clear land for agriculture, unwittingly substituting their own homes for termites to live in and on.

Termites are master architects, building nests of wondrous design and symmetry. In Australia, Asia, and Africa, from underground nests, they build tall mounds that are the termite equivalent of skyscrapers. In some areas of the world they are a valued source of food. People tap on the mounds to simulate the sound of rain in order to entice the termites out and provide a meal.

Sometimes called white ants, termites are often mistaken for ants, particularly carpenter ants, who also make their homes in wood, grow wings, fly off, and establish new colo-

Termites

nies. Termites, however, are more closely related to cockroaches. A termite has a thick waist, whereas an ant has a pinched, or wasp, waist. Ant antennae are elbowed, while those of termites are not. The wings of termite reproductives (potential kings and queens) are bigger, too, almost twice as long as their bodies, and their two sets of wings are equal in size. Winged ants have pairs of wings of unequal sizes. (For controlling carpenter ants, see *Ants*.)

If you do see a termite, chances are it will be the winged form—the only stage at which one ever leaves its nest. Inside the nest, the worker termites are much lighter colored, and their wingless, segmented bodies look wormlike. In fact, their name comes from the Latin word *termes*, which means "wood worm."

Thanks to central heating, termites, which are tropical insects, have migrated steadily northward, and they are now in every state except Alaska. The two major house-damaging types of termites in the United States are the subterranean termite and the dry-wood termite.

A new termite colony forms when a number of winged termites, called reproductives, or alates, exit from the colony and fly away. This is the only time in a termite's life when it will experience light, sight, and flight. These colonizing flights take place in the fall, early spring, or summer (depending on the species), generally just after a rain, when the earth is damp and soft. They can also be precipitated by heavy watering or irrigation. In our city, Santa Barbara, termite flights are most common on the first clear day after the first heavy rain of the season.

Any home, even a home that has recently been tented and fumigated for termites, is vulnerable to these random landings of winged immigrants. Fortunately, termites on the wing are highly vulnerable to predators. Birds and dragonflies eat them by the thousands. And once they come down to earth, they are preyed on by ants, frogs, spiders, mantids, lizards, and snakes. When they do come to earth, a male and female pair up, break off their wings, run about in tandem, and burrow under a rock or into a hole in the ground. They then seal themselves in, now mated for life.

The colony will grow very slowly at first. As it develops, it will come to include workers, who take care of the young and provide all the food, and soldiers, who protect the colony. The workers, whose jaws have saw-like edges, do all the damage. They usually tunnel into wood that has been wet and damaged by fungus.

Ironically, termites cannot digest wood. They harbor colonies of microscopic, one-celled protozoa in their guts, which break down the cellulose for them and make it digestible. Because they are born without these protozoa in their intestines, they must acquire them by eating each other's fecal matter. They also eat the skins they shed, as well as their own dead and dying.

Subterranean Termites   These termites live in huge underground colonies, which may number a quarter of a million insects. Because they have to have regular contact with moisture to survive, they build distinctive tubes to travel between soil and wood. In the winged stage, termites are brown to brownish black. Workers can forage considerable distances, so your house could be infested by a colony from your neighbor's next door.

If you don't have anything else to worry about in the middle of the night, worry about the Formosan subterranean termite, which first appeared in the United States in the 1960s. Now found in more than a dozen states, from Virginia to Hawaii, it is similar to other subterranean termites but is more aggressive, eats a wider variety of wood, does more damage, and does it faster. A colony can consist of several million individuals and can take up more than an acre of land. They are pale yellow, and the soldiers have oval-shaped heads instead of square ones. Colder temperatures may limit its dispersion in the northern states.

Dry-Wood Termites   Found predominantly on the West Coast and in the southern coastal states, dry-wood termites are larger than subterranean termites and live in much smaller colonies. Winged termites are reddish brown. They build their nests right into wood, in locations removed from soil, and do not need much moisture. Because their colonies are much smaller, they can be moved from one area to another in lumber.

Dry-wood termites occasionally push their fecal pellets, called frass, out of their nests through "kickholes." Little piles or sprinkles of these dark-colored, granular particles are a good indication that termites are busy chomping away in the wood right above the pile.

Damp-Wood Termites   Damp-wood termites are similar to dry-wood termites, except that they are found in wet, decaying wood. They are large, up to an inch long, with even bigger wings, and are found up and down the Pacific Coast.

DETECTION

The wood destroyers' greatest advantage is that they are hidden from sight. We need to be vigilant around our homes to detect them. Have at least one thorough inspection of the house every year, on your own or by a professional.

All homeowners should be on the lookout for the exodus of winged termites and for signs that they have entered the house. Sometimes they accidentally emerge into a brightly lit room instead of outdoors. Look for masses of their transparent wings, which they tear off before starting to burrow.

Subterranean termites, which cannot survive without moisture, live entirely underground. If you open up a termite nest or burrow and expose it to air, their soft bodies will dry up and they will die.

Because they must have moisture at all times, they can't simply crawl out of the earth and climb up the side of a building. Naturally, wood that sits right on the earth is ideal for them. Never, never build so that this condition exists—anywhere. In many cases, termites stream up through cracks in the foundations to get to the wood. They can travel though a crack as fine as one-thirty-second of an inch.

Termites frequently build tunnels, called shelter tubes, that get them over concrete foundation walls and up through cracks to the wood. They will also build shelter tubes over treated wood to avoid it. These tubes are made from particles of dirt and wood and a cementlike substance that the termites secrete. They look a little like dribbled sand and are quite distinctive. Sometimes a tube, called a drop tube, can be seen suspended from wood, hanging down in midair.

Keep an eye out for these shelter tubes. If you see one, knock it apart. If it is rebuilt within a few days or a week, you know that termite activity is going on.

If you destroy the shelter tubes and keep them from being rebuilt, the subterranean termites in the house will die, because they have to be able to return to their underground headquarters to replenish their moisture. Destroying the tubes will also give their enemies, the ants, a way to get at the termites.

Another way to check for the presence of subterranean termites in your yard is to drive untreated and weathered wooden stakes (like pine) into the ground. Pull them up every month to see if they have been attacked by termites.

Inside the house, check for wood (especially flooring) with a slight rippling or pebbled look or darkened patches on it. Use an ice pick or screwdriver to tap the wood; if the termites have been at work it will easily give way. Test windowsills and window frames also.

Sometimes the clicking and chewing sounds of termites will alert people. Knock on wood and listen for the warning ticking sounds made by soldier termites. A stethoscope comes in handy for this.

Money spent on a professional inspection (provided you are not pressured into using poison treatments) is a good investment. A truly complete inspection is a laborious feat and requires poking into the farthest recesses of the attic (for dry-wood termites) and crawling around dirty, dank crawl spaces. Sometimes the physical evidence of termites may be old, and yet the house will get treated over and over just because this evidence was never removed. An inspection should detect only living insects.

▶ CONTROL

The greatest enemy of the termite is the ant. By being barricaded in wood, termites escape this mortal adversary. One of the most foolish things a homeowner can do is spray a ring of poison or set out a series of poison ant stakes around the house. If you see ants crawling up and down the walls of the house and they're not bothering you in the kitchen, leave them alone.

If you suspect a termite colony is in the ground near your house (wood in the woodpile, tree stumps, or fence posts show signs of being eaten), get out a shovel and start digging. You can't totally expose a very large colony, but you can create access to it for ants and other termite enemies.

Traditionally, the treatment for subterranean termites has been to inject insecticides into the soil around and beneath houses. Chlorinated hydrocarbons such as chlordane were used routinely for termites (and ants) in millions of homes. A known carcinogen, chlordane remains active for twenty-five years. It is no longer on the market, but its use (and overuse) may be one of the twentieth century's great pesticide disasters.

People commonly buy and sell at least one or two homes during their lifetime, and renters move even more frequently; but little information is kept on the pesticide-use history of a dwelling. How are you to know, when you move into a house, that it has been treated with gallons of chlordane, not once, but over and over again?

When a house is tented and fumigated, methyl bromide or sulfuryl fluoride (Vikane) is pumped into it. These are among the most toxic and hazardous pesticides used today, a dangerous source of pesticidal air pollution that may result in unsafe exposures for people living nearby. Moreover, a United Nations scientific panel estimated that methyl bromide is responsible for from 5 to 10 percent of ozone depletion worldwide. In 1995, almost 600,000 pounds of this chemical were injected into thousands of California homes and businesses. Furthermore, according to Californians for Pesticide Reform, methyl bromide levels *outside* homes under fumigation may exceed the California safety standard sevenfold. And methyl bromide can be detected inside other closed houses up to 100 feet away from a fumigated structure. Passersby beware! Hazardous vapors drifting through empty pipes into neighboring houses have killed a number of people.

Used much more frequently than methyl bromide, Vikane is an extremely toxic nerve poison. Researchers have found that it can be absorbed by many household materials and released for up to forty days after fumigation.

Fumigation only kills the termites in the house and does not affect underground nests. Houses can be reinfested immediately afterward, although evidence that a colony exists then may take a few years to show up. And often after pesticides are used, people do not attend to the important tasks of monitoring and detection.

People twenty years ago might be forgiven for using hazardous substances to "save" their homes. But today a variety of nontoxic treatments for termites are available. Call around to locate exterminators who use them and give them your business. The more we demand safe treatments that will not poison our water and air, the more operators will begin to use those treatments.

Biological Controls One of the most promising biological treatments available to pest control operators and individuals uses bait blocks saturated with termiticides that are safe to humans. These include insect growth regulators (Recruit) that interfere with molting and poisons that inhibit termite respiration (Subterfuge and Firstline). Because termites forage unpredictably, they have to be located before the baits are placed. This is done by prebaiting with pine stakes, or cardboard in a bait station, about every twenty feet around the home and checking monthly for termite activity. Once a colony has been located, a bait is placed at that spot. This method is environmentally safe, but it could take months to eradicate a colony. Aboveground bait stations are also available.

Another treatment uses nematodes—microscopic parasitic organisms (little worms)—that attack termites by invading them through their body openings. They are poured into the soil in a water mixture. Termites eat their own dead and also pass their food around, so it doesn't take too many nematode-infected termites to infect a whole colony. They must be applied close to the termites and require loose, moist soil.

Inside structures, an innovative and effective treatment consists of injecting a fungus (BioBlast) into active termite galleries. It does not affect humans.

Heat The environmentally advantageous method for treating insect infestations with heat was pioneered by Charles Forbes and Walter Ebeling. Marketed by TPE Associates, mostly in Southern California, the San Francisco area, and southern Florida, the process uses a portable propane heater that blows hot air into a tented house. When the temperature of the wood reaches 130°F for thirty-five minutes, the termites die. Some objects in the house must be removed—computer equipment, plants, medicine, some food, and most plastics. The process costs more than fumigation because it is more labor-intensive, but it is completed in less than a day. Every other bug in the house dies, too. Best of all, it releases no toxins into the air.

Another company, Tallon, uses flexible heat strips to release high heat into specific infestations.

Cold   A simple idea, based on the fact that there are no termites in the cold climate of Alaska, led to the development of a technique that freezes dry-wood termites. The Blizzard System (in California and Florida) uses liquid nitrogen pumped into small holes drilled in the walls of infested areas. This chemical drops the temperature within the wall to 20° below zero. A majority of the earth's atmosphere is composed of nitrogen, so this gas is entirely harmless to humans (unless they breathe it exclusively, without oxygen). Operators use fiber-optic scopes to locate the termites' galleries. The treatment comes with an eleven-month reinspection and a two-year guarantee. Tallon, the company that pioneered it in 1987, has had remarkable success with it.

Electricity   For more than a decade, Etex has manufactured and leased an appliance called the Electro-Gun, which kills dry-wood termites and powderpost beetles by zapping them with electricity. Because the insects themselves and their tunnels are slightly moist, the arc of electricity goes directly into the burrow and travels along the galleries, killing the termites. The operator can easily return and treat places where new termites are discovered, and it is safe to use. Its only limitations are that it can't be used in any part of the home that the operator can't get to, and it is impractical if the infestation is really widespread.

Barriers   Subterranean termites have been successfully prevented from getting to a building by the use of sand barriers. The termites find it impossible to tunnel through coarse sand, because their galleries won't hold up. The sand is the kind used in sand blasting; beach sand is too fine. The installers either lay down four inches of sand beneath the foundation, or create an eight-inch trench around the house. This method has been widely tested in Hawaii, where it has even been incorporated into some building codes. Wire-mesh or steel barriers can also be used.

Wood Treatments   Look for safe new products that penetrate wood and make it repellent and deadly to termites and wood-destroying fungi. These include boron compounds or diffusable sodium borates (Bora-Care, Jecta, Termite Prufe, Tim-bor) and orange oil (Power Plant), all of which are injected into galleries or sprayed or painted on bare wood. Tallon is also researching the use of salt under houses as a safe termiticide.

Dusts   Dry-wood termite reproductives often enter attic areas through vents, then crawl around on the floor until they choose a spot to burrow into. Have silica aerogel dust or boric acid blown onto floorboards in the attic and into spaces between walls. These dusts can be applied during new construction, but you can also drill holes into walls to have it blown in. These dusts will kill termites if they crawl over it, but they are better for prevention than for treatment.

▶ PREVENTION

- Do not let the exterior paint on wood structures deteriorate. Unfinished wood is the termites' welcome mat.
- Inspect wooden porches and steps that touch the soil, as well as wooden trellises and planter boxes next to the house. These provide perfect access for termites. If possible, no wood should ever come in contact with the soil.
- Remove all wood, firewood, scraps, stumps, building material, and unfinished building projects away from the house. Firewood should be stacked on a poured concrete foundation, or stored eighteen inches above the ground. If you find termites in the wood, burn it, or soak it in soapy water or water laced with ammonia.

- Crawl spaces and areas under buildings should have adequate ventilation, using screened vents, to keep them dry.
- Cut back shrubbery and vines from around the outside of the house to keep vents open.
- Patch and repair cracks in concrete or masonry, which provide good access for termites.
- Check areas where pieces of wood join together or abut—corners of houses and walls or up under eaves. These are good entry places for insects, particularly if they have shrunk or split.
- You are more likely to have termites (and wood-destroying fungi) if you provide them with moisture. Check to see if you have leaky pipes or a leaky roof. Is there condensation anywhere? Is there a leaking shower pan or moisture around the base of the toilet?
- Keep gutters clean. Make sure downspouts direct water away from the structure. The soil line around the house should slant downward, so that water runs away from the house. Make sure sprinklers are not dampening the sides of the house during watering.

If you are remodeling or building a new house, consider alternatives to wood. Besides never having to worry about termites, you will be conserving one of the earth's finite resources.

WOOD-BORING BEETLES

Detection, control, and prevention for beetles is very much the same as for termites. You should always inspect any used furniture, wood, or firewood for beetles before bringing it into the house. Removing the bark from firewood outdoors is also a good idea.

Powderpost Beetles   After the female lays her eggs in hardwood furniture, flooring, or paneling, the larvae eat out small winding tunnels. They cause rapid and extensive damage, usually not discovered until you see their tiny ($\frac{1}{32}$ to $\frac{1}{16}$ inch) round exit holes. Their frass has the consistency of talcum powder. Once they emerge, they fly to light, and you might see them crawling on window sills or on the floor.

Furniture and Deathwatch Beetles   These anobiid beetles will attack both hard and soft woods. Their exit holes (1⁄16 to 1⁄8 inch) are round, and their frass has a gritty feel. Deathwatch beetles make a ticking sound at night.

Old House Borers   In some areas, this beetle is second only to termites in the damage it inflicts. Despite its name, it prefers softwoods that are less than ten years old—as in new homes. It spends two to ten years as a cream-colored, rather large (11⁄4 inch) larva with dark-colored eye spots on the sides of its head. You may be able to hear its chewing. Exit holes are oval and a quarter of an inch in diameter.

TICKS, CHIGGERS, AND MITES

Ticks, chiggers, and mites are all Arachnida, related to spiders, and it's perfectly all right to have arachnophobia about these appalling little creatures, which attach themselves to our bodies and feed off us, leaving calling cards that range from the agonies of itching to serious illnesses.

TICKS

Most ticks like a long, slow feed of our blood. Although frequently painless and even unnoticed, their bites can cause reactions ranging from severe pain to paralysis. Ticks are also very dangerous vectors of dozens of serious and debilitating animal and human diseases. In the first century A.D., Pliny the Elder called them "the foulest and nastiest creatures that be." In this country, they are considered more dangerous than fleas and mosquitoes. Because they get their start in the great outdoors and only attack humans who venture into their territory, controlling them is a seemingly impossible task.

Ticks have very few predators, but few animals on earth are immune to a bite from one of the 800 species of these bloodsuckers. They feed on birds, as well as mammals, and will even live on reptiles. Because they feed from a variety of hosts, they pass diseases between these hosts. After a female has had a good blood meal, she drops off her host and lays thousands of eggs. Ticks pass any disease they are carrying to their eggs, so the next generation of ticks are ready-made disease carriers.

Ticks hatch in the spring or summer and attach themselves first to birds or small mammals such as rodents and squirrels. Not until they have reached the nymph or adult stage do they climb up onto tall grass or bushes and wait for larger hosts, like deer and humans, to pass by. After climbing up the vegetation, they hang on with their back legs and wave their forelegs in the air. They can't jump or fly; when a host walks by, alerted by its carbon dioxide, they drop or grab onto it. And if a host doesn't happen by that day, they wait. And wait. Even if it takes months.

Once a tick gets on a human being (usually around the ankles or shoes), it wanders around, taking its time to find a suitable spot to feed. A tick can move with a very light touch and often causes no sensation at all when it bites. This is why looking for and spotting ticks is our foremost defense.

Once it selects its site, the tick grabs on with a set of curved teeth and begins to secrete a cementlike substance to help it stick. Into the skin it goes, head first like an ostrich. It feeds very slowly, often taking several days to finish, sometimes swelling to ten times its size, to the size of a pea or a small grape. Once embedded, a tick is very hard to dislodge and will readily leave its mouthparts in the skin if pulled away. This can cause an infection in its victim, but the tick gets away scot-free and regenerates the mouthparts it lost.

Ticks can be classified as either *hard* or *soft*. Hard ticks have a "shield" on the back and are more common than soft ticks. Since they feed longer, they tend to be found more often. The following kinds of ticks give diseases to people.

Lone Star Tick   Named because of the white mark on its back, this large, reddish brown tick is found in the southern United States and feeds on both deer and humans. It transmits tularemia (rabbit fever) and Rocky Mountain spotted fever.

(Left) Dog tick; (right) deer tick

American Dog Tick   Common in the East, but also found in the Midwest and West, this is a large tick, between one-quarter and one-half inch long, and brown with silvery gray markings on its back. Although it prefers dogs, it will also feed on humans. It carries Rocky Mountain spotted fever, as well as tularemia, and causes tick paralysis.

Rocky Mountain Wood Tick   Also called the Rocky Mountain spotted fever tick, this resembles the dog tick. Found west of the Rocky Mountains, it transmits the disease it is named after, as well as tularemia, Colorado tick fever, and tick paralysis.

Deer Tick   Infamous for transmitting Lyme disease, this tick gets its name from its primary host in the East, the white-tailed deer. In the Midwest, it is known as the bear tick. It is extremely small. As a nymph, it looks like the period at the end of a sentence, and when it first matures, it is little larger than a poppy seed. Most people don't even know they've been bitten by it.

Western Black-Legged Tick   Found in the West, this is the cousin of the deer tick, which it resembles, even in size. It also transmits Lyme disease. It is reddish brown, with black legs.

DISEASES TRANSMITTED BY TICKS

For many years, Rocky Mountain spotted fever was the worst disease given to people by ticks. If untreated, this illness has a high mortality rate—around 20 percent. Other common diseases spread by ticks include relapsing fever, tularemia, and tick paralysis. Tick paralysis mostly affects animals and children who have been bitten around the back of the neck.

Lyme disease has now become the most serious disease carried by ticks. First identified in the Northeast, Lyme disease (or Lyme arthritis) is now carried by ticks in forty-eight states and continues to spread. An early symptom of the disease (besides flulike symptoms in some) is a target-like (or bull's-eye) red rash expanding from the bite locus. This is followed by flu symptoms and aching muscles. If untreated, it escalates to symptoms that mimic meningitis and rheumatoid arthritis. It can also cause permanent damage to the joints, heart, and nervous system of its victims. Some say that had it not been for AIDS, Lyme disease would have been called the plague of the 1990s.

▶ CONTROL

Do not be passive when it comes to ticks! The season for ticks is early summer to early fall, so be prepared for careful and constant vigilance during this time. Also, in certain areas of the Pacific Coast, ticks can be active during the winter.

Animals are prime hosts of ticks and should be examined daily for infestation. Check your pets while they are still outdoors, so they don't carry ticks into the house. Look especially carefully around the head and neck and between the toes of your animal. A flea comb can be used to remove ticks on dogs and cats. Lint cleaners, made of a roller with sticky masking tape (available from hardware and large drugstores) can be used to remove ticks from cats. Animals can also be treated with nontoxic shampoos (see *Fleas*).

Some ticks brought in by animals will breed indoors. Remember, this can mean thousands of eggs. This means constant vacuuming and washing pet bedding.

To find out if an outdoor area is infested with ticks, tack one end of a large piece of white flannel to a board attached to a rope and drag it around on the ground. Turn it over and you will be able to see the ticks that have jumped on. If you see a lot of them, leave the area.

Another way to trap and monitor ticks is to spread out a cloth and put on it a colander with a chunk of dry ice in it and a lid on top. Or use a styrofoam box with holes drilled in the side. Ticks will be drawn to the carbon dioxide given off by the dry ice and will travel (actually run) over the cloth, where you can pick them off. The dry ice container can also be placed on a board with flypaper or some sticky substance around the edges.

If you find the area is heavily infested, you can treat it by spraying with insecticidal soap or diatomaceous earth. This would only be practical near the house, of course. Treating large areas with toxic insecticides, as has been done in the past, has probably done more harm than good.

When you are outdoors in an infested area, try to avoid walking in tall grass, brush, or shrubbery. Avoid narrow paths commonly traveled by animals—that is where ticks hang out.

Ticks are more visible if you wear light colors, but these also attract them. Wear long sleeves and long pants, preferably tucked into socks or boots. Some people wrap masking tape around the bottoms of their pant legs, as this is one of the most common entry points for these marauders. Check for ticks on your clothing every thirty minutes.

Even though products containing DEET are sold to repel ticks, they are not as effective as they are with mosquitoes, and they have also been known to cause allergic reactions, blisters, convulsions, seizures, and even death. More effective are products containing permethrin (a chemical form of pyrethrum), which will repel and kill ticks when sprayed on clothing.

Many flea repellents (including garlic) will also repel ticks. Dr. Bronner's peppermint liquid soap can be combined with water, one tablespoon to a cup, and used as a spray repellent on clothing and skin. Citronella, Avon Skin-So-Soft bath oil (see *Mosquitoes*), eucalyptus oil, and pennyroyal are tick repellents too; they should also be diluted with water. Some hikers put cloves of garlic in their shoes. Try walking with an herbal flea collar on your ankle.

On returning to the house after walking in an infested area, remove all clothing and put it immediately into the washing machine. If you have picked up a tick, it may be wandering around on your body, still searching for a feeding site. Do a thorough tick check of your entire body, especially the groin and armpit area. Get a friend to look in places where you can't see, or use a mirror. Take a hot, soapy shower or bath, then check again. These frequent inspections are important, because diseases carried by ticks usually require that the tick be attached for two to eight hours before the infection begins to take place.

If you have ticks in your area, examine your children every day, especially the back of the neck and under the hair.

Keep long grass and weeds cut short around your property. Eliminate underbrush around trees. Remove leaf litter and prune trees so that sunlight can dry the soil. Ticks thrive better in a humid environment.

Reduce the rodent population so that ticks have less to feed on. Some people set out permethrin-soaked cotton (Damminix) in little containers around their property. Small mammals collect it as nesting material, and it later kills ticks.

Since the presence of deer—especially in the Northeast—has been associated with disease-carrying ticks, exclude them, as well as other stray animals, from your property (see *Foragers*).

Consider planting molasses grass around the circumference of your property. The tiny, sticky hairs on this plant are believed to trap the ticks and keep them from climbing up it. Fewer ticks are also said to be found where sage, pyrethrum, and lavender grow as ground covers.

Removing Ticks To best remove a tick, take a pair of blunt, curved tweezers or forceps, grasp the tick very close to the skin, and pull it gently, firmly, and steadily out. Do not twist it! Some recommend putting petroleum jelly, rubbing alcohol, or nail polish on the body of the tick to make the procedure easier. If you use your fingers to remove a tick, cover your skin with tissue or wear gloves to avoid infection. Never touch or crush one with your bare hands. Drop it into alcohol or soapy water. Clean the bite area with an antiseptic and wash your hands with soap and water.

CHIGGERS

As with ticks, the modus operandi of chiggers is to wait patiently on grass and brush for likely victims to pass by. Next to chiggers, which look like tiny red specks, ticks seem gigantic. Small as they are, chiggers are actually mid-sized mites.

Chiggers are found in the midwestern, southern, and southeastern areas of the United States. They are also known as jiggers, red bugs, and hot weather bugs, because they flourish in the summertime. People can pick them up from grass, weeds, brambles, and even their gardens.

If bloodsucking sounds like a bad way to make a living, chiggers have even worse habits. Once they get on your skin, they inject an enzyme that literally causes cells to disintegrate. Then they suck and slurp up the juice. It can cause unbelievable itching, but the reaction usually comes long after the mites are gone. After feeding, they don't stick around but drop off, burrow into the ground, and molt.

The adult chiggers are harmless, but the bright red, blind baby chiggers attack anything that gives off carbon dioxide—people as well as numerous other mammals, rodents, reptiles, frogs and toads, and even turtles. They usually jump on people around their feet and make their way up the body until they get past an obstruction like the tops of socks or a belt, and then they start to feed.

▶ CONTROL

If you have chiggers in your area, cutting down high grass and brambles may help. Also wear tight-fitting clothing. The best treatment for chiggers is to take a hot, soapy bath as soon as you come in from outdoors. This will kill them before they have time to do a lot of damage.

Some people recommend dusting areas known to be infested with chiggers with sulfur. You can also dust your clothing with it, using a duster, but wear a mask and goggles when applying the dust.

SCABIES AND OTHER MITES

Ranging in size from nearly invisible to half an inch long, mites inhabit land, water, and air. Of the 300,000 or so known species (there may be a million), a full half live as parasites on other animals. One mite species lives exclusively in the ears of moths. Humans are hosts to a number of mites besides chiggers. (Ticks are not mites, but they belong to the same order.) One of these, the hair follicle mite, swims around in the oily sea that surrounds facial hairs. Some even live in eyelids. Whether these mites are harmful or beneficial has never been established. We can only be grateful that they are nearly invisible, because, like lice, they look like little monsters.

House Dust Mites   These are probably the most numerous of the mites who live off us. A favorite habitat is the hollows in mattresses, where they wait for bits of skin to float through the sheets. These mites are thought to be the cause of many allergies and asthmatic attacks, and they are one more reason to get out the vacuum cleaner as frequently as possible. Vacuum slowly, preferably with a water-filter vacuum. Dust mites can't survive in low humidity. Air purifiers with electrostatic filters can be used to reduce dust.

Bird Mites   These mites can be very tiny and pale or dark. Frustrating, almost invisible and rapidly moving, they sometimes switch to human blood after birds have vacated nests near homes. Look for birds' nests attached to the house. The best defense is to caulk and seal all cracks and crevices and vacuum well. If you must spray something, use an insecticidal soap or a citrus-based cleaner.

Scabies, or Itch Mites   These mites are particularly virulent. Also called seven-year itch, or mange, scabies mites can spread with great ease from person to person. You can get scabies from shaking hands or from clothing and sheets that have been infested. Because it can take weeks or months to develop a sensitivity to scabies, you can spread it unknowingly for quite a while. After infested people become sensitized, they develop a rash and unbearable, excruciating itching. But because cortisone ointments are now readily available, many cases of scabies go undiagnosed.

The larvae of scabies mites travel freely over the skin looking for a spot to settle in, but they don't start burrowing until they are adults. When they do burrow, they choose the most delicate, sensitive skin, like that found between fingers, at the bends of elbows and knees, or around private parts. Females live for several months eating and laying eggs under the skin. The tunnels they make, as they proceed to nibble along, look like whitish hairs on the skin, and the mites can actually be removed with a needle. Under a magnifying glass they look something like a hairy turtle. If you suspect you have scabies, you can diagnose it by digging the mites out with a sterile needle or sharp blade, but you might prefer that a doctor do this for you.

▶ **CONTROL**

Those who have scabies should avoid any physical contact with others. Traditional treatments for scabies have included soaps containing the insecticide lindane. Avoid this dangerous pesticide (see *Lice*).

Treatment consists of frequent hot baths or showers—which will kill scabies mites crawling on the surface of the skin. If you can, take a sauna.

Changing and washing linens every day and washing all clothing in hot water are also advised. Scabies mites only live a few days away from people, so any items that cannot be washed can be sealed in plastic for a week.

Nontoxic lice shampoos (e.g., Not Nice to Lice) and various preparations containing sulfur are also available.

OCCASIONAL INVADERS

At one time or another, we may experience temporary insect infestations that are more annoying than pestiferous. Nobody likes to have their space invaded, but insects don't have a clue that we feel this way.

ASIAN LADY BEETLES

Multicolored Asian lady beetles get their nickname, Halloween beetles, from their orange color (with black spots) and the fact that they make their appearance in huge numbers around the end of October.

Introduced from Japan to control tree-inhabiting aphids, they have spread rapidly in the East. In many areas, pecan growers are no longer troubled by pecan aphids and have even stopped spraying pesticides. But in the fall, as they get ready to hibernate, the beetles can mass in huge numbers on the sunny southwest sides of pale rocks or houses. Presumably, they wintered in limestone cliffs in Asia and are thus genetically drawn to light-colored structures.

When they do get in, they can be a real nuisance, crawling into smoke alarms, computers, beds, food, even noses, and qualifying as a bona fide invasion.

The best protection consists of making sure that houses are well caulked, that windows are weather-stripped, that screens are in good repair, and that all vents have screens.

If you try to squash them, you'll be sorry, because they will leave orange stains. When stressed, these beetles actually bleed from the joints in their legs

We've heard of people hanging flypaper in a little-used room and keeping the lights on all night to draw them in and trap them.

A more beneficial solution would be to vacuum them up and take the bags to a protected spot outdoors, where they can remain until spring and then go on their way. Houses are actually too warm for them. *Organic Gardening* advises putting them in a paper bag with a little water and keeping them in the refrigerator to release in the garden in the spring.

BOXELDER BUGS

So named because they live on boxelder trees, these dark brown or black insects are easily recognizable by the red markings on their wings. You can't miss them when they congregate on the sunny south and west walls of your house (or on fences or trees or rocks) in the fall or on warm winter days. And, it being the nature of bugs to crawl into cracks, they inevitably get into any house that has not been well caulked, screened, and weather-stripped.

To control eggs and larvae, attract lacewings, ladybugs, or mantises. In early spring or summer, spray neem on the trees.

If they are congregating on the wall of the house, you can spray them with soapy water or neem to kill them. Or use diatomaceous earth as a barrier.

Once they get inside, boxelder bugs are not harmful to people, but they can be annoying, because their fecal pellets will spot the walls, shades, and curtains. You will have to vacuum them up; when crushed, they leave a colored stain. Keep in mind that, unlike many other bugs in your house, they won't eat a thing. And they actually smell rather nice—like flowers. They've even been called a "six-legged air freshener."

Some people recommend getting rid of boxelder trees, which seems a shame—we should be planting trees, not cutting them down. You can, however, encourage or release lacewings or ladybugs to prey on eggs and nymphs.

CENTIPEDES

In this country, house centipedes will sometimes come indoors, especially into basements and damp areas of the house. There they prey on insects like cockroaches, clothes moths, silverfish, and flies—doing these good deeds at night and keeping out of sight during the day. A centipede's "bite," although painful, has rarely been fatal to humans.

They can easily be vacuumed up. Also, use a dehumidifier and check for plumbing leaks, because they are drawn to moisture.

CLUSTER FLIES

Cluster flies can be a major annoyance in the house. The adults who happen to emerge in the fall often head indoors for the winter; they crawl into tiny holes in buildings and hibernate in walls, attics, or even dark closets. Then, on warm days, out they come—and come and come. Little horrors, they look just like house flies, but fuzzier. They can be hidden deep within a structure, so they can be very hard to rout out at the source. They've even gotten into air-conditioning equipment and shown up in hospital surgical rooms.

Don't feel bad about killing them, even though they won't be after much in the house. In their other lives (as maggots) they enter the bodies of live earthworms and live off them. The vacuum cleaner may be best for huge numbers, although it can get tedious.

Try sprinkling diatomaceous earth down into crevices where they hide. Soapy sprays will kill them on contact, of course. You can buy cute window traps that hide the flies captured by sticky paper behind decorative sleeves.

If they are getting into attics, try leaving lights on, day and night, to repel them.

Cricket

CRICKETS

Folklore has it that the sounds of a cricket in the house foretell death, but far more traditions, including old Celtic ones, hold that a cricket on the hearth is good luck. The Chinese have kept them in cages as pets for the same reason and appreciate them as "watchdogs" too. For when a cricket stops chirping at night, an intruder could be in the house. The Chinese have also used them in "real" cricket matches. Unpleasant in shape, if pleasing in sound, crickets are familiar in this country as pet food, live bait, and cartoon characters, but we aren't very happy to see them indoors.

Caulk and seal all possible entrances. Use diatomaceous earth and desiccant dusts in cracks and crevices and voids where you suspect crickets may be. Instead of pouring poisons around the perimeter of the house—the usual practice—sprinkle a layer of diatomaceous earth around the foundation. (If it gets wet, it has to be replaced.) Or use neem. Crickets are related to cockroaches and grasshoppers, so you can use similar tactics to discourage them.

EARWIGS

Earwig

Earwigs sometimes invade houses, where they behave somewhat like cockroaches, hiding in crevices by day and foraging by night. They may hide in basements, crawl spaces, storage areas, and chests of drawers. With their repulsive rear-end pinchers, they look more fearsome than cockroaches, but they are quite harmless. They tend to come indoors in times of drought.

To keep them out in the first place, trim plants so that they don't touch walls, and create a dry bare border on the ground around the house. Caulk all cracks and weather-strip doors.

Diatomaceous earth and other desiccants can be used in cracks to kill earwigs. Also, they can easily be vacuumed up.

Will they crawl into your ears at night and damage your brain, as folklore has it? Not very likely. However, a medical dictionary from the 1800s advises that earwigs "being dried, pulverized, and mixed with the urine of a hare, are esteemed to be good for deafness." Isn't progress wonderful?

MOTHS

Old superstition held that moths were the souls or ghosts of the dead, trying frantically to get into the homes of the living by throwing them-

Moth trap

selves at their windows. Sometimes light-attracted moths do manage to get into the house, where they flutter around lights and lamps. Like flour moths and clothes moths, they can be annoying, although they pose no threat to food or clothing.

To make a simple trap for these night-flying, light-attracted moths, take a night-light, the kind that plugs into a wall socket and uses a 15-watt bulb. Plug it into an extension cord and set it on a counter. With little blocks of wood—or even books— build a small enclosure around it. Then place a small glass bowl on top of the blocks so that the night-light, shining from below, lights up the bowl. Fill the bowl with water and a little liquid soap or Windex (which seems to attract them). We have caught dozens of moths this way.

SCORPIONS

Scorpions are the oldest known arachnids. Hundreds of millions of years ago, ancient forms included a giant water scorpion that was almost ten feet long, possibly weighed hundreds of pounds, and has been called "the fiercest predator of the primal seas."

Scorpions have always aroused fear and loathing in humans. Also many misconceptions. Old superstition held that smelling basil could engender scorpions in your brain. Through the ages, there have been an astounding number of remedies for the pain of their sting: from sitting on an ass backward to the use of pigeon's dung or "house mice cut asunder" as a salve. Dried scorpions have also been put to amazing uses, from "curing colicky pains" to "driving out worms miraculously" and curing lunacy and the plague.

On that note, we move on to the relatively harmless scorpions that sometimes make themselves at home in houses in parts of America. Although all scorpions sting, often quite painfully, of the forty species in the United States, only one, found in Arizona and New Mexico, has venom that is dangerous to humans. Antivenom has reduced mortality, however.

If these fast-moving, rarely seen nocturnal predators are in your house, they are ridding it of vermin. They kill and eat clothes moths, book predators, bed bugs, spiders, carpet beetles, and other scorpions. Inasmuch as they themselves are eaten by mice, toads, snakes, lizards, and birds, they may actually be safer indoors. But because they prefer high temperatures and are not even very active when the temperature falls below 70°F, they will for the most part avoid the relative coolness of houses in the summer. However, sometimes flooding of their habitat outdoors will precipitate a household invasion.

In areas where scorpions might come indoors, be sure to wear shoes at all times. They seek out small enclosed spaces to hide, so shake out clothing, towels, shoes, and slippers before using.

If you are really paranoid, get an ultraviolet or black light and go searching with the lights off. Scorpions glow like little neon astrological signs in this light.

Use diatomaceous earth or silica gel in cracks and voids and anywhere you suspect them to be hiding.

PART 2

TINY GAME HUNTING
IN THE GARDEN

THE HEALTHY GARDEN

THE FALLACY OF PESTICIDES

We have actually bred armies of superbugs that our poisons can't kill. In 1938, there were seven insect pests known to be resistant to at least one chemical; now there are 535 resistant insect species. There are also 210 weed species resistant to at least one herbicide. Most of the "bad bugs" were around long before chemical pesticides. And after all these years of spraying (CAUTION!), dusting (WARNING!) and soaking (DANGER!), the same bugs are still coming around to see what's growing and to get as much of it as they can. The general failure of chemical pesticides to eradicate these insects is a good reason to give them up, given the inherent danger they present to all of us.

Birds in particular are the living— and dying—proof of the fallacy of using garden and lawn pesticides. The bird lover who puts out a bird feeder and then sprays his lawn with commonly used garden chemicals might as well sit outside and shoot the birds that show up.

Our policy is identify the enemy, assess the damage, and call in the troops—the good bugs. Chemical

Superbugs that poisons can't kill

warfare has too many casualties; it's like dropping bombs on innocent civilians.

Think of it as a game. The bad bugs may be crop connoisseurs, but you're smarter than they are. And you don't have to get rid of them entirely. All you have to do is make sure that the level of damage they inflict is within a tolerable range. If they get a plant or two, plant two more. Some say that a plant cannot be considered lost to the insects until more than a quarter of it has been eaten.

Another reason you don't have to obliterate every single one of the bad bugs is that the natural predators have to eat. If they don't have anything to prey upon, they will go away and won't be there when the next inevitable pest invasion arrives. Treat your allies well.

Regular inspection tours of the garden are essential for the tiny game hunter. Know when the enemy is starting to advance and become familiar with the signs of encroachment. When you spot an infestation in your yard, study the situation carefully. Is that green worm on your rosebuds really a threat to the perfect flower you had hoped to get, or is it a hover fly larva hunting down the rose aphids alighting from the sky? If you mistakenly spray your friend (the green worm, the hover fly larva), more aphids will land successfully, and they will reproduce ever more rapidly.

If you know your insects and all the options available, you can be on the front line of defense. Above all, experiment! The various remedies provided here have been culled from both scientific and nonscientific sources and may not all work every time. If you have a pest in your strawberry patch, apply one treatment to one part, another treatment to another part, and leave one part alone. Check them every few days. Observe carefully and take notes. That's how Thomas Jefferson worked, and he had a remarkable orchard and garden.

BETTER SOIL FOR STRONGER PLANTS

Bullies attack weaklings; insect pests are the bullies of the garden. Some biologists believe that distressed plants release chemicals that are picked up by insects searching for food. Insects may even be performing a beneficial function in the garden by getting rid of ailing or feeble plants, thereby allowing the healthy ones to flourish. We should observe insects and let them reveal to us which plants need better care.

Strong, healthy plants, on the other hand, resist bugs and can survive surprisingly well even when insects are feeding. Using chemical nitrogen fertilizers makes plants grow fast, but it does not give them the strength or range of nutrients they need to resist insect attacks. In fact, nitrogen feeding actually attracts some insects. The best way to get healthy, vigorous plants is to provide them with good soil.

Good soil consists of four things: **organic matter** (humus) from plants and animals, **inorganic matter** from rock and mineral particles, **air**, and **water**. A soil rich in humus is full of beneficial bacteria and fungi; chemically treated soil is lifeless. Organic matter is the magic ingredient—loosening heavy soil and binding sandy soil, making it easier for water and air to move through it. Vegetables grown in soil containing good, rich humus have been found to contain 400 percent more minerals than those grown with chemical fertilizers.

The healthy garden is one in which the gardener gives back to the soil that which has been taken out. The best way to return nutrients to the soil is to add organic matter through compost, mulch, organic fertilizers, and cover crops. This giving back literally "grows" soil, a radical departure from standard mechanized agriculture, which is depleting the world's soil at an alarming rate.

COMPOST

Composting means speeding up nature's process of changing once-living material into the soft, crumbly, rich soil conditioner known as "black gold." Like cooking, compost has its expert practitioners, with their own favorite recipes, tools, and temperature gauges, but it also attracts those whose method is to simply throw something together and forget about it. Although it might be considered both a science and an art, as its devotees like to say, "Compost happens." However you go about it, adding compost is probably the most important thing you can do to achieve a healthy garden.

Composting requires the following ingredients: raw **organic material** (green and/or dry vegetation, kitchen scraps, etc.), **nitrogen** (grass clippings, fresh or dried livestock manure), sufficient **moisture** to make it feel like a slightly dampened sponge, and some **bacteria** (from good soil, compost, or a commercial activator) to start the breaking-down process. In aerobic composting, the pile is turned regularly so that oxygen-consuming bacteria can break down the organic material. Anaerobic, or airless, composting can be done by leaving the pile alone and forgetting it for many months, or by putting it into sealed compost bins or plastic bags.

Compost piles reflect the individuality of their creators. They can be located in an out-of-the-way corner of the garden where leaves and clippings are piled in a heap, or started in sleek mail order compost bins. Bins can be made from concrete blocks, chicken wire, slatted wooden shipping pallets (which are discarded in landfills by the millions), or snow fencing. Many people have a series of bins: one for filling, one for aging, and one for emptying around the garden. The process can take from two weeks to three years, depending on moisture, heat, frequency of turning, and how finely shredded the raw material happened to be. The smaller the particles, the faster they decompose. Once the magic transformation has taken place, you can dig the compost into the soil or use it as a top dressing one inch deep around the garden.

Good books on composting include *Let It Rot,* by Stu Campbell; *The Urban/Suburban Composter,* by Cullen and Johnson; and *The Rodale Book of Composting.*

EARTHWORMS

Sometimes called the "intestines of the soil," earthworms perform the invaluable task of literally eating their way through earth, digesting organic matter and minerals, and transforming it into richer, more usable soil. These underground tillers also break up and aerate the soil. Soils without them are hard and difficult to work. Earthworms also attract birds, which then eat insects. Charles Darwin concluded that no other animal had played as important a part in the history of the world.

By all means, order earthworms and disperse them in the garden so that they can go to work. However, be sure to add organic matter to the soil to give them something to work with, or they will go elsewhere. Earthworms cannot tolerate chemical fertilizers, and they are killed by slug and snail poisons.

PUTTING WORMS TO WORK

To get the benefit of rich earthworm castings for your garden, consider vermiculture, or vermicomposting. You can acquire earthworm boxes and hundreds of red wrigglers for a nominal cost, set them up in an out-of-the-way spot, and let them go to work for you, turning kitchen wastes into a marvelous source of nutrients and soil conditioners. This can be especially practical in cold climates, where winter brings composting to a halt. Earthworms may turn out to be the best pets you ever had—fascinating to children, quiet, and capable of being left home alone for weeks, and they even clean up after themselves.

Many community waste management programs now provide information and even bins for vermiculture (and composting too), as do mail order suppliers. Plan on one square foot of surface area per pound of garbage produced per week, and about two pounds of red worms for each pound of daily garbage. Worm suppliers can be located in garden magazines and mail order catalogs. All you need to do is supply damp bedding (shredded paper, but no colored ink) and a little bit of dirt.

After about four months, you can push everything to one side, add fresh bedding and start adding garbage to the new area. The worms will gravitate there and you can harvest the castings. You can get three-layer bins in which the worms move progressively up to the top, which makes collecting the castings less messy.

MULCH

Mulch consists of a layer of organic matter spread around the plants right on top of the soil. A good mulch keeps down the weeds, holds moisture in the ground, regulates the ground temperature, creates a favorable habitat for earthworms, protects plant roots, and adds organic matter to the soil. As Ruth Stout describes in *Gardening Without Work*, mulching also cuts down on gardening chores, namely digging, hoeing, weeding, and watering. Although Stout used salt hay at least eight inches deep, or garden leaves covered with hay, any number of materials can be used for mulch: compost (probably the best), bark, wood chips, alfalfa hay, buckwheat hulls, cocoa shells, shredded oak leaves, coffee grounds, corncobs, grass clippings, evergreen branches, hops, peanut hulls, peat moss, pine needles, sawdust, wood chips and shavings, ground cork, ground seashells, seaweed, and newspapers.

ORGANIC FERTILIZERS

Organic fertilizers contain a much wider spectrum of nutrients than petroleum-derived chemical fertilizers. Some organic fertilizers consist of soybean meal, hoof and horn meal, bonemeal, alfalfa meal, or worm castings (earthworm manure). Fish fertilizers are among the best.

Seaweed has been used for hundreds of years by farmers. A magic bullet in the garden, it contains hormones, fifty-five trace minerals, and soil conditioners. Composted into the soil, it reportedly adds nutrients, such as trace elements, plant enzymes, and growth hormones, that are difficult to find from other sources. As a mulch, it helps retain moisture, while gradually adding nutrients to the soil.

A good organic fertilizer can be made by combining one part bloodmeal, two parts bonemeal, three parts wood ash, and four parts compost. Dig small amounts into the soil around plants and water well.

Seaweed meal can also be worked into the soil. Spraying kelp on plants as a foliar fertilizer (a fertilizer absorbed through the leaves) strengthens the leaves, making them more resistant to pests. Kelp provides the plants with the means to develop their own arsenal against pests.

Another foliar feeding spray consists of a compost tea made by filling a bucket half full of compost (or well-rotted manure) with water. Wait a few days, stirring occasionally, then strain and spray. Use the leftovers as mulch.

To make instant blender fertilizer, throw all your kitchen scraps into a container by the sink. Stale bread, leftover cereal, vegetable parings, eggshells, fruit peelings—anything that would go down the garbage disposal, except grease and meat scraps. In the morning, throw it into a blender and fill with water. Liquefy it, then take it out and pour it around your plants. To keep peace in the family, you may want to buy a used blender and keep it just for this purpose.

Limestone, phosphate rock, gypsum, crushed eggshells, greensand, granite dust, and wood ashes can also be added to the soil in small amounts to provide additional minerals.

It's a good idea to have your soil tested to determine its unique weaknesses and needs. Contact your local agricultural cooperative extension office or look in the yellow pages for professional labs.

COVER CROPS

Sometimes called green manure composting, cover crops add nitrogen to the soil while improving its structure and adding organic matter. Seed an area with plants like vetches, clovers, legumes, alfalfa, beans, peas, barley, buckwheat, or rye. After they have matured, turn or dig them into the soil and wait a month or six weeks for them to decompose.

COMPANION PLANTING

If you plant certain species together, they help each other thrive and they repel insects. This also adds to the variety of plants—which is the way nature's gardens thrive. The more interplanting you have in the garden, the less chance that a particular pest population will get out of control. This has been called the pointillist approach to gardening successfully against pests. We add another battle cry: "Diversity!" Many pests are fairly specific about what they will eat and will voluntarily starve rather than eat a different plant, although there are notable exceptions, of course, such as grasshoppers.

Champion insect-repellent plants can be found in members of the onion family, including garlic. You probably can never have enough of these, and they are particularly good as borders. Other "protector" plants include tansy, coriander, wormwood, rue, thyme, sage, and members of the mint family. Flowers include nasturtium, marigold, petunia, geranium, and chrysanthemum. More than one plant is generally needed to have much effect against insects, so be liberal.

Rotate plants every year to remove them from the sphere of influence of pests living in the soil. Buying resistant varieties will also save a great deal of time in the trenches.

THE TACTICS OF TINY GAME
HUNTING IN THE GARDEN

If gardening means war, we have only ourselves to blame. We plant delicate seedlings and then are amazed when they tantalize the taste buds of hungry slugs. We try to grow the sweetest, best-tasting corn and expect the raccoons to ignore it. We lovingly nurture spectacular roses and are horrified when aphids find them attractive too.

Although the era of DDT, the wonder poison, ended in the 1960s in the United States, its spirit lived on. DDT was superseded by more and more poisons, all promising the perfect kill. However, the quick fix of bombing the house and nuking the yard to get rid of everything that scurries, crawls, climbs, digs, or flies may be losing its appeal.

In the new battle plan, we try to design the healthiest garden possible, prepare the richest soil, and grow the strongest plants. Then we enlist nature on our side, using her own soldiers in our cause. After all, no one understands aphids better than the ladybug whose life revolves around eating as many of them as possible. There are no better insect hunters than the beetles and spiders who devote their entire lives to trapping and devouring them. Simply by understanding who is on our side and who isn't puts us on the road to success. Along the way, we use the following tactics.

HANDPICKING

Handpicking is the first line of defense. You can't find an older method of pest control. Bugs never develop resistance to it either.

Gardeners used to like to put the bugs they handpicked into kerosene—we're not sure why, unless people have always had an urge to mix their insects with strong, foul concoctions. A jar with soapy water will do just fine.

Handpicking in the early morning, when the bugs are still cold and sluggish, can bring rewarding results. Be sure you know exactly what you are picking, however. If in doubt, put the insect in question in a glass jar and take it to your local natural history museum or agricultural extension agent. Or consult an insect guidebook with colored illustrations.

Shaking insects out of hiding is a way to pick them off by the dozen. For small plants, use a light-colored umbrella. Slip it under the plant, then give the plant a couple of shakes or whack it with a stick. When trees are infested, place white sheets under the branches and shake them. You'd be amazed at what the poor tree was putting up with. You can also use a hand-held vacuum cleaner to mechanically handpick bugs.

Some of the worst garden assailants are the tiniest, and a magnifying glass can be an invaluable tool. Use it to first see if any predators are at work. Try gluing a magnifying mirror onto the flat end of a spatula and hold it under the leaves. This works particularly well with whiteflies.

One gardener we know heard that birds have eyesight equivalent to seeing through binoculars. Now he imitates birds and looks for his bugs through binoculars.

HOSING

If bugs are assaulting your plants, counterattack by turning a strong stream of water on them. A good, adjustable hose nozzle is all it takes. This is especially good for dealing with insects that are too small to see or handpick effectively, such as aphids, thrips, and spider mites. Don't forget to get the undersides of the leaves, where they tend to hide out. Many will be unable to get back on the plants to resume their feasting, and it can even kill some of them outright. A handheld Rainbird is particularly effective.

TRAPS

Traps can be used for flies, moths, yellow jackets, aphids, beetles, slugs and snails, and many more. They can be made from old jars, milk bottles, cans, plastic bags, boards, whatever. Baits can be whipped up from molasses, fruit, eggs, honey, beer, fish, and meat scraps. Fermenting liquids made from yeast and sugars or fruit also make good baits. Sticky products and pans of soapy water become death traps when cleverly manipulated. All it takes is a little imagination and some knowledge about the habits of the pests. For instance, when fruit trees are just starting to bloom, coat pieces of white paper with a sticky substance and hang them in the trees. Later, when the fruit begins to set, use red or orange sticky-coated balls.

Pheromone traps that use chemical attractants for specific pests are now readily available. Contact your local farm advisory or university extension service to ask if pheromones are manufactured for the particular insect you want to trap.

Because many pests are attracted to chrome yellow, sticky traps can be made from yellow-painted cans hung on stakes around the garden. Coat the cans with a substance such as Stikem Special, Tanglefoot, or petroleum jelly. The insects will land on the can and get stuck. Instead of coating the can itself, you can cover it with a clear plastic bag and put the sticky substance right on that. When the bags are full of bugs, discard them and use fresh sticky-coated bags. You can even buy huge strips of sticky sheeting to encircle plant beds.

A more ornamental version of this trap can be made by cutting heavy yellow paper into flower shapes, coating them with a sticky material, and "planting" them around the garden.

Always monitor the traps to make sure they are not catching beneficial insects.

Electric bug zappers catch and sizzle all kinds of insects—good and bad—and for that reason we do not recommend their use outdoors. Besides, a germ-laden fly that gets zapped spreads those germs beyond the trap.

BARRIERS

Barriers run the gamut, from surrounding the garden with copper stripping to keep out snails to encircling each plant with its own little paper collar to keep out cutworms.

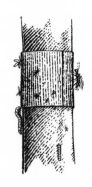

Sticky tree-trunk barrier

Barriers around tree trunks can be highly effective, because many pests in trees either get there by crawling up the trunk or eventually crawl down it. An old method of collecting moths and beetles on tree trunks was called "sugaring." It consisted of mixing stale beer, brown sugar, and crushed bananas in a thick consistency and smearing it on the tree trunk. Tree trunks can be wrapped in expandable cloth (tree wrap) and smeared with grease or a sticky substance like Stikem Special or Tanglefoot. Because some insects, like ants, are adept at getting through tiny crevices, the tree can first be wrapped in cotton batting. Or simply wrap the trunk with strips of sticky tape, like masking tape, alternating sticky side out adjacent to sticky side in.

Row covers placed over plants will keep insects away. Best used when the plants are first set out in the spring, they can be made of old screens bent in half and sealed at the ends. Cheesecloth or porous polyester fabrics let in water, air, and sunshine, while keeping out pernicious flying insects that attempt to lay their eggs on the plants. The fabric should cover the entire plant, with the edges buried in dirt.

SOAPS

Soaps were once a common weapon for combating insects, both in the home and outdoors, and they have made a welcome return to the gardener's arsenal. We like them because we've never managed to spray anything in our lives without getting some spray on ourselves.

Insects are very sensitive to soap sprays, which seem to make it impossible for them to breathe through the tubes on their sides. Wasps on guard at their nest will tumble helplessly to the ground when hit with a soap spray. Soaps may also act to destroy the insects' nervous system. (No one really understands exactly how they work, however.) They must be sprayed right onto the insects to kill them. Remember, most insects are found on the undersides of leaves. Soap sprays are particularly effective on aphids, earwigs, psyllids, sawflies, leaf miners, spider mites, thrips, scale, and whiteflies.

Soaps are biodegradable and largely harmless to honey bees, ladybugs, and parasitic wasps who visit the plant later—although not if they get sprayed directly.

Because soaps break down rapidly, they have to be used repeatedly—every few days in some cases. The label will give instructions. Water well before using and spray when plants are in morning or afternoon shade. Don't use them when it's hotter than 85°F. Some soaps should be rinsed off the plant about an hour after using.

We like to use a soap spray made by putting two tablespoons of liquid dish soap into a gallon of water. Other gardeners use soap flakes, Murphy's Oil Soap, Dr. Bronner's liquid soap, or Basic H. The same quality that makes soaps effective at cutting grease allows them to cut down wax-coated pests.

Most garden centers carry insecticidal soaps (e.g., Safer's) formulated to harm plants as little as possible. (Homemade soap solutions may burn the plant leaves if the mixture ends up too strong.) Soaps can also be mixed into other sprays to make them stick to the plants better and add an extra whammy.

One grower we know mixes Safer soap with fish emulsion and kelp to provide protection, nutrition, and some repellence for his plants. To one gallon of water he adds two tablespoons fish emulsion, two tablespoons powdered kelp, and two tablespoons soap.

Soap spray for aphids

Enzyme cleaners are now also being marketed as insecticides (e.g., Kleen Kill). They dissolve the insects' exoskeleton and are biodegradable. You can also find preformed (salmonella-free) enzyme cleaners at swimming pool, plumbing, and janitorial supply houses.

HORTICULTURAL OILS

Horticultural oils have been used successfully for hundreds of years. They went out of favor when newer chemicals took their place. But the older methods are effective and safer than modern controls. These oils work particularly well on mealybugs, aphids, scale, mites, whiteflies, beetles, and the eggs of many tree pests, particularly caterpillars. They work by suffocating the insect or egg, and they destroy the insect *before* it has a chance to do any damage. Insects have not developed resistance to them because they do not survive them, and they do absolutely no harm to the environment or to us.

Horticultural oils on the market today do not damage the leaves of plants and can be used all year round. However, be sure the plant or tree is well watered before you spray. The label on the oil should tell you which plants are suitable for treatment and when to treat them.

To make your own oil spray, simply mix a cup of vegetable oil (corn and olive oil are good) and a tablespoon of liquid soap into a gallon of water. (The soap helps emulsify the oil.) Shake well and spray. For smaller amounts, put two or three teaspoons of the oil/soap mixture in a cup of water, shake well, and spray.

DUSTS

If you have ever seen an animal giving itself a dust bath, it was probably using the dust as a form of insect control. Dusts are some of the most useful (and underrated) products that can be enlisted in the war against insects, because of both their durable insecticidal properties and their general harmlessness to people. The one precaution that must be followed when using a dust is to wear goggles and a mask, because dusts can irritate eyes and lungs.

Diatomaceous earth   This dust comes from the mined remains of fossilized one-celled diatoms that lived 30 million years ago. It kills insects mechanically, not chemically, because its sharp, silica edges puncture their soft, waxy covering. Death is by dehydration. Considered safe for humans, it is added to animal feed to control intestinal parasites and used on stored food to deter pests. Birds that eat insects killed by diatomaceous earth are not affected. It can kill individual bees but won't contaminate the hive. Furthermore, it won't kill earthworms.

Diatomaceous earth makes an excellent barrier in gardens, where it deters caterpillars, slugs and snails, borers, leafhoppers, and thrips, among other bugs. It can also be mixed in water and sprayed against aphids and spider mites. When the water evaporates, a thin coating of the dust will remain on the leaves. Try not to spray it on blossoms where bees will be landing.

Some people sprinkle diatomaceous earth on manure around barns and stables to keep down the fly population.

Note: Do not use diatomaceous earth that is treated for swimming pool filters. Only use horticultural grade diatomaceous earth.

Silica aerogel   Another desiccating dust, silica aerogel can absorb hundreds of times its weight in moisture. When an insect comes in contact with it, the moisture from the outer surface of the insect's body gets absorbed and the insect dehydrates and dies. Two commercial products that contain mostly silica aerogel are Dri-die and Drione.

Boric acid   This product is a formulation of borax, a mined mineral. It is one of the most effective and safest ways to kill cockroaches and can also be used for ants, crickets, silverfish, termites, and caterpillars. It was once a common household item, used as eyewash. You can buy it in powders, sprays, and baits, specifically for use as an insecticide. Remember, it is poisonous to people if ingested.

Sulfur   One of the oldest known pesticides in the world, sulfur is another gardening remedy that has gained new respect. Its use actually goes back thousands of years; the Egyptians fumigated their granaries with it. Homer even wrote about it in the *Iliad*.

Although growers use it mostly as a fungicide, sulfur also controls mites and chiggers. Additionally, it plays a vital role in plant nutrition and can be used to lower the pH of soil that is too alkaline.

You can get sulfur in a powder form for dusting, a wettable powder for spraying, and a liquid spray. If you use it as a dust, be sure to wear protective clothing, goggles, and a face mask, because it can be quite irritating to mucous membranes.

Lime   Calcium carbonate, or lime, comes from limestone, marble, or chalk. Often used to change the pH of the soil to make it more alkaline, it also acts as a good pest repellent or pesticide. Another formulation is called quicklime, or hydrated lime. All draw water out of the insects on contact and thus dehydrate and kill them. It should be handled with care, as it is caustic.

BIOLOGICAL CONTROLS

As the saying goes, "My enemy's enemy is my friend." Biological control means using the natural enemies of the pests to fight them. These include microbes (bacteria, viruses, fungi, protozoa, and nematodes); parasites and parasitoids (parasitic wasps and flies); and predators (beneficial insects and animals). Nature itself keeps organisms in balance in this way. The biologist Paul DeBach called biological control "intellectually satisfying, biologically intriguing, and ecologically rational." More and more farmers and citizens are turning to biological controls, which are insect-specific, biodegradable, and nontoxic to humans and the environment.

Bacterial controls   These include the use of disease-causing bacteria to kill pests. In other words, germ warfare. Probably the most widely used bacterial insecticide, *Bacillus thuringiensis,* or Bt, occurs naturally. First discovered in 1901 as a silkworm pathogen, it has been widely manufactured since the 1960s. Pathogens like Bt are quite selective, so even though they infect hundreds of garden pests, especially caterpillars, they won't harm plants, animals, humans, or most beneficial insects. A little nibble of a leaf treated with Bt is enough for a pest to get a lethal dose, but it has to be eaten. The caterpillars must be in the leaf-chewing stage, not the moth or butterfly stage.

Other formulations of Bt include Bti, which kills mosquito larvae, one of the major pest problems of the world, and Bt San Diego, for the Colorado potato beetle.

Milky spore disease   This is the common name for *Bacillus popilliae,* a naturally occurring bacterium that wipes out the grubs of Japanese beetles, rose chafers, and May/June beetles, among others. The grubs ingest the spores as they move through the soil. This disease causes their normally clear blood to turn milky, thus the name. As they sicken and die, they release millions more spores. Although it can take a few years to get established in a lawn, the treatment is self-perpetuating and can last for fifteen to twenty years. The trick is to get all your neighbors to use it, too, so that their beetles don't come wandering onto your grass or plants.

Growth regulators and pheromones   These controls use the insects' own hormones and sex attractant chemicals to maim, trap, confuse, and otherwise stymie them. For instance, a juvenile hormone for fleas, methoprene, keeps them from ever attaining their fertile maturity. Another hormone, 20-hydroxyecdysone (Intrepid), sends target larvae into a lethal premature molt.

Since many insects spend most of their lives in isolation, and they don't see well enough to find mates visually, they are highly dependent on scent or pheromones to find each other so that they can reproduce. These sex attractants can be quite effective when used in traps to catch otherwise elusive critters. Or they can be used without traps to confound and confuse mates trying to find one another. They are also providing scientists with challenging problems: one scientist, Dr. Robert Yamamoto, spent nine months "milking" ten thousand virgin female cockroaches to get $\frac{1}{2,500}$ of an ounce of their sex attractant so that it could be synthesized in the lab. Good work, Doctor.

Biological fungi and viruses   This is a fairly newly exploited family of biologicals that attack specific pests. All insects are susceptible to fungal and viral diseases, and they often decimate populations of pests spontaneously. Currently, fungus pathogens are available commercially to control cockroaches, aphids, whiteflies, mosquito larvae, crickets, and grasshoppers. Viruses available commercially mostly attack moth larvae. This is a promising area of pest control that targets only specific pests.

Parasites, parasitoids, and predators These creatures are the tiny game hunter's living troops. Parasites and parasitoids generally attack only one specific victim. For instance, one tiny parasitoid wasp only goes after the alfalfa seed weevil. (Their cocoons are quite something—they jump!) Predators are insects or animals that get their nourishment from devouring other creatures. Most such predators eat many, many insects in the course of their life span, and their appetite can be amazing. Toads can eat 3,000 insects a month. Predators also attack a great number of insect species.

For more about acquiring or attracting predatory insects, which work so hard, so unwittingly, and so selfishly for us all, see *Good Bugs*.

BOTANICALS

Plants have evolved chemical defenses against insects for millions of years. In fact, pesticides made from plants with insecticidal properties were commonly used before chemical insecticides usurped their place in the gardener's arsenal. A classic botanical is made from tobacco.

Just because they are made from plants, however, doesn't mean all botanicals are safe. We actually consider these botanical pesticides as a last resort. Some are harmful to fish and other aquatic life, and so they should never be used around bodies of water. Some are also harmful to honey bees, so if you do use one, spray in the evening after the bees have departed. A good rule of thumb is to hold off on using botanicals unless more than 25 percent of the plant's leaves have been damaged.

On the brighter side, they do work. They break down easily in the environment, are not stored in living tissues, and don't pose a danger to future generations of humans and wildlife.

Be familiar with the names of these botanicals so that you can buy them instead of the much more dangerous pesticides. Often there is nothing on the label to differentiate them. If you do purchase a botanical, make sure it hasn't been mixed with other chemical pesticides or synergists such as piperonyl butoxide (PBO), which is toxic.

Neem The neem tree is an evergreen tropical plant known for its insecticidal properties. It grows in Asia, Malaysia, the African tropics,

Florida, and Southern California. We advise anyone living where this tree grows to plant one. The insecticides produced from the extracts of the tree are known to repel or disrupt the development of at least 200 insects, including cockroaches, grasshoppers, mosquitoes, corn earworms, Mexican bean beetles, and armyworms. Termites won't even eat the wood. Because it is both a repellent and an insecticide, insects stand less chance of developing resistance to it, and it doesn't seem to harm beneficial insects. The fruit produces an oil traditionally used as folk medicine in India.

Sabadilla   An organic pesticide made from a Mexican lily, sabadilla has been used since the sixteenth century. This same plant has also been used for years to lower blood pressure, so people on blood pressure medication should avoid it. It is a contact killer and is toxic to bees, beneficials, fish, and frogs—do not use it where runoff may occur. When applying it as a dust, use a mask and goggles and avoid skin contact. It works well on hard-to-kill insects, especially when applied directly onto the bug. In sunshine it breaks down in about two days.

Pyrethrum   This product comes from the dried flowers of various chrysanthemums. One of these, *C. cinerariifolium*, used to be called the insect flower or insect plant and is thought to have been used hundreds of years ago by the Persians against body lice. It can be used as poison and to repel flies, roaches, termites, aphids, fleas, thrips, leafhoppers, whiteflies, and some kinds of beetles. It breaks down very quickly and is considered so safe for people that it used to be dispensed by doctors for intestinal worms. However, bees and ladybugs are killed along with the pests, so take great care when using it.

Pyrethrum consists of the powdered, dried flowers; pyrethrin is the active ingredient in the flower; pyrethroids are synthetic forms of pyrethrin. Pyrethrum has a fast knockdown effect, which is good when you want pests to stop eating immediately. Sometimes, however, the bugs are only paralyzed and manage to recover. Pyrethrum is often combined with synthetic pesticides because of its quick action. Do not buy any of these combination products.

Chrysanthemum plants have caused an allergic reaction in some people—the same people who get hay fever may be sensitive to pyrethrum.

Ryana   This substance is made from the roots of a South American plant. It was discovered in the early 1940s and has proven good for control of codling moths in apple, pear, and quince trees. Sometimes it doesn't kill the pests but puts them into a kind of nonfeeding stupor.

Rotenone   A stomach poison for insects, rotenone is made from extracts of tropical plants—mainly derris and cube—and has been used for centuries in Asia and South America. It can be dusted (wearing a mask and goggles) or sprayed to control beetles, caterpillars, weevils, borers, and other bugs. It kills a wide range of pests but is also toxic to fish, frogs, toads, and bees. Of all the botanicals, rotenone is probably the most toxic to humans, so think of it as a last resort. Care must be taken to apply it after dusk, when bees are no longer active. It breaks down in the environment after three to seven days and may not be as effective if mixed with alkaline water.

Nicotine   Nicotine is an old, old botanical spray. It can be purchased as a dust, or a spray can be made from the tobacco plant (especially the stems) or even from plug tobacco, cigars, or strong cigarettes. Nicotine is highly toxic; even though it breaks down fairly quickly, it is one of the most toxic insecticides mentioned in this book, and we strongly recommend doing without it. The nicotine sulfate form is less toxic. Nicotine can also be used as a pesticide in its smoke form (see *Houseplant Pests*).

REPELLENTS

Many plants have their own brand of chemicals that combat or resist insect attack, and some of the following repellent sprays use those properties. Some of these sprays are so repellent, they kill the insects.

Adding dish soap or a little vegetable oil (one teaspoon to a quart of liquid) to the spray makes it stick to the plant better. Soap will also coat the bodies of the insects and kill them even faster.

Some of these repellents are made from plants like garlic and onion that we use to flavor our own food. It's hard to believe that insects find them that awful. Others, like quassia spray, have an intense bitterness and make more sense to us. A different kind of repellent is made by adding two tablespoons of artificial vanilla to a quart of water and spraying it around the stems of squash and cucumber plants. It masks the innate bitter smell of the plant that attracts the insects in the first place.

Note: Repellents need to be reapplied after a good rain or overhead watering.

Don't worry too much about using the exact ingredients for these sprays. As with cooking, adjust them to suit yourself. Many concoctions require straining, which can be done well through old panty hose or coffee filters. Many of these sprays are now manufactured commercially, with certain advantages: hot pepper spray (e.g., Hot Pepper Wax), formulated with paraffin to stick better; and garlic (e.g., Garlic Barrier), formulated to use as a systemic.

Here are our favorite all-around repellent sprays:

Mish-Mash Spray

A good general repellent spray with something distasteful for everyone. This is especially good for cabbage loopers, imported cabbageworms, and other caterpillars.

1 cup spearmint leaves
1 cup onion tops
½ cup hot red peppers
1 small horseradish plant—roots and leaves
2 teaspoons liquid soap
water

Grind the first four ingredients in a blender or food processor with enough water to liquefy them. Add the liquid dish soap and a quart of water. This is the base and should be refrigerated. When you want to use it, add half a cup to one quart of water and strain into a spray bottle.

Tomato Leaf Spray

Tomato leaves have insecticidal properties, which can be explained by the fact that they are related to the tobacco plant.

> 2 cups tomato leaves and stems
> water

Chop the plant parts coarsely and process in a blender with two cups of water. Let the mess stand overnight. Strain and add two more cups water, then spray onto your plants. Excellent for aphids.

Hot Pepper Spray

New York transit officials once tried using hot pepper on turnstiles to keep teenagers from sucking out the tokens. Hot chili peppers have also been used to repel roadrunners, rats, and even underwater zebra mussels. We use this spray to keep chewing insects such as tomato hornworms and other caterpillars from enjoying our plants. It is also good against cucumber beetles.

> ½ cup hot peppers
> 2 teaspoons liquid soap
> water

Mix the peppers and two cups of water in a blender. Let stand overnight, then strain and add the soap and six more cups of water. This can also be made with a quarter cup of ground red pepper, the hotter the better. Dissolve the pepper in boiling water first; then let it cool before spraying.

Another way to make use of chili pepper's incendiary properties is to dampen plants with a mist of water (or wait for a dew) and sprinkle the plants directly with powdered hot red pepper. This treatment is good for caterpillars, cabbageworms, and ants, among other bugs, and it will not harm the plants.

Garlic Spray

Garlic has wonderful repellent qualities, as anyone who has been around someone with a penchant for eating raw garlic on toast knows. Besides planting garlic—a lovely plant—around the garden, you can use it as a seed dressing to keep birds and rodents away. Dampen the seeds before planting and sprinkle them with garlic powder. Try this on bulbs, which mice sometimes like to nibble on. Garlic powder can be substituted for fresh garlic in the following recipes.

More than a repellent, garlic also works as an insecticide and has been proven to kill large numbers of mosquitoes, aphids, and onion flies when used as an emulsion with oil. It can also control fungus, mildew, scab, and other pathogens.

> 3 whole garlic bulbs (not cloves)
> 3 tablespoons mineral or olive oil
> 1 tablespoon liquid soap
> water

Separate the cloves of garlic, but you needn't bother to peel them. Chop in a food processor. Put them in a jar with the oil and let stand for twenty-four hours. Add the liquid soap and three cups of water. Store in the refrigerator in a glass jar. When ready to use, strain and dilute, using half a cup of the concentrate to a quart of water. Spray on plants to kill or repel cutworms, wireworms, slugs, and whiteflies.

Garlic-Pepper Spray

> 1 garlic bulb (not clove)
> 1 tablespoon hot red pepper
> water

Finely chop the garlic. Add the hot red pepper and a quart of water. Let steep for an hour. Strain and spray. Good for aphids and spider mites.

Hot Pepper-Onion-Garlic Spray

This spray operates under the assumption that if one is good, three ought to be better.

> 2 hot chili peppers, or 2 teaspoons of powdered hot red pepper
> 1 onion
> 6 cloves garlic

1 teaspoon liquid soap
water

Grind the first three ingredients in a blender or food processor with four cups of water. Let stand for twenty-four hours, then strain and add the liquid soap. Spray on plants.

Citrus Peel Spray

According to *Science News*, limonene, an essential oil extracted from citrus peels, has been found to deter pests such as fall armyworms and cotton boll-worms. Chop the peels of citrus fruit and pour boil-ing water over them to release the limonene. Blend the mixture in a food processor, let stand overnight, then strain, dilute, and spray on plants. It has both repellent and insecticidal properties.

Hot pepper spray

Glue Spray

This will really stick it to them. Mix a tablespoon of ordinary liquid pa-per glue or rabbit's skin glue (from an art supply store) with three or four cups of warm water. Spray on plants to make the leaves inedible and to coat insects' bodies and suffocate them. Use it against scale and mites. As the glue dries, it flakes off the plant and the dead insects go with it. Some people use a spray-on adhesive—this works, too, but it's detri-mental to the ozone layer.

Quassia Spray

Quassia may be one of the safest of all botanical sprays. It harms soft-bodied pests like caterpillars and aphids but won't hurt bees and lady-bugs.

Cover a pound of quassia chips (available by mail order from some garden supply centers) with water. Let soak overnight. Strain. Dilute with water at a ratio of 1 to 10, adding a little dish soap to the spray water.

Wormwood Spray

This is like making a tea, and the method can be used with any plants you want to make a repellent spray from.

Cover two cups of wormwood leaves with two cups of boiling water. Let steep for one hour. Strain and add to two quarts of water. Spray at once. Wormwood is very, very bitter, and insects like flea beetles and cabbageworms don't like the taste of it.

Other plants to make a tea spray from:

Rhubarb leaves. Poisonous if eaten, because they contain high concentrations of oxalic acid. That is why people eat the stems and not the leaves of this plant. But no point letting the leaves go to waste.

Coriander. Good for aphids.

Chinaberry leaves. This tree is well known for its insecticidal properties.

Tansy. A strong tasting herb, once used as a salt substitute. (It is not recommended for eating, however, because it is mildly poisonous.) Ants, Japanese beetles, flies, striped cucumber beetles, and squash bugs dislike it.

Other plants and herbs suitable for sprays include elderberry leaves, eucalyptus, pennyroyal (for ants), cedarwood, sassafras (for aphids), rose geranium, lavender, bay laurel, feverfew (sometimes confused with pyrethrum), mint (for aphids and ants), and onion skins.

Essential Oil Sprays

In *Gardening Without Poisons,* Beatrice Trum Hunter wrote of the insect-killing properties of essential oils, such as oil of lemon grass, mint, coriander, geranium, lavender, and sage. Mix these oils with water and use in place of botanical tea sprays.

ALLIES IN THE AIR
AND ON THE GROUND

We have long recognized movement in the garden as a source of beauty, and garden lovers have traditionally achieved this with fountains. But movement also comes from a hummingbird darting into sight, a bee crawling over a flower, and the hop of a frog. Make your garden more beautiful with living things. The wildlife you welcome will also become your allies as tiny game hunters.

These predators are not as attracted to perfectly manicured gardens. They do better where the grass is a little longer and where there is plenty of native vegetation, a small rock or woodpile to hide in, a pond to hunt around, a few dead branches for nests, and a working compost heap in which to forage for bugs. They also need a good variety of plants, trees, and shrubs. These should take up at least half of any given yard in relation to the lawn area. Consider planting "islands" of native shrubs, tall grasses, and small trees right in the middle of the lawn. And don't use any chemicals on the grass. These are deadly to birds and other wildlife.

Here are some of the wild tiny game hunters that you will want to welcome.

BATS

If birds were once considered pests in the fields, bats were thought to be the devil incarnate and as such have been treated far worse. And for much

Bat with prey

longer, too. We are only just beginning to reverse our long-standing prejudices against these odd and marvelous little mammals, the only ones that fly.

Bats are among the most important predators of night-flying insects. When birds go to sleep, the bats come out—and remember, this is when mosquitoes are on the move. One bat may eat up to 3,000 mosquitoes in a night! A good-sized colony of about 250,000 bats can eat two to four tons of insects each night. Besides being among the best tiny game hunters we know, bats pollinate vital plants and disperse seeds, mostly in tropical forests. Frankly, we need bats.

Because they breed very slowly and tend to congregate in large numbers, bats have been extremely vulnerable. With great folly, they have been shot, poisoned, burned, and dynamited by the millions. Pesticides have taken as great a toll on bats as prejudice, and DDT and other insecticides have exterminated untold numbers.

Fortunately, an organization called Bat Conservation International has done a great deal to educate people about the true value of bats. Many believe that bats pose a great menace because of rabies, but although some are infected, and no bat should ever be touched with bare hands, dogs with rabies create far more problems for humans than bats do.

Bats sometimes set up housekeeping in the attics of homes for the warmth and shelter provided there. They can go unnoticed for years. We advocate exclusion only when they have become a problem.

Using pesticides to get rid of bats in houses risks poisoning the human residents too. Bats can be effectively excluded by figuring out which holes they are entering and exiting from. Then bird netting can be tacked over the hole. The netting should be larger than the hole and left open at the bottom, so the bats can leave but can't get back inside. Do not do this when there is danger of baby bats being stuck inside the dwelling to die, generally from late May to July. Once all the bats have been excluded, seal up the holes.

If you find a bat in a room, don't panic; they are one of the gentlest animals on earth. Keeping the bat in sight at all times, close all the doors to other rooms, and open as many windows and doors to the outside as possible. The bat may leave when it detects the currents of fresh air. You can also trap it by putting a can or box over it and sliding cardboard underneath. Do not touch it without wearing heavy gloves.

Bat house

Many people have begun to put up bat houses to attract these marvelous hunters to their neighborhood and to make up for the loss of bat habitats through urbanization. You can order a bat house specifically designed to meet bats' need to roost in tight crevices from Bat Conservation International, which also sells inexpensive plans for making your own bat house (see *Resources and Mail Order*).

People have had the greatest success when bat houses are placed near bodies of water, on poles or the sides of buildings, between ten and twenty-five feet high, and facing east or southeast. Some people have reported that after they had put up a bat house, the bats were literally lined up on the tree waiting to get in. Others have found that it can take as long as a year or two for a bat house to be occupied. But the reward of having the bats hunting for tiny game, night after night, certainly makes it worthwhile to welcome and protect them.

BIRDS

Before the turn of the century, farmers firmly believed that birds were eating their crops and could not be persuaded that many were only eating insects. As a result, many beneficial birds were shot almost to extinction by the late 1800s. In fact, the passenger pigeon and the Eskimo curlew were totally exterminated.

Today it is common knowledge that birds are among the most important predators of insects. Swallows have been observed eating hundreds of leafhoppers in a day, and a house wren will feed a hundred bugs to its young in one afternoon. Without birds, our insect infestations would be greatly magnified. And hummingbirds are major pollinators.

So it makes sense to try to welcome as many birds as possible onto your property (unless they are crows, which eat baby songbirds).

Birds can be greatly encouraged to visit a garden by providing them with water, food, and shelter. A shallow birdbath can be placed out in the open where the birds can see their enemies. Be sure to find one with a rough surface; the smooth ones don't permit a good footing. Birds are attracted by a fine spray of water or dripping water, so prop a slowly dripping hose over the birdbath. Or make a small hole in a bucket, fill it with water, and hang it over a galvanized pan or a metal garbage can lid set on bricks. The sound will attract birds from far away.

Another way to welcome birds is to provide them with a dust bath. Birds probably keep down their own vermin (mites and lice) with dust baths, which they thoroughly enjoy. Dig out a spot about three feet square and six inches deep and line it with bricks or stones. Fill it with a mixture of equal parts sand, loam, and sifted ash. Put it where you can enjoy watching them frolic.

The purple martin is one of the best insect eaters, and the best way to attract it is to build a martin house—or martin condos, a whole row of them. To attract many kinds of birds, put up a variety of houses and nesting boxes.

Some birds do best if they build their own nests, so provide them with materials such as hair, string, yarn (pieces four to eight inches long), feathers, or cotton rags. Tack these to bird feeders or place them in a box and hang it from a tree. Don't put out bright-colored material, as the nests are best camouflaged.

Bird feeders can be as simple as a dish on a deck or a wooden tray with sides, nailed onto a post. Nail sheet metal onto the post to make an upside-down funnel to keep cats or squirrels from climbing up. Like birdbaths, bird feeders should be out in the open so that cats can't wait in ambush. It's only fair

Welcome birds in the garden

if you are attracting birds to your garden that you keep the cats away. Put a bell on your cat's collar to warn birds.

The more kinds of food you put out, the greater the variety of birds. Hang a suet feeder in a fruit tree to attract woodpeckers, who will eat the caterpillars. Many birds like suet (hard beef or mutton fat); put it into net bags or melt it and pour it into a coconut shell and hang it in a tree.

BIRDS AS PESTS

Sometimes birds wear out their welcome, such as when they won't leave your cherry tree alone. However, they may be eating cherries because they are thirsty. Giving them water may be a solution. Spraying your cherries with a mild solution of salt water will also deter them.

If you want to keep birds away from sweet berries, provide them with tart berry bushes, which they actually prefer.

If you think the birds are taking an unfair share of your corn, give them the benefit of the doubt. They may be after the corn earworms instead. Put paper cups on the ears just in case. When the corn is tempting them, be sure the bird feeders are full. You can also soak unpopped popcorn overnight and throw it on the ground around the corn plants for the birds.

Netting thrown over trees and strawberries will keep birds out. Timing is important: put the netting on before the fruit ripens, so that the birds don't have a chance to discover what they are missing. Because it is so hard to cover certain trees with netting, some people simply use heavy strong black thread, tossing a spool back and forth over the branches until a good amount of thread crisscrosses the tree. Birds dislike getting entangled in it.

Other items that can be hung in trees to repel birds include sliced onions, empty milk cartons, inflatable plastic owls or snakes, pinwheels, thin strips of black plastic stapled to paper plates, and crumpled balls of aluminum foil. Birds become accustomed to them fairly quickly, however.

In the past, people would hang a stuffed hawk in a tree or put out potatoes with feathers stuck in them. We know one fellow who hangs a dead crow in a tree and successfully keeps other crows at bay.

To keep birds out of the strawberry patch, cut up an old garden hose into two- or three-foot lengths and place these around the plants. The idea is to fool the birds into thinking the hose is a snake. Plastic snakes or old cassette tape can be strewn around the plants too.

Before strawberries ripen, paint hazelnut or walnut shells red and strew them around the beds. Birds will quickly learn to avoid them.

Planting specifically for birds is one thing that homeowners can do to counteract the frightening and very real loss of their habitat, caused by never-ending development. Large-acreage farming has also led to the loss of vital fencerows and woodlots for birds. Garden books, local botanic gardens, and master gardeners will have lists of plants and trees that will attract birds in your area.

Don't forget, birds will eat ten times as many insects as they will other types of food, so sharing some fruit with them may be a good price to pay for their presence.

LIZARDS

Lizards love insects. The only trouble is, cats love lizards, and they will hunt and eat them just as they do birds. So the presence of a cat can be a deterrent in a garden that would accommodate wildlife. We know of one gardener who conditioned neighborhood cats to stay out of his yard by luring them into metal traps baited with tuna fish and then turning the hose on them.

Lizards have a few advantages over snakes—they don't frighten people, and they don't eat toads. They need sunny spots in gardens and are drawn to the shelter of rock walls or rock piles with cracks and crevices to hide in. They are also attracted to logs and dead branches. We find they take refuge under our juniper bushes. You can keep a few shallow containers in the shade and fill them with water for lizards. Remember, the wilder and less cultivated your garden is, the more wild species will be at home in it.

In subtropical regions, many lizards, including geckos, are welcomed into houses, where they are appreciated for their pest control, particularly of mosquitoes and cockroaches.

SNAKES

We do not admit to any great love of snakes, but because they are so use-ful and eat so many rats, mice, and insect pests, we have to put them in the tiny game hunters' hall of fame. More than two hundred species oc-cur in North America. Of these, only four (rattlesnakes, copperheads, water moccasins, and coral snakes) may harm humans. All snakes, in-cluding the poisonous ones, are constantly at work for us cutting down pest populations. It's a pity so many snakes are killed on sight out of fear and ignorance.

Bull snakes and gopher snakes eat gophers and do an adequate job of controlling them in the wild. When housing goes up in an area, how-ever, snakes tend to disappear, leaving the gophers free rein. Garter snakes are a great ally in the garden, because they feed so readily on slugs. How-ever, they also eat earthworms and frogs. King snakes are especially use-ful, because in addition to feeding on rodents, they also kill poisonous snakes.

TOADS AND FROGS

Like snakes, spiders, and bats, toads have been vilified and associated with witchcraft and evil in ways they don't deserve. Toads eat hundreds of in-sects every night. One toad will eat 10,000 to 15,000 bugs in a season. As Ruth Shaw Ernst wrote in *The Naturalist's Garden:* "If there is a toad on your property, cherish it. There is nothing a toad relishes more for breakfast, lunch, or dinner than a slug, unless it is a caterpillar, cutworm, or other horrid grub."

Like snakes, toads and frogs only eat insects that move. Sometimes a toad and its prey will play a waiting game of eerie stillness. As soon as the quarry moves, the toad's tongue darts out so fast you can hardly see the insect disappear. Toads eat mosquitoes and termites as well as stan-dard garden pests.

Toads can be mistaken for frogs, which also consume insects. Frogs have smoother skins than their bump-covered cousins, and they look wet-ter. They also need to live closer to water. Frogs also have much longer hind legs and jump around energetically, while toads seem more lethar-

Frog

gic. In fact, toads are so slow, they can be sadly vulnerable around power mowers.

People often import toads into their garden for tiny game hunting chores—certainly more frequently than they bring in snakes. For one thing, toads are fairly easy to catch in the wild near ponds. When you bring one home, it may have to be kept in a cage or an upside-down crate for a while until it loses its homing instinct. Try to capture a young one, which will be more likely to settle in. While it's in its cage, provide it with plenty of live insects, either handpicked from the garden or from a pet store.

Toads do best if they have access to a shallow pool with a sandy bottom. If you can't provide one, make sure they have a shallow pan of water or a ground-level birdbath in a shady place. Toads and frogs don't drink water but absorb it through their skin. They also need moisture to breathe. If you want the toad to breed, it will need a small pond.

Provide your toad-in-residence with shady, moist havens around the yard. An overturned clay pot sunk into the ground makes a nice toad house. Chip a hole in the clay for a doorway. Or dig out a special toad hole for your new friend a few inches deep and covered with a board or encased with rocks. Put sandy soil in the bottom to make the little creature comfy. A small piece of concrete drainpipe can be used for the entranceway.

Rigging up a low-watt light or a footpath light and having it on for several hours after dark will attract insects for the toad's delight. Place it near low vegetation to give the toad a place to lie in ambush. Some toads have inhabited gardens for dozens of years.

Toad

GOOD BUGS

The average square yard in a typical garden contains more than 1,000 insects. They can't all be gluttonous garden destroyers, or we'd have only bare dirt. Actually, less than 1 percent of all insects are considered pests, and virtually all have predators and parasites of their own to contend with.

Ours is truly a bug-eat-bug world, and here we sing the praises of the best of the tiny game hunters, those that live to eat our pests. Insects have always done a much better job of controlling other insects by eating them than we have done with poisons. So get to know your bugs—and stop killing the wrong ones.

The idea of deliberately manipulating insects for pest control is not a new one. In 1800, Charles Darwin's grandfather, Erasmus Darwin, suggested deliberately breeding lacewings and ladybirds to control aphids. At the time, people didn't take him up on it, but today the idea has become a reality. Suppliers of beneficial bugs are doing business all over the country. Take advantage of them. Not only will they send you the right insect for the job, many of them also give advice on the best way to manage particular problems. (See *Resources and Mail Order* for suppliers.)

MAIL ORDER MERCENARIES
• • • • • • • • • • • • • • •

When ordering and using beneficial insects, stop using any residual pesticides for at least a month and maybe more before the "good guys" are brought in. These bugs seem to be much more sensitive and vulnerable to pesticides than the pests. And remember, you must have some pests for the beneficials to eat—and the pests will eat some of your plants. That's life.

Make your garden more attractive to desirable insects. Many beneficials feed on nectar and honeydew while in the adult stage, so plant flowers—especially flowering herbs and wildflowers—to give them something to eat. Plants like cosmos, daisies, white sweet alyssum, sunflowers, black-eyed Susan, oleander, yarrow, and tansy will attract them. Jerusalem artichokes, strawflowers, and clover also give encouragement and good harborage, as do plants such as wild carrots, parsnips, and angelica. Damselflies like the shelter of a nice nasturtium blossom. Parasitic wasps, which have the tiniest of tongues, need the smaller blossoms of herbs and flowers such as wild Queen Anne's lace, coriander, dill, fennel, baby's breath, lovage, and parsley.

When your mercenaries arrive, follow the directions for their release, especially regarding timing and temperature. They generally prefer a garden with high moisture or some access to water. A 2,000-square-foot garden should have at least four or five permanent sources of moisture. Pans or birdbaths filled with gravel and water will do. Change the water often to keep the algae and mosquito wrigglers out.

A solution of honey and water can be sprayed on plants to satisfy the predators' craving for sweets. Commercial preparations of nectar-type food (e.g., Bio-Control, Honeydew, Wheast) are also available.

The following pest predators can be delivered to your door.

GREEN LACEWINGS
With its golden eyes and long diaphanous wings, this glorious insect looks incredibly fragile—like some exotic pet from a fairy kingdom—but it is one of the most practical and effective of the beneficial insects.

Some adult green lacewings feed on insects, but most feed on honeydew. Their larvae, however, have voracious appetites and eat aphids with such gusto that they are called aphid lions. (The larvae of the brown lacewing are called aphid wolves.) They also devour other soft-bodied insects such as red spider mites (another favorite), mealybugs, thrips, and scale, as well as the eggs of many worms.

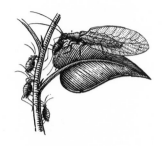

Lacewing eating aphids

Like ladybug larvae, lacewing larvae look like little alligators with pincers. They use these hollow mandibles to impale their prey and suck out its juices. Some of them then toss the carcass remains onto their back.

Lacewing eggs

So greedy are lacewing larvae, they have a tendency to cannibalism. The female lays each egg on the end of a fine, hairlike strand, thereby separating them at birth and preventing this.

When you order lacewings, they will arrive as eggs, packed in a feeding material such as rice hulls, in case they should hatch. They are so tiny that you may need a magnifying glass to see them; a thimble would hold thousands. If you detect any movement at all, the eggs are hatching, so disperse them right away, or the larvae might eat each other up. If you can't disperse them immediately (and it's not a good idea to do so if rain is imminent), the eggs can be refrigerated for a few days to delay their hatching.

Sprinkle the eggs on foliage around the garden on a warm day wherever pests are present. Or distribute them in little paper cups stapled to leaves. The lacewings can travel up to a hundred feet in search of food, and they may be better at finding potential pest problems than you are.

To hold them in the garden, make sure that the adult lacewings are supplied with nectar, honeydew, or pollen.

LADYBUGS

Everyone is familiar with spotted ladybugs, ladybirds, or lady beetles (which is what they really are), one of the few insects that inspire universal affection. They are considered harbingers of good luck in many countries. The "lady" in "ladybug" refers to the Virgin Mary, and such sacred allusions are found in many languages. In Sweden their name translates to "the Virgin Mary's golden hen," and in France they are called *bêtes à bon Dieu*, "the Good Lord's creatures."

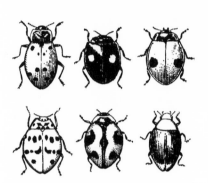

(Left to right, top to bottom) Convergent ladybird, two-stabbed lady beetle, two-spotted lady beetle, ashy gray ladybird, vedalia, and mealybug destroyer

There are around 400 species in North America, of which the **convergent lady beetle** is one of our most important predators. They love to eat aphids but also devour scale insects, leafhoppers, thrips, eggs, and the larvae of harmful insects, including many moths. Another ladybug, the **vedalia beetle**, achieved fame when it was imported from Australia in the late 1880s and successfully saved the California citrus industry from devastation by cottony cushion scale. After a disastrous wipe-out by DDT applications in the 1940s, ladybugs are back at work in orchards today.

Their orange eggs, which are laid under leaves and can be seen standing on end in clumps of five to fifty, hatch in the spring. The larvae resemble tiny, black, spiny alligators with orange spots, and they may eat about 400 aphids as they grow up. An adult ladybug can go on to eat thousands, insinuating its body into tight little buds and other places that sprays can't reach. It may also produce several generations of predaceous offspring in one summer.

A lot of people faithfully buy ladybird beetles, bring them home, and release them, only to find no trace of them the next day. Because they were gathered in hibernation, they may simply need to fly away to burn

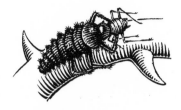

Ladybug larva eating aphid

Ladybug eating aphid

off stored fat. We actually recommend lacewings as the more reliable predator to purchase and release.

If you do succumb to the ladybug's charms, plan to release them in the evening in a well-sprinkled garden; they are less likely to fly away at night. It's a good idea to refrigerate them for a few hours first. Handle them gently; too much agitation causes them to fly to safety. Place them at the base of plants, but not too many at one spot—a tablespoon per plant or shrub will suffice. They can be stored in the refrigerator for two weeks and doled into the garden a few tablespoons at a time—think of them as garden vitamins.

The real trick is to get them to stay long enough to lay eggs, for their larvae will stick around and dine exceedingly well for you. Some people put them in loose mesh bags that enclose an aphid-infested branch—with full release a day or two later. You can also provide them with something to eat immediately: spray the plants with a 10 percent sugar or honey solution or a commercial nectar. You can also purchase lures with kairomone scent to keep them around. Ladybugs require high humidity and water to drink, so keep the garden moist.

Ladybugs have few enemies, because of their bitter taste, but they are highly vulnerable to poisonous sprays.

MEALYBUG DESTROYERS

An Australian relative of the ladybird, the mealybug destroyer is, of course, a mealybug and scale predator. In its larval stage, it quite resembles a mealybug. The adult, a black, shiny insect with a reddish head, will eat other pests if there aren't any mealybugs around. If you order them, be sure to keep the ants away, or they can't do their job.

PARASITIC NEMATODES

It's a good thing that nematodes are literally invisible, because these microscopic roundworms are incredibly fearsome looking. They're quite lethal, too—to their underground victims. In many areas they have become one of the most effective, as well as safest, ways to take care of pests such as cutworms, armyworms, root maggots, borers, wireworms, and cabbage loopers, as well as soil-dwelling grubs such as Colorado potato beetles, Japanese beetles, and June beetles. In fact, beneficial nematodes will kill more than 200 species of insects, but they will not harm earthworms or plants. (Other nematodes, such as root-knot nematodes, are harmful to plants.) Some beneficial nematodes can also control subterranean termites.

Nematodes may live in the soil for months. Like awful creatures out of science fiction, they enter their victims through their mouth or body openings. Some kill by introducing bacteria into their victims, others by slowly eating their tissue.

Building a healthy, humus-rich soil always leads to an increase in beneficial parasites. When you buy nematodes, they come in a form that can easily be sprayed or poured onto the surface of the soil. A small package containing millions of these organisms will go to work destroying harmful pests. Although they don't last in the ground forever, they're not that fragile, but don't spray them onto the soil in direct sunlight.

PARASITIC WASPS

Our tiny allies on the big bug battlefield, these insects give wasps a good name. They sting neither humans nor animals, and different species can kill as many as 200 kinds of pests—mostly caterpillars, although some also go after the eggs or larvae of beetles and flies. There are literally thousands of species, very diverse in shape, and all extremely tiny.

Aphidius wasp

One wasp may parasitize as many as 100 pest eggs during its lifetime. When the eggs hatch, they feed on the contents of their host eggs, killing them and later emerging as well-fed adults. Entomologists call parasites such as these "parasitoids," because the host never survives but is completely consumed from within. And they effectively prevent pests from even starting to do any damage. They search out many of the pests (or their eggs or larvae) in the garden, lay their eggs in them, and force them to switch roles—from pests to terminal incubators of more wasps.

The following wasps are available through mail order suppliers.

Trichogramma wasps   This is the wasp most commonly bred by commercial insectaries. They are tiny, with a wingspread of about one-fiftieth of an inch. When you purchase them by mail, they arrive inside the host eggs. Keep them in a warm, humid place. Timing is important when dispersing them, because it must be done when the moths are laying their eggs. Start releasing them in stages, near where the moths are laying, the moment you first see them in your garden.

Encarsia formosa   Another parasitic wasp, *Encarsia formosa* is also known as the whitefly parasite. It lays its eggs right in the scales of immature whiteflies; as the wasp grows, it feeds on the whitefly and kills it. When an egg is laid on a scale, it turns black, so you can actually watch the process working.

Braconid wasps   These can be observed as little white ricelike attachments on the backs of caterpillars or beetle larvae. The tiny silken bags are the cocoons of the next wasp generation. The larvae themselves have already spent some time inside the body of the caterpillar, consuming its tissue without quite killing it. Some braconids, such as ***Aphidius* wasps,** are avid aphid eaters; they leave dead aphids with little holes in their backs. Adult braconids can look like flying ants.

Braconid wasp

Ichneumon flies   These are really wasps, with very long ovipositors (egg-depositing devices) that look like formidable stingers, but they actually use them to bore through bark and lay eggs on caterpillars and wood-boring beetles hiding deep within the bark or wood of a tree. They may find their victims by sensing them through vibrations.

PARASITES OF FLIES

Highly specific parasitoids, which can be either flies or wasps, prey on flies that hang out around livestock. People do not even notice their presence. They lay their eggs inside fly pupae, killing them before they can emerge. These filth fly parasites are quite effective where flies are in abundance, particularly around manure in stables, kennels, feedlots, barns, and big composting operations.

Fly parasites have to be released continuously throughout the fly season, because flies steadily move in from elsewhere. And just because you're using them doesn't mean you can give up good sanitation. Traps should be used along with the parasites, because the flies are much faster breeders than the parasites. A program using fly parasites may take weeks or months to get going, but it does work, often quite dramatically. As with other biological controls, parasitic flies are much more vulnerable to insecticides than their hosts.

PREDATORY MITES

Predatory mites, bigger than their prey and faster breeders, too, can be ordered through the mail and released to control spider mites, especially in greenhouses. They can't be dispersed if residual pesticides have been used in the previous two or three weeks. The pest mite population should be controlled with insecticidal soap as much as possible before releasing the predators. Since they don't fly, they can't fly away—a big plus for you.

GOOD BUGS GRATIS
• • • • • • • • • •

Many other beneficial bugs appear in the garden on their own without benefit of insectaries and postage. Learn to recognize and appreciate them, and leave them alone.

"TRUE" BUGS (*HEMIPTERA*)

Some true bugs, like bed bugs, plant bugs, and lace bugs, are definitely pests. Others, including assassin bugs, big-eyed bugs, soldier bugs, ambush bugs, damsel bugs, and pirate bugs, eat a wide range of pests and their eggs. Some have adhesive pads on their legs covered with thousands of sticky hairs—like Velcro—that enable them to get a good grip on their victims. They visit flowers with lots of pollen. Provide them with wild weedy patches for harborage. Big-eyed bugs and pirate bugs are strongly attracted to alfalfa.

Beneficial bombardier beetle

Big-eyed bugs, minute pirate bugs, and spined soldier bugs are now available commercially.

BEETLES

Beetles make up the largest order of all living things—almost 300,000 species. There are so many kinds that it's often hard to determine which are good and which are bad. One old rule of thumb from gardening lore is, if it's moving slow, stomp on it; if it's moving fast, it's probably after another bug, so let it go. You can always tell a beetle by the straight line going down the center of its back, where its hard front wings join.

Ground Beetles There are 40,000 species of ground beetles, but they are mostly nocturnal, and hardly anyone seems to be expert at identifying them. Most are black, but some are iridescent. Their bodies may be shaped like shields. Sometimes called caterpillar hunters, fast-moving ground beetles are very valuable in any garden. They eat ants, aphids, cutworms, flies, gypsy moths, mosquitoes, slugs, snails, spider mites, termites, and many other pests. Some even climb trees to hunt their prey. One of these, the European ground beetle, was imported to help control gypsy moths

Fast-moving ground beetle

in the East. Most ground beetles emit noxious vapors when attacked, so be careful about picking them up.

Rove Beetles   This slender insect doesn't look like a "real" beetle, but more like an earwig without the pinchers. Very active and quite speedy, it sometimes raises the back end of its body when running around. It preys on mites, aphids, nematodes, snails, slugs, and fly eggs and maggots, including cabbage maggots. Common in compost piles, it scavenges in decaying material and is an important predator of cabbage beetles.

Rove beetle

Soldier Beetles   With their rectangular shape and brownish color, soldier beetles, also called leather-winged beetles, somewhat resemble fireflies with the light turned off. Although their larvae are all insect predators, the adults of some varieties no longer soldier, but spend their days on flowers.

Soldier beetle

Tiger Beetles   These master hunters are beautifully colored, iridescent blue, green, and bronze, and big— three-quarters of an inch long. A truly fast-moving beetle, the tiger beetle goes after ants, aphids, caterpillars, and other bugs. The larvae live in vertical tunnels in the ground, where they position themselves with their heads blocking the tunnel entrance; then they stretch out and grab passing prey.

Tiger beetle

A FEW GOOD FLIES

It would not be fair to omit these insects from any good-guy list. Although they are vastly outnumbered by their pestiferous relatives and are not available through mail order, you should know them when you see them and try not to harm them.

Robber Flies Robber flies, some of which look like bumblebees, will attack their prey in flight. Some even run down prey such as small grasshoppers. The larvae feed on other insect larvae in the soil.

Syrphid Flies (Hover Flies or Flower Flies) These colorful, yellow-striped flies are noted for their striking protective mimicry; some look like bees, some like wasps. Their appearance keeps them safe from birds and predators, although they are actually quite harmless. Some can be as large as half an inch and remain motionless in flight like humming-birds. Like hummingbirds, too, the adults feed on nectar, and they are also important pollinators. The larvae eat aphids, scale, leafhoppers, and thrips, among other pests. That small green, sluglike worm on your rose-bud may well be a syrphid maggot hunting for aphids, so take care.

Tachinid Flies Parasitic insects that closely resemble extra-large, hairy house flies, tachinid flies glue their eggs onto many kinds of caterpillars or onto the leaves that the victim might eat. One species can parasitize 100 kinds of caterpillars, including European corn borers and gypsy moths. Others live off grasshoppers and true bugs.

DISTINGUISHED NATIVE BENEFICIALS
• • • • • • • • • • • • • • • • • • • •

ANTLIONS
As an adult, this insect resembles the damselfly. The larvae, which are sometimes called doodle bugs, are wonderful hunters and trappers. They dig little pits in dry earth or sand and wait for their victims to tumble in. Then they throw up sand to confound them, pounce on them, par-alyze them, suck out their insides, and toss the dry shells out of the pit.

DAMSELFLIES
Damselflies are a smaller relative of dragonflies, and they prefer insects with soft bodies. A damselfly can hover motionless in midair while pick-ing off aphids one by one from a bud or leaf. Like dragonflies, they are

daytime hunters and usually patrol near bodies of water. The nymphs of both dragonflies and damselflies eat mosquito larvae practically nonstop. A water garden will attract these marvelous hunters.

DRAGONFLIES

Fossils of ancient "dinosaur" dragonflies show them to have once been giant insects of the air, with up to twenty-nine-inch wingspans, and some are still quite impressive today at around five inches. Also known as mosquito hawks, bee butchers, horse stingers, and devil's darning needles, they are magnificent fliers, with fabulous 360° vision. Tennyson called them "living flashes of light."

Dragonfly and prey

Dragonflies scoop up their prey, with their hairy legs forming a "shopping basket." They devour their victims in flight, sucking them dry and discarding the carcasses. They can eat their weight in food in half an hour. A dragonfly was once reported to have had as many as 100 mosquitoes in its basket of legs at one time.

In one of the more amazing transformations of the insect world, the dragonfly changes from an underwater creature to one that spends most of its time in the air. The only thing that remains the same is its insatiable appetite for living, moving insects.

FIREFLIES

Sometimes called lightning bugs, although they are no more true bugs than they are flies, fireflies possess a luminous segment near the end of the abdomen, which is the basis of an elaborate mate-signaling behavior. As larvae (glowworms), they eat cutworms and small insects. They also have a way of eating slugs and snails by injecting them with digestive juices and then drinking the newly liquefied tissue.

HONORABLY DISCHARGED

• • • • • • • • • • • • • •

PRAYING MANTISES

This is one of the silliest-looking, most oddly affecting insects you will ever make friends with. It's also one of the insect world's great ambush predators. Lying patiently in wait for its victims, looking for all the world like the soul of religious contemplation, the mantis can suddenly attack with lightning speed and grasp its victim in a sawlike clamp. It consumes its prey alive and then delicately grooms and cleans itself. Aggressive and gluttonous, it can eat vast quantities of insects, including beetles, caterpillars, and grasshoppers. Some even attempt to attack small frogs, lizards, and birds. Unfortunately, it will also devour beneficial insects, including bees and others of its own kind, so we do not recommend buying it for pest control. It might best be ordered as an entomological adventure for children.

In Europe, women used to collect mantis egg cases under a full moon to use them for toothaches or chilblains. In Africa, some people believed they could bring the dead to life! If you get praying mantis egg cases through the mail, attach them on low-growing twigs in the fall. It can be a lot of fun to watch them hatch, although the event is easy to miss. Most will fall prey, when they first hatch, to ants, lizards, and other predators—their own kind included. You can put the egg case
in a paper bag secured with a paper clip. Place it in a sunny spot
on a windowsill, but don't let it
get hot. Check it daily to see if
any are hatching (it could take
up to eight weeks). As soon as
they start to emerge, take them
outside and let them go.

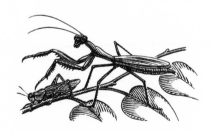

Praying mantis

GARDEN PESTS

CHOMPERS

• • • • • •

CABBAGE LOOPERS
AND IMPORTED CABBAGEWORMS

Although separate species, the one being a moth and the other a butterfly, these two caterpillars have many similarities. In addition to munching on cabbage plants, they will both attack almost any vegetable you care to grow: broccoli, cauliflower, beans, radishes, turnips, peas, mustard, potatoes, tomatoes, brussels sprouts, some leafy greens, and even a few flowers. They chew big holes in the leaves and then bore right into the vegetables.

The cabbageworm, a pretty pale green caterpillar, turns into a white butterfly with black spots on the wings. It's not hard to catch in a butterfly net. Or take out an old tennis racket and whack it before its offspring start whacking at your plants.

Cabbage looper

The cabbage looper moth is brown and gray and has a couple of silver spots on its wings. The caterpillar gets its name from the funny loopy way it draws itself up as it moves, which is why it is sometimes called the measuring worm, or "inchworm." For once, this is a pest that lays its eggs (little white ones) on the tops of leaves.

These two caterpillars both have several generations a year, and they can be summer-long nuisances. The following controls work for both of them.

▶ CONTROL

Cabbage pests tend to get worse year after year, so be sure to rotate plants around the garden. Clear away all garden and crop debris in the fall, because this is where the eggs will overwinter. When you put in new crops, watch for the butterflies. As soon as you see them, cover the plants with fabric row covers or other protective barriers.

Keep an eye out for their eggs under or on top of leaves. If the caterpillars are at work already, you will see chewed-up leaves and even their green droppings at the bottom of the leaf. They can be knocked off the plants into jars of soapy water.

Some people spray their plants with seawater. (Plants in the cabbage family can tolerate a little salt.) The salt water kills the eggs and keeps the caterpillars from eating the leaves. Garlic spray can also be used.

As with hundreds of other pestiferous caterpillars, *Bacillus thuringiensis* (Bt) is a most effective treatment. Start spraying it once a week after the butterflies or moths appear. Try Bt before using botanical sprays like sabadilla or rotenone. Bt is a pathogen that attacks only leaf-eating caterpillars, so it doesn't pose any risk of harming beneficial insects.

Repellents   If you find these pests infesting heads of cabbage, pour sour milk into them. You can make milk sour by adding a little vinegar to it (four teaspoons per cup of milk). Mish-mash spray (see *Tactics of Tiny Game Hunting in the Garden*) makes another good repellent.

For another tried-and-true repellent, mix a quarter of a cup of salt with half a cup of flour and dust the plants lightly with it. Ruth Stout (*Gardening Without Work*) simply sprinkled her cabbages with a saltshaker a couple of times during the growing season. Wood ashes sprinkled on the leaves act as a repellent. (If you don't believe this, try sprinkling ashes on your own salad.) Diatomaceous earth can also be sprinkled onto the plant. All these dusts must be reapplied after rain or watering.

Cabbageworms can also be deterred by placing geranium leaves over the growing cabbage.

Natural Enemies Parasitic wasps and tachinid flies are natural parasites of caterpillars, so grow herbs and flowers near your vegetables to attract them. Yellow jackets and ground beetles will eat great numbers of them. Although many gardening experts advise keeping weeds out of the garden, ground beetles like a few weeds around, so plant some ragweed or lamb's quarters just for these predators.

COLORADO POTATO BEETLES

Up until the 1870s, the Colorado potato beetle was a fairly innocuous beetle living near the Rocky Mountains, happily eating a wild plant called buffalo bur and its relatives. These plants happen to be in the nightshade family, so when immigrants began to plant potatoes (also in the nightshade family), the beetle found brand-new pastures.

Perhaps because one female can lay as many as 1,000 eggs, and there may be four generations a season, this is one of the most difficult and persistent pests of the garden, going after eggplant, peppers, and tomatoes as well as potatoes, chomping away until leaves are lacy shreds.

The potato beetle is easy to identify by its black-and-yellow-striped body; even the larvae are colorful—red or orange, with rows of tiny black spots along their sides.

▶ CONTROL

Look for yellow-orange egg masses on the undersides of leaves and destroy them. Handpick larvae and adults too. Wear gloves.

A good thick mulch of straw may keep them from climbing up your potato plants. Repellent sprays like pepper-onion-garlic spray may also deter them. Sprinkle damp plants with wheat bran to deter eating.

Dig a deep trench around the garden and line it with plastic. Destroy beetles that fall in and can't get out.

Soap sprays will kill the larvae on contact. A formulation of Bt (Bt ssp. *tenebrionis*) can also kill larvae.

Lacewings, ladybugs, soldier bugs, toads, and predatory wasps all go after potato beetles.

As a last resort, use rotenone or pyrethrin spray.

CUCUMBER BEETLES

Is it the cucumber beetle's fault if the plant it feeds on starts to wilt, stem by stem, until the whole thing collapses in a dead heap? It certainly is. These beetles carry the dreaded bacterial wilt and other plant diseases in their digestive tract, but even disease-free, they can decimate plants.

A number of beetle species share the name. The **spotted cucumber beetle** (also known as the southern corn rootworm) is greenish with black spots. The **striped cucumber beetle**, yellowish orange with black stripes, can be found virtually everywhere and gets the award for being the greatest enemy of the cucumber.

Striped cucumber beetle

All cucumber beetles and their bacteria hibernate over the winter months in garden debris or weeds or under logs or leaves. Although the adults feed on just about any plant, their larvae are more picky; they need cucurbit roots or corn roots to develop. In addition to cucumbers, cucurbits include vines like squash, pumpkin, melon, and gourd, so the beetles have plenty of choices in a well-stocked vegetable garden. They lay their orange-yellow eggs in the soil at the base of plants. Little whitish wormy grubs hatch and go after the plant roots. Both the grubs and the adults pass along incurable diseases to the plants.

▶ CONTROL

Tilling or cultivating the ground in early spring or late fall helps kill the eggs in the soil. Use a good thick mulch to prevent beetles from laying their eggs there in the first place.

Radishes, marigolds, catnip, and nasturtiums repel cucumber beetles.

Some gardeners literally ring their plants with radishes. Be sure to rotate crops defensively.

In the spring, cover your seedlings with barriers like cheesecloth, floating row covers, or screen cone covers to keep the beetles away. Bury the edges well—don't leave a single spot where the little marauders can crawl under and get to the plant. Just in case, plant extra seedlings as insurance against losing your produce.

You can handpick these bugs, and you should, too, but they are really small, only a quarter of an inch long. One of the best places to look for them is inside the blossoms. If you take a big funnel with a plastic bag attached to the bottom by a rubber band, you can hold it under the plants and knock the bugs right into the funnel.

A traditional treatment for cucumber beetles is to mix a quarter of a cup each of wood ashes and lime in a gallon of water and spray it on the plants. Make sure the undersides of leaves are sprayed too. The plants can also be sprinkled with hot red pepper, lime, or chalk powder. Be sure to mist the plants first so that the dust will adhere. If the situation is desperate, spray the plants with neem or pyrethrum.

The bitter essence (curcurbitacin) of the cucurbit family strongly attracts cucumber beetles. Although repellent to other insects, it's like a drug to these beetles, and they eat compulsively when they get around it. Certain varieties of plants have had the bitterness bred out to some extent, providing some resistance to the beetles. You can disguise the bitter essence of the plants by making a spray out of water and vanilla extract or artificial vanilla flavoring and spritzing the plants with it.

You can also take advantage of the beetles' addiction to this particular flavor. Take cucumber peels, let them dry out, and sprinkle them with rotenone or pyrethrum, which will poison the beetles, or with diatomaceous earth, which will puncture their outer membrane. The nice thing about this trap is that other insects will not be attracted to it, although there is always the possibility that you might attract the neighbors' cucumber beetles.

Cucumber beetles' frenzy for the bitter quality in these vegetables (especially for the buffalo gourd) can make experimenting with these traps fun. Try coating a piece of yellow board with a sticky substance and placing cut-up cantaloupe rinds on it. Or use a shallow bowl with water, a little liquid soap, and some cantaloupe rinds or cucumber peels. Be on the lookout for commercial traps too. Some suppliers now carry a pheromone trap for these beetles.

Natural Enemies These beetles may be formidable, but they're not without enemies. Beetles, toads, and beneficial nematodes will consume them. Tachinid flies will parasitize them. Lacewings and ladybird beetles will devour their eggs. Grow dill to attract these fine hunters.

CUTWORMS

These obnoxious, greedy little devils can be black or dull brown in color. Look for them on the ground, curled up under bits of leaves or dirt right at the base of your seedlings. They curl up on purpose; perhaps you'll think they are dead. Don't be fooled. At night, while some feed on leaves, others go around biting off the stems of plants just above or just below the soil line. They are really vicious and not too smart, since they kill off the poor plant entirely and have to go find another one the next night.

▶ CONTROL

Cutworm collars, a good, sensible line of defense, can be made from toilet paper tubes, bottomless paper cups or tin cans, or lightweight cardboard or screen stapled around the plant stem. Press these collars at least an inch or two into the dirt around the plant. Aluminum foil or newspaper can also be wrapped around the stem; the newspapers will eventually disintegrate into the soil.

Before the advent of tin cans, stems were wrapped with hickory or walnut leaves, which probably acted as both repellent and barrier. Some people still like to anchor the ends of a couple of long onion or garlic tops in the hole before setting the plant in, then take the tops and wrap them around and around the stem of the plant.

Cutworm at work

Another cutworm foil consists of sticking a twig, nail, or straw into the dirt next to the stem. This keeps the cutworm from doing its boa constrictor number on the plant. When the plants get older and tougher, they aren't as appealing to cutworms.

Take a flashlight out at night and look for these caterpillars. Sometimes you'll even find them chewing on the edges of leaves. During the day you may find them resting under the soil right next to the stem— especially if they've just mangled that plant. Scrape away a layer of dirt or poke viciously around the soil with a sharp skewer. If you find one, put it in the bird feeder. Birds like cutworms a lot. So do toads, moles, and predatory beetles. They can also be parasitized by tachinid flies, trichogramma and braconid wasps, and nematodes.

Cutworms dislike the prickly quality of an oak-leaf mulch. Eggshells are another sharp deterrent; crush them and mix them into the soil near the plant. Or sprinkle diatomaceous earth or wood ashes in a circle around the plant. Ruth Stout wrote in *Gardening Without Work* that if her thick hay mulch was close enough to the stem of the plant, she was never bothered by cutworms.

Gardening literature from the early part of the century advised putting soot and lime around the plant; this probably worked, not because it hurt the cutworm, but because it gave the plant a chance to outgrow it. (Soot can be collected by scraping the inside of the fireplace chimney.)

Onion plants and tansy are said to repel cutworms, but a dusting of Bt will kill them. However, since they spend their days buried in the soil, you'd have to do this at night. Nematodes would be more effective.

Armyworms, or army cutworms, are one of several hundred species of cutworms. They get their name from their tendency to move in masses to "greener pastures." Handpicking provides good control, as do nematodes. Stop migrating masses with aluminum barriers. Use parasitic wasps or flies. Spray with Bt if necessary.

FALL WEBWORMS
AND EASTERN TENT CATERPILLARS

Fall webworms are quite gregarious. All the caterpillars that hatch from eggs laid by one moth on a tree stay together and spin a kind of waterproof pavilion for themselves. They travel back and forth between this home base and the leaves of the target tree. There may be between 50 and 300 caterpillars in a single web, and they can completely defoliate a tree in a very short time.

Tent caterpillars also spin webs for themselves in the crotches of trees or forks of branches. They mostly favor fruit trees. Unlike with webworms, their webs do not cover leaves and the ends of branches. With both of these caterpillars, however, the combination of insects and web makes for quite an infestation. But at least they're easy to spot.

▶ **CONTROL**

An old superstition held that if a woman walked disheveled and naked around the perimeter of a garden, it would cause the caterpillars to "fall off from the tree." Gardeners in the 1790s hung wet seaweed in the crotches of trees in the spring to repel the moths. The seaweed would also make a good mulch as it disintegrated.

Look for the egg masses on the trees during the winter months and cut off or scrape away any you find. Spray with horticultural oil. Later in the year, the tents or webs can be torn out manually with a stick or long pole (hammer nails around the tip of the pole for more grab) and the caterpillars can be destroyed. If the caterpillars are already crawling about on the tree, spray them with Bt.

Because they crawl down the tree before they pupate, you can set up traps for them around the trunk. Wrap the trunk in burlap or flannel, check it daily, and pick out the caterpillars.

Tent caterpillars and webworms share a number of predators, including birds, praying mantids, and parasitic wasps. They are even eaten by some species of beetles bold enough to climb trees and invade their nests.

FLEA BEETLES

When disturbed, these shiny little black or bronze bugs jump just like fleas. For such a little pest (one-tenth of an inch long), they make an awful lot of their distinctive round holes in leaves. Usually worst in the spring, these beetles generally won't kill your plants; they just ruin their looks. Some people actually tolerate them with a good deal of equanimity.

It's such a relief sometimes to deal with a pest that maims but doesn't murder.

They feed on the leaves of dichondra, eggplant, broccoli, cabbages, and cauliflowers, among other plants. They've really taken to California cuisine—they love arugula. Many vegetables have their very own species of flea beetle.

▶ CONTROL

Adult beetles lay eggs on the soil when they "awaken" (emerge) in early spring. The less garden debris and weeds left in the garden from last fall, the fewer the beetles in the spring. Flea beetles have several generations a year in the South. Cultivate the soil around plants regularly to kill or expose their eggs. Drenching soil with nematodes also gets rid of the grubs, which feed on roots.

Adult beetles feed on weeds while waiting for the good stuff to appear in the garden. They especially like young plants, so in the spring cover new plants with fabric row covers or screen covers. Like other pests, they seem to favor the weakest plants, so be sure that your plants have the advantage of a rich soil with a high organic content. Interplanting also helps foil them.

These hopping beetles dislike moisture, so first zap them with a hard spray of water. Other sprays that can be tried against them include garlic spray, onion spray, wormwood tea, soap spray, and neem.

Friendly plants that seem to repel these beetles include elderberry, mint, catnip, and wormwood.

Flea beetles are said to be attracted to traps baited with beer. They can also be trapped with white or yellow cards smeared with a sticky substance. Placing a drop of mustard oil in the center of the card will enhance the attractiveness. Sometimes all you need to do is hold the card over the plant and jiggle it to get the flea beetles to hop onto the trap.

GRASSHOPPERS

Grasshoppers and locusts (some people also refer to cicadas as locusts) were once thought to be two separate creatures, until the startling discovery that under certain circumstances, including food shortage, some species of solitary grass-hoppers actually metamorphosed into gregarious locusts, multi-plied unbelievably, and took off in swarms of inconceivable numbers.

Grasshopper

Before the twentieth century, the arrival of locusts (sometimes described as "grasshoppers gone crazy") meant that famine and death were sure to follow. Desert people called them "the teeth of the wind." American settlers in the 1800s called them hoppers, fighting them off with little success and great losses. Locusts would literally darken the sky when they appeared, accompanied by a great roaring, crackling sound. Where they landed, they ate every-thing except native grasses—including the paint off houses. Locusts have contributed much to the idea that insects are our enemies, and every year is the year of the locust somewhere in the world.

Mormon settlers had a similar problem with shield-backed grasshop-pers, termed "Mormon crickets." However, seagulls appeared and gorged themselves on the invaders, after which the Mormons erected a monu-ment to the gull in Salt Lake City.

Grasshoppers in the home garden can be great pests, because they eat so much. They range from an inch to two and a half inches long and are dark gray, green, yellowish, brown, or black. Their powerful hind legs enable them to jump twenty to thirty inches, and they can fly long distances.

▶ CONTROL

Look for clusters of creamy or yellow eggs in the shape of rice. Destroy them by digging up the soil in the fall to kill the eggs or bury them so deeply—at least six inches—that the hatched grasshoppers can't make it to the surface in the spring. A good thick mulch will also make it hard for them to come above ground.

Grasshoppers can be picked off at night by going out with a flashlight and getting them while they sleep. Or you can handpick them in the early morning while they are still lethargic. Wear gloves or use an extra pair of kitchen tongs and drop the bugs into a jar of soapy water.

Spray hot pepper spray or pepper-onion-garlic spray right on the plants to keep grasshoppers from eating them. Sabadilla dusted on wet leaves will also deter them. Covering plants with cheesecloth or fabric row covers will keep grasshoppers from getting to them. Leave enough room for the plants to grow under the fabric, securing the corners with rocks.

An effective biological control for grasshoppers, *Nosema locustae*, is a naturally occurring spore or parasite that infects the insects as a killing disease. It has to be ingested by the grasshoppers and comes in the form of baited wheat bran (Grasshopper Attack, Nolo Bait). When a grasshopper eats the bait, the spore is activated inside its digestive system, slowing its ability to feed and eventually killing it, although it may take weeks. The disease spreads from grasshopper to grasshopper, because they are cannibalistic. Timing is important. Grasshoppers should still be young—one-quarter to three-quarters of an inch in length—when the bait is applied, so it's best to start in early summer.

Natural Enemies   Here is a lazy way to get rid of grasshoppers: Make a solution of molasses water, using one part molasses to ten parts water. Fill wide-mouthed containers or dishes half full of this solution and set them around the yard. The grasshoppers will go after the sweet concoction, and birds, especially jays, will go after the grasshoppers. Other predators include praying mantises, spiders—if they get them in their webs—snakes, toads, skunks, and chickens. Ground beetles and blister beetles will devour grasshopper eggs—another reason not to use pesticides.

In addition to using molasses in water to trap grasshoppers, you can also try other ingredients, such as citrus juices, vanilla, beer, and vinegar.

GYPSY MOTHS

After the accidental release of gypsy moths in Medford, Massachusetts, in 1858, by a French astronomer and naturalist who should have known better, the voracious caterpillar descendants of this prolific moth went on to defoliate millions of trees. The hapless man who brought them to this country had been hoping to breed them with silkworms to help the French silk industry. In only twenty years, the infestation built to truly tremendous proportions. By the 1880s, the caterpillars in Medford were described as coming down the street in a black tide.

The female moth lays her eggs in large clusters of several hundred to a thousand, covered with hairs from her body. These clusters overwinter under stones, on tree trunks, and on many other kinds of surfaces—patio furniture, planters, cars, trucks, and campers. People have unknowingly transported many an egg cluster to a new location. When the eggs hatch, the caterpillars climb the trees.

The female moths themselves don't fly. The hairy little caterpillars travel by hanging themselves from the trees on silken threads they spin, until the wind picks them up and carries them aloft. They can easily go half a mile, and a strong wind will take them farther.

Gypsy moths prefer oaks and other hardwoods, but they will feed on over 400 plant species. Although they completely devour all the leaves on a tree, they kill few of the trees that they infest. They weaken them, however, and when an entire forest loses its leaves in the summer, its ecology changes.

Over the years, an incredible barrage of pesticides has been sprayed but has failed to control gypsy moths or even stop their spreading. Three million acres were sprayed with DDT in the Northeast in the 1950s, killing songbirds, fish, and crabs and forcing beekeepers out of business. This spraying probably made the problem worse by getting rid of the moths' enemies.

▶ CONTROL

Gypsy moths have been called "pests of people," not of trees, mainly because they do not destroy forests so much as they outrage homeowners by crawling all over their backyards, causing skin rashes and ruining the looks of their best trees. Rather than mass spraying, we advocate that each person fight his or her own moths simply to bring them within a personal tolerance level.

Eggs can be scraped off surfaces and dumped into ammonia or soap solutions. Tie a piece of burlap or wool to the tree and fold it over to make a double layer, with the fold at the top. The caterpillars, which are nocturnal, will crawl under it, seeking shade in the daytime. Then you can shake them out over a large pan of soapy water.

To keep the caterpillars out of the trees, band the trunks in late May and June with a sticky substance or sticky tape. Remember, these caterpillars travel; if kept out of one tree, they will simply move to another.

Spraying Bt on the caterpillars will be effective if done at the right time. Use a commercial sprayer available from garden catalogues, or hire a tree company. Be careful, though; some Bt strains can harm other insect larvae, such as those of butterflies. Bt is not used widely on forests, because it has to be reapplied every two weeks and hence is too expensive. Neem has also been used successfully against gypsy moths, however, and new fungus sprays are appearing on the market.

Pheromone, or sex attractant, traps are available for these moths. Pheromones can also be sprayed to cause general mayhem, confusion, and nonperformance among the male moths.

Natural Enemies   Infestations seem to come and go and have peak years—in 1981, gypsy moths infested and defoliated almost 10 million acres of forest. Ultimately, however, when the moths reach peak populations, a virus kills off most of them, quite spectacularly, and then the cycle starts all over again.

Numerous predators have been imported against this moth from all over the world, including flies, wasps, a white-footed mouse, and a large ground beetle that, in defiance of its name, climbs trees, where it feeds on moth larvae and pupae. Braconid wasps and tachinid flies are among the insects that parasitize gypsy moths.

Birds are wonderful predators of the caterpillars, as are moles, shrews, skunks, chipmunks, and squirrels, so the more such animals live in your yard, the better off you are.

If your trees are attacked and turned into the ugly ones on the block, do not abandon them. To bounce back they will need nurturing— adequate water and good feeding of the soil.

JAPANESE BEETLES

What a mess these beetles can make of people's gardens. The Japanese beetle invasion took place in New Jersey in 1916, when they hitchhiked in on some plants from Japan. That has been the time-honored way that some of our worst pests got their start here, while their natural predators missed the boat. After its arrival, the Japanese beetle flourished far better than it ever did in Japan, gradually spreading west.

Japanese beetle

These attractive beetles, with their metallic green bodies and bronze-colored wings, will devour more than 200 varieties of plants, including your favorite roses. Alighting on leaves, they go for the choice meat between the veins, leaving the leaf in lacy shreds. They also group feed, often in alarming clusters, on flowers and ripe fruit. Later, they lay eggs in the grass, and the C-shaped grubs root around under lawns, where they also do a great deal of damage.

▶ *CONTROL*

The adult beetles are fairly easy to handpick. In the early morning, before the sun makes them active, they can be shaken out of bushes and plants onto a cloth or an opened umbrella laid on the ground. Later in the day, they are so busy eating that they will hardly notice when you pick them up and throw them into a can of soapy water, or water and rubbing alcohol. White geraniums or primroses can be planted as trap crops for easy handpicking. Vacuuming works too.

Japanese beetles are so easy to trap, placing commercial traps in your yard may draw beetles from all over the neighborhood. These traps generally consist of a funnel over a jar or bag baited with a pheromone or a scent the beetles find attractive. Put them downwind and well away from the plants you want to protect. Since many people believe pheromone traps are too effective, you could try experimenting with some less potent ones. Make your own trap by taking stiff yellow construction paper and folding it into a cone with a hole at the bottom. Staple or tape it to a plastic bag into which you have poured a little rose-scented essential oil or anise- or fennel-scented oil (anethole).

Japanese beetle trap

Here is another trap. In a small container, concoct fermented bait by combining mashed ripened fruit, water, sugar, and a little yeast. Place it on a block in the middle of a yellow bowl or pail filled with soapy water to just below the top of the container. Place it about twenty-five feet from the plants that need protection. The beetles zero in on the smell of the fruit, fall into the water, and drown.

If you start getting brown patches of dead grass, suspect Japanese beetle grubs. Dig up the sod and look under it; if the grubs are there, you'll see them. Because they spend ten months out of their one-year life cycle as grubs, the best control is milky spore disease (*Bacillus popilliae*), which attacks them at this stage. It can easily be applied to grass by the teaspoonful (it comes in a powder) and then watered into the soil.

Although it takes several years for the spore disease to accumulate in the soil, it will last for several decades. Milky spore disease is harmless to humans, animals, plants, and earthworms. It does kills June beetle grubs, but that is all to the good. Try to get all your neighbors to apply the treatment too, so that their beetles won't show up in your yard.

Nematodes can be purchased and applied to the soil. Moles, skunks, and birds will also devour the Japanese beetle grubs. Dry weather and an alkaline soil tend to keep their population down. And those spiky sandals that aerate the soil do double duty by impaling the grubs.

MEXICAN BEAN BEETLES

The Mexican bean beetle is known as the rotten relative of the beneficial, insect-eating ladybird beetle. It doesn't seem quite fair that it got this bad reputation just for being a vegetarian in a family of meat eaters. You can distinguish it by the sixteen—no more, no less—spots on its round, copper-colored body. True to its name, this insect loves the members of the bean family, specifically the leaves, which it eats until nothing is left except limp skeletons.

Usually a female lays around 400 eggs, but she can lay as many as 1,500, so a small problem can rapidly escalate into a large one. Even before it turns into a hungry adult beetle, it does a lot of damage as a weird, fat orange grub, covered with spines. Commonly found east of the Rocky Mountains, the Mexican bean beetle overwinters right in your garden under woodpiles or among plant debris.

Mexican bean beetle

You may mistake a **bean leaf beetle** for a Mexican bean beetle. That's okay. Even though it belongs to an entirely different family, the bean leaf beetle looks and behaves quite a bit like the Mexican bean beetle and deserves the same treatment.

▶ CONTROL

Interplanting potato plants with bean plants helps keep the beetles away. This planting arrangement also protects potatoes from their nemesis, the Colorado potato beetle. Marigolds, summer savory, rosemary, radishes, nasturtiums, and garlic are also good companion plants for bean protection.

Floating row covers will hold bean beetles at bay. Garlic spray will repel them, and, as a last resort, pyrethrum, neem, or rotenone will kill them.

Don't hesitate to handpick these beetles and their spiny orange larvae and drop them into a can of soapy water. Even more important, try to get the orange-yellow eggs on the undersides of leaves.

You can order the parasitic *Pediobius* wasp from suppliers. Praying mantises, ladybugs, and the spined soldier bug will also eat these beetles. The nymphs of spined soldier bugs eat hatching bean beetles, and the adults move over to eat cabbageworms.

TOMATO HORNWORMS

There is nothing subtle about this gargantuan caterpillar. With its impressive three-to-four-inch size, chlorophyll green color, delicate white stripes, and distinctive horn protruding from its rear end, it's hard to miss. All over the United States, it goes to work stripping tomato, eggplant, pepper, and potato plants. A similar caterpillar, the tobacco hornworm, prefers tobacco but also attacks tomato plants.

▶ CONTROL

Handpicking the hornworm is a must. To foil its excellent camouflage, place light-colored fabric, such as old sheets, under the tomato plants. In a few hours, check for little piles of caterpillar droppings, then look straight up from the evidence to find the culprit (fecal pellets can only fall straight down). Don't worry about its horn—it seems to be for little more than show. But take a good look at the caterpillar first. If it has little white cocoons stuck to its skin (they look like pearls of rice), leave it where it is; it will not live to reproduce. The cocoons are those of parasitic braconid wasps, which will soon emerge and find other hornworms to lay eggs on.

A trap crop of dill, which hornworms like, can make handpicking easier, because the caterpillars show up so well on this plant.

We like to toss the hornworms onto the lawn for our friendly jays to consume.

Planting borage, basil, and marigolds in the garden is said to keep hornworms away. They can be dissuaded from eating plants by spraying with hot pepper or citrus peel spray (see *Tactics of Tiny Game Hunting in the Garden*).

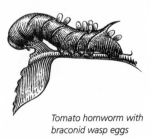

Tomato hornworm with
braconid wasp eggs

If hornworms are a serious problem, consider using a light trap at night for the adult moths, called hummingbird, sphinx, or hawk moths, which are large and grayish brown and sport a five-inch wingspan. They appear soon after sunset and feed on nectar from blossoms.

They then lay eggs on your favorite plants—unless, of course, they get caught in your trap.

Predators include trichogramma wasps, ladybugs, and lacewings. Bt works very well, killing hornworms rapidly after they take a bite of leaf sprayed with the pathogen.

ROOT DESTROYERS
• • • • • • • • • • •

JUNE BEETLES

Also known as Junebugs and May beetles, these beetles mostly show up (sometimes in swarms) in May or June. They make bumbling but persistent attempts to fly into porch lights and through screens. When not attracted to light, they munch irregular holes in leaves of trees by night and then hide out all day.

They only spend two months as adult beetles in a cycle that can be as long as three years. For much of the rest of the time, they live as C-shaped white grubs in the soil, where they do their worst damage, eating roots and ruining turf grass, especially on golf courses. They can also damage the roots of corn, potatoes, and strawberries. Digging up the soil, plowing, or tilling allows the birds access to them. In the past, people used to run hogs in fields to "grub" for them.

▶ *CONTROL*

Because they are related to Japanese beetles, milky spore disease will kill the grubs, as will parasitic nematodes.

Attract beneficial wasps, which parasitize them, by growing flowers such as Queen Anne's lace.

Moles, skunks, toads, and ground beetles will devour June beetles, which are also said to make excellent fish bait.

NEMATODES

Bad nematodes are really bad. These minuscule-to-microscopic translucent roundworms attack the root systems of plants, making it possible for bacteria and fungi to invade. Fortunately, only a small percentage of all nematodes are harmful. Most are quite beneficial and attack grubs and other harmful pests in the soil.

You won't know you have nematodes until the plant shows signs of damage—stunting, wilting, or yellowing leaves. Root-knot nematodes cause galls or bulbous swelling or small growths along the roots. Others are harder to identify; you may have to pull out the plant, put it in a bag along with some of its soil, and take it to your local agricultural extension office, which can send it to a laboratory for identification.

It seems that the smaller the pest, the better it can reproduce. Nasty nematodes are no exception, for a female root-knot nematode can lay from 300 to 3,000 eggs in one gelatinous mass near the roots.

▶ CONTROL

Fumigants and nematode-killing chemicals are extremely toxic. Many that were used for decades have now been removed from the market. One of these, DBCP, was banned in 1977, after being linked to sterility and cancer. This same chemical has now been found in hundreds of wells across the state of California. Methyl bromide, another extremely dangerous fumigant, is widely used in strawberry fields. And don't forget, using these kinds of chemicals also kills every beneficial organism.

During hot, sunny weather you can kill nematodes with solarization. The best time to do it is during July or August, when the temperature is high and the chance of rain is low. Prepare the soil for cultivation, then water thoroughly until the ground is saturated. Cover the soil with heavy-duty *clear* plastic and secure the perimeter with dirt and rocks. The temperature under the plastic can heat up to 140°F. In about four to six weeks, this heat will cook out the nematodes, as well as many insect larvae and a significant amount of weed seeds.

Some people advise clearing all plants from a nematode-infested area and keeping anything from growing there for at least three years. Who wants to do that? A more ornamental (but still drastic) treatment consists of planting the entire area in marigolds, which give off a chemical from their roots that is toxic to nematodes. When the marigolds have finished blooming, dig them into the soil.

Asparagus plants also produce chemicals that are inimical to nematodes. Every time you cook asparagus, try pouring the cooking water back into the garden. Other plants believed to discourage nematodes are dahlias, salvia, calendula, hairy indigo, velvet beans, and garlic.

Sugar apparently draws moisture from the soil and dries out the nematodes. To kill them with sweetness, dissolve a cup of sugar in two cups boiling water, add it to a gallon of water, and pour into the soil.

Rotating plants regularly and planting cover crops will also help. Nematodes are both host-specific and homebodies, so they will starve if you move their favorite plants to another spot in the garden. A farm bulletin from the 1950s recommended using half the property for a garden and half for a henyard and switching them every year or two.

The higher the organic content of the soil, the better protected your plants will be. In nature, nematodes have plenty of enemies, including other cannibalistic nematodes and worm-catching, nematode-trapping fungi, both found in a soil rich in organic matter. Use lots of good compost and heavy mulch in the garden.

Apply fish emulsion, and don't forget to try seaweed, which is said to make plants more resistant to nematodes. Seaweed (extract or dried) can be added directly to the soil or used as a foliar spray.

ROOT MAGGOTS

Gardeners can develop a real distaste for these pests. The fly, which looks all too much like a house fly, lays its eggs in the dirt. When the young hatch, the white worms (maggots) burrow down among the roots and feed voraciously. By the time the plant starts to wilt, it's usually too late to save it. Pulling it up by the roots and finding the little white worms will convince you that, with this pest, the best defense should have begun a good deal sooner.

Two common root maggots are the **cabbage root maggot** and the **onion root**

Cabbage root maggot

Onion root maggot

maggot, but others attack the roots of cabbages, broccoli, cauliflowers, radishes, turnips, onions, leeks, shallots, and chives. Still another fly, the **carrot rust fly**, attacks carrots, leaving rust-colored tunnels in the vegetable. Root maggots are more likely to attack young seedlings, but they can go through several generations and torment the plants throughout the season.

▶ CONTROL

Save used tea bags and mix the tea leaves into the planting mix as a repellent to the maggots. We have also heard of people who mix fresh ground coffee into their planting mix to deter carrot root maggots.

The traditional means of control is to make root maggot mats to keep the maggots from penetrating the soil. People have used tar paper for this. Or you could use pieces of carpeting or foam, cut into squares with slits to slip around the plant stem. Seal the slits with masking tape.

Take a big container to a popular breakfast restaurant and ask the cook to throw all the eggshells into it. Crush the shells into sharp little fragments and mix them into the soil to keep the maggots from getting through in one piece. A good mulch of oak leaves will do the same thing, as will mixing diatomaceous earth into the soil. Sawdust also serves as an impassable barrier. It has to be at least two inches thick and extend six inches out from the plant. Pile the sawdust right up against the stem.

Sprinkle wood ashes around the base of plants. Or make a mixture of equal parts lime, rock phosphate, and bonemeal, add the same amount of wood ashes, and mix this into the soil around the plant, or even put it into the hole when planting. It's bad for the maggots, but good for the plants.

You can soak a third of your seeds before planting them with the unsoaked seeds. The soaked seeds will sprout first, get eaten by the maggots, and leave the later plants to flourish. (This sounds clever, but it does amount to feeding the enemy.)

Hide onion plants from maggots by interplanting them around the garden. In fact, hide all your plants by covering them with fabric row covers or cones made of window screens and keep the flies from laying eggs near the plants in the first place.

Get others to do the work: parasitic nematodes, chalcid, and trichogramma wasps can be ordered from suppliers and released. Rove beetles are the great unsung heroes in the cabbage maggot root wars. But if you use pesticides, there won't be any beetles to do battle for you.

WIREWORMS (CLICK BEETLES)

Wireworms, the larvae of click beetles, are hard-shelled, segmented, wormy creatures, usually a yellowish to reddish brown. They feed underground on seeds, roots, tubers or bulbs of potatoes, beets, beans, peas, onions, carrots, and cabbages, among other things, and they are quite destructive. They look a bit like millipedes, but they have only three pairs of short legs, up near their head. Unlike most other insects, they live a long time—from two to five and sometimes even eight years. They were excommunicated for their bad deeds by the bishop of Lausanne in 1479, which did nothing to curb their appetite.

Click beetles (the adults) have achieved fame because of their odd acrobatic abilities. A click beetle can right itself when it is on its back by flipping in the air while making a clicking sound. This has earned it the nicknames skipjack and snappy beetle.

▶ **CONTROL**

You can use the wireworms' attraction to potatoes to trap them. Cut potatoes in two and bury them cut side down in the ground. The wireworms will burrow into the potatoes, and then you can dig them up, pull them out, and dispose of them. Whole carrots with the tops on will also work. Place the traps two or three feet apart, mark the spots with stakes, and dig them up in the evening a couple of times a week.

Click beetle and its larva, the wireworm

183

Cultivating the soil after harvest allows predators, especially birds, to get to the wireworms. Because wireworms seem to like soggy ground, add humus to improve soil aeration. Withholding water will slow them down. Beneficial nematodes will kill wireworms. Many gardeners plant marigolds to deter them.

SLIMERS

• • • • • •

SLUGS AND SNAILS

Probably the most loathed pests in the garden, slugs and snails both eat large ragged holes in plants. They'll eat the whole plant if it's young and tender, and their destructive chomping and silvery trails are a dead give-away to their presence. Classified as gastropods, meaning "stomach foot," they're fun to hate and easy to kill, but maddeningly difficult to control. Because many species came from elsewhere, there aren't enough natural predators to cope with them in North America, and we humans have to step in.

The chief difference between a slug and a snail is that slugs lack the spiral shell that snails tote around. The brown garden snail was introduced in this country in San Francisco in the 1850s by a Frenchman who thought he could get people there to eat them. He was wrong, and if they didn't catch on as food in San Francisco, there was surely no hope of them doing so in the rest of the country. Undaunted, the brown snails set out on their own to conquer America and have succeeded so far in becoming the most common snail pest in California.

Several species of slugs range from a quarter of an inch to six inches in length and are gray, brown, yellow-ochre, and spotted. Since each slug is both male and female, they have no trouble finding mates, and both of them can get pregnant! They can lay 100 eggs in a season, and in dry times they can hibernate for years. They are capable of eating thirty to forty times their body weight each day. They range throughout North America.

Snails are mobile creatures and can travel a mile in about fifteen days (although they don't). Slugs are almost twice as fast, able to travel the same distance in eight days. In your garden, a snail may travel a hundred feet for a meal.

Both slugs and snails hide during sunny days in shady, preferably moist spots under leaves, rubble, stones, and garden debris. They congregate and breed in certain plants, among them agapanthus, lilies, irises, ice plant, ivy, nasturtiums, jasmine, and strawberries. They also favor soft, moist mulch.

▶ CONTROL

Barriers   Keep in mind that slugs and snails have their place as food for other animals and birds. They are also recyclers (even of dog droppings), and they produce humus. So barriers are perhaps the most benign form of control. The tender, soft, slimy bodies of slugs and snails need a fairly smooth surface on which to travel. (Can you imagine trying to navigate your garden on your tongue?) Their trails, in fact, are self-created roadways laid down with mucus, which is why barriers can stop them.

Good barriers can consist of wood ashes, crushed oyster shells (from feed stores), crushed eggshells, diatomaceous earth, sawdust, lime, short hair clippings, powdered ginger, bran, and ammonium sulfate. Make sure the barrier is at least three inches wide—the wider the better. If a powder barrier gets wet, it will need to be replenished. A border planted with low, spreading rosemary is another one they won't want to cross.

Garden centers sell snail barriers, some of which resemble strips of sandpaper; others have salt embedded in the material. Copper strips make the best barriers. When the slimers touch the copper, it shocks and repels them. These strips are also effective as barriers on trees. Snails love citrus trees and can be real pests in orange groves. Copper comes in sheets, strips, and sticky-backed tape. One gardener glues copper pennies around her pots.

A good mulch of oak leaves will also repel slugs and snails. Gather seaweed and spread it around as a mulch. Not only does it makes a good barrier, but it

Snail and slug

will also be good for the soil. If you use decorative mulches, choose cocoa hulls or crushed rock, which are quite inimical to slimers.

To protect new seedlings from voracious slugs and snails, cover each one with a topless plastic soda bottle with the bottom cut off.

Old window screens (or new screening) can be cut into snail barriers. Copper screen would be ideal. Make a slit from one corner of a ten-inch square of screen and cut out an opening for the plant. This is even more effective if you shred the edges of the screen by removing a few wires from the perimeter.

Handpicking   For major snail or slug infestations, the best method of control is handpicking. Because these creatures are nocturnal, begin collecting them about two hours after sundown. Watering late in the afternoon will make them more active. Get your family together and give everyone a strong flashlight. Children are easily motivated by a monetary reward in these matters.

For handpicking slugs, use tweezers, kitchen prongs, an iced-tea spoon, or latex surgical gloves—cheap and disposable. Equip everyone with buckets or jars filled with water and a little vinegar or ammonia. Then dump the critters on the compost heap. (Salted or soapy water will also kill them.) Or crush the snails and bury them where they will add nutrients to the soil. Even better, if you have a pond with turtles and fish, heave them in.

At first go out several nights in a row. Not all slugs and snails venture out to pillage every night. When the infestation has been controlled, you will only need to go out about once a week.

Salting and Squirting   If slugs are your chief problem, and you don't feel up to handpicking them, tape closed all the holes of a saltshaker except one. Sprinkling a slug with a few grains of salt will cause it to crawl out of its slime coat. Then apply a second time—this is the lethal one. If you are worried about adding salt to the soil, try sprinkling the offenders with ammonium sulfate, which both kills them and fertilizes the soil.

A squirt bottle filled with a mixture of equal parts water and vinegar or water and ammonia will finish slugs off in one squirt. It works on snails extended out of their shells too.

Traps   One of the most time-honored ways to get rid of slugs and snails is the beer trap. Take a small container like a cat food can, or—if you are convinced your garden is infested with giant snails—a pie tin. Bury it so the top is level with the ground and fill it with beer.

The brand of beer does make a difference. We once bought the cheapest beer we could and succeeded in catching exactly one slug with the six-pack. An entomologist at Colorado State University, Whitney Cranshaw, conducted a beer tasting for slugs in 1987, killing 4,000 of them in eight weeks in the name of scientific inquiry. Kingsbury Malt Beverage attracted the most, but Michelob and Budwieser fared well too. The yeast in the beer is what attracts the varmints, while the alcohol befuddles them and makes it harder for them to climb out. Beer is most effective in the first twenty-four hours.

Another trap makes use of yogurt or cottage cheese containers with one-inch holes cut out around the sides, several inches from the bottom. Pour in the beer and wait for the creatures to crawl in. The lid on the container means the beer won't evaporate, and the dog won't be able to lap it up.

Another way to keep the dog out of the beer is to use a beer bottle with a little beer in it, laid on its side with the lip at ground level. This is best for slugs and smaller snails.

Here's a bait that is cheaper than beer and takes advantage of the slimers' attraction to yeast. Mix two tablespoons of flour with a teaspoon of baker's yeast and a teaspoon of sugar in two cups of warm water. Or take two cups of grape juice and add a teaspoon of yeast and fill a con-

Beer trap for snails and slugs

tainer. One thing about these traps that is horrid but effective: slugs and snails are attracted to the dead bodies of their own kind.

If you provide slugs and snails with hiding places that they will seek out when morning comes, you can go and pick them off at your leisure. They will more likely go into your shady traps if you eliminate the other hiding places and debris that they favor. Traps can be made from shingles, small boards, or overturned clay pots propped up a little on one side. Two-gallon nursery pots can be stacked together and laid on their side, with a little space between the bottoms. Plastic lawn and leaf bags or damp burlap can also be used to attract slugs and snails. It helps if you dampen the ground underneath first.

Set out grapefruit or orange rinds, propped up a with a small stone. Or use banana peels; slugs will be attracted by the odor and crawl underneath. Other suitable hiding places include cabbage leaves, lettuce leaves, and potato slices. Slugs and snails are also drawn to raw bread dough, dry dog food nuggets, and fallen hibiscus blossoms.

Long boards laid down between garden beds and slightly propped up with pebbles will attract slugs and snails. An effective trap devised by entomologists at the University of California at Riverside consists of an untreated board (between twelve and fifteen inches square) with one-inch wooden strips nailed on two sides to prop it up. Redwood makes a very durable trap. Crushing a few snails on the underside of the board will draw in others.

Many slugs hide in the soil, so rototilling is a good way to get rid of them.

Natural Enemies   Many beetles prey on slugs and snails, including rove beetles, carrion beetles, soldier beetles, and a big impressive specimen called the devil's coachman. In a greenhouse where slugs are a problem, the ground beetle can be brought in to do slug duty. This beetle hunts all night and hides during the day.

Outdoors, other natural predators of snails and slugs include chickens, ducks, and geese. Toads (the best), frogs, box turtles, skunks, shrews, opossums, rats, moles, birds, snakes, and lizards will also eat slugs and snails. Certain flies will prey on them, as will centipedes.

Birds will be more likely to eat snails if you provide them with a big flat stone that they can use to crack the shells on. Scatter birdseed around the garden to encourage birds to poke around.

Decollate snail attacking a garden snail

The decollate snail, *Rumina decollata*, a somewhat smaller snail whose shell looks like a seashell, is the most effective natural enemy of the brown garden snail. In Southern California, a number of gardeners and citrus growers have successfully imported these snails to control the brown garden snail. Check with suppliers; they are not allowed in some California counties.

Decollate snails have the same requirements for moisture and the same nocturnal habits as the snails they prey upon. They may eat an occasional tender leaf in contact with the ground or a fallen bruised fruit, and they can be hard on some low-growing plants. But this snail actually prefers decayed vegetation, and it will not eat the healthy leaves in your garden. It does not do well in dry places, so if you order these snails, try to provide some sort of damp haven, just as you would for a toad or frog. The decollate snail does its best job on smaller snails, so you will still need to handpick the bigger snails in your garden. And it may take them a few years to eradicate the brown snail, so use barriers, not poison!

Poison Snail poisons and bait in the form of powders, pellets, and goo have been dumped on yards, gardens, and public landscaping by the ton. The empty snail shells leave proof that these poisons work. But what else are you killing when you kill snails in this way? Earthworms, for one thing, are very vulnerable to certain snail poisons. And earthworms are said to deter slugs and snails, because their castings are inimical to them.

Birds have been other victims of snail poisons. Starlings, for example, which eat garden snails, seem to avoid gardens where poison is used. You also run the risk of poisoning your own pets and even children, since some pellet baits are attractive to them. Furthermore, certain poisons are absorbed by plants that we eat and can thus poison us.

Look for snail baits containing metal aluminum ions or iron phosphate. They take several days to work, however, so don't use them the same day you set out your tender new seedlings.

Resistant Plants   Here is a list of some of the plants that snails and slugs don't seem to like: azaleas, basil, beans, corn, daffodils, ferns, freesias, fuschias, geraniums, ginger, grapes, holly, lavender, mint, parsley, rhododendrons, roses of Sharon, sage, and sunflowers.

SUCKERS

• • • • • •

APHIDS

Aphids are probably the commonest pest in your garden, and they may be the most prolific of all insects. Thomas Huxley claimed that the descendants of a single aphid might at the end of one summer equal the population of China. Moreover, pesticides kill off the beneficial insects that prey on aphids. For instance, aerial sprayings of malathion in California to kill the medfly have led to tremendous aphid proliferations.

Winged aphid

Aphid

Small—less than a tenth of an inch long—pear-shaped, and soft-bodied, aphids come in many colors: white, green, pink, gray, red, brown, and black. Woolly aphids have a fluffy coating. Aphids love the tips, buds, and tender stems of plants, and the 4,000 or so species infest a wide variety of plants. They are often called plant lice (or green fly), and there are few plants that are not attacked by one kind of aphid or another. Hundreds of aphids may be found on a single plant, but with a little diligence—and an eye out for ants—they are really not that hard to control.

When aphids go to work on a plant, they insert their piercing mouth into the stem or the underside of a leaf. The sap starts to flow, and they just suck the day away. The leaves curl up or turn yellow, growth stops, and the plant may die. But the worst thing aphids do to your plants is transmit diseases through their salivary secretions.

To extract the nutrition they need—namely, nitrogen—aphids have to draw out huge amounts of the plant's juices. (Using a high-nitrogen fertilizer to induce quick growth is often an invitation to aphids.) They excrete the excess in the form of a sticky-sweet liquid called *honeydew*, often producing many times their own weight of the stuff in one day. Honeydew coats the leaves of the plants, making them look slightly silvery in the light. Sometimes the honeydew nourishes a black, sooty-looking fungus.

Ants milk aphids for this sweet honeydew, stroking the aphids' abdomen to get them to release it. Some ants move aphid nymphs to new plants, and into their own nests during bad weather, and they assiduously guard their aphid cows from their natural enemies. If you see aphids or signs of aphids, look for ants traveling up and down the stem of the plant, and then keep the ants away, using sticky barriers, diatomaceous earth spread around the base of the plant, or a boric acid bait (see *Ants*).

▶ CONTROL

If you have an aphid infestation, the first thing to do is direct a strong stream of water at the insects. Once knocked off the plant, aphids usually can't get back on. You can also simply brush them off, crush them with your hands (wearing gloves), or use a little rubbing alcohol to kill them.

Other methods of aphid control include spraying with soap spray, garlic-hot pepper spray, or limonene or linalool sprays; but try the water first. Spray fruit trees in early spring with dormant oil spray.

Sticky yellow traps can be used, but they only work for flying aphids; if aphids are on the wing, they will likely alight on these traps. Or place bright yellow bowls filled with soapy water around plants so that the aphids will fly into them.

Plant nasturtiums around plants that tend to get aphid infestations. Garlic plants work as an aphid repellent.

Another deterrent is to place strips of aluminum foil underneath plants particularly susceptible to aphids. Light reflecting off the foil confuses

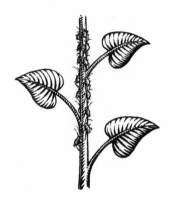

Aphids (on stem)

Hosing off aphids

them and prevents them from landing on the plant.

Too many aphids is a sign of something amiss—too much fertilizer, or an imbalance in the soil. Have your soil tested.

Natural Enemies   When ants aren't keeping them away, the best natural predators for aphids include ladybugs, ladybug larvae (which look like little alligators), birds, lacewings, lacewing larvae (called aphid lions), earwigs, hover (flower or syrphid) fly larvae, soldier beetles, and parasitic wasps. If you order predators, lacewings are best.

If you observe an aphid that is swollen and metallic, dull brown or blackened, it is a mummy, an aphid that has been parasitized by a wasp. Leave it alone so that the wasp larva can develop. Remember: if you don't have any aphids at all, there won't be anything for their predators to eat, and they will go elsewhere. The FDA considers forty to sixty aphids in a serving of brussels sprouts to be perfectly acceptable.

LEAFHOPPERS

Some species of leafhoppers, or "sharpshooters" (there are thousands), are pests to over 100 plants, tapping into the large veins on the leaves and sucking out the juices. They not only weaken the plants but inject substances that cause "hopperburn," which means wilting, curling, and discoloration. And as if that weren't enough, they also pass along plant diseases. Two of the worst are the potato and the bean leafhoppers.

Whether slender and pale green or yellowish green and wedge-shaped, leafhoppers can escape their enemies by great leaps. They will also run sideways to confound predators.

Leafhopper

▶ **CONTROL**

Row covers are the first line of defense for young plants. Plant geraniums and petunias as repellents.

Spray infested plants with a strong stream of water; leafhoppers dislike moisture. Soap sprays will kill them on contact, if they don't jump out of the way first. Diatomaceous earth can also be sprayed on plants.

Try using yellow sticky traps to trap leafhoppers.

Attract predators such as big-eyed bugs, wasps, damselflies, and green lacewings. Spiders are also leafhopper predators.

MEALYBUGS

Mealybugs can be found all over the United States but are especially common in the South and on houseplants—probably because their predators can't get into the house. Some give birth to live young, whereas others lay hundreds of eggs, which they cover with a white coating similar to the one they themselves hide under.

These plant-sucking insects look like little fluffs of white, greasy or waxy cotton snuggled down into the crevices between stalks and stems or clamped onto the undersides of leaves. These may look wimpy, but they are one tough little bug. They don't move around much—they just stick their mouthparts into the plant and suck out its juices.

The more water and nonorganic fertil-

Long-tailed mealybug

izer a plant gets, the higher its nitrogen content, and the more this pest is attracted to it. Furthermore, a small infestation can rapidly become a large one, and if unchecked will kill the plant.

▶ CONTROL

If the infestation is not too severe, pick mealybugs off with a toothpick or a pair of tweezers. Or use a small paintbrush or cotton swab dipped in rubbing alcohol (or nail-polish remover) and swab the mealybug. The alcohol or acetone destroys the insect's protective waxy cover and then kills the bug itself. Sometimes it takes more than one treatment to really get them. Try not to get any of the liquid on the plant leaves.

A strong jet of water can be used against mealybugs outdoors. Homemade soap spray, Safer's insecticidal soap, horticultural oils, or neem can also be used, as can quassia spray, an old remedy. As a very last resort, use a pyrethrum spray.

Encourage the predator population in your garden. Buy and disperse lacewings. Ladybugs and mealybug destroyers, a kind of ladybug, are wonderful mealybug predators. Syrphid flies and chalcid wasps search out mealybugs and destroy them by laying eggs on them.

Use organic fertilizers.

Like aphids, mealybugs excrete honeydew, so ants may be protecting them from predators. Use sticky barriers to keep ants away from these plants (see *Ants*).

SCALE INSECTS

There are many kinds of scale insects, around 1,700 species, and all can be tricky adversaries. Using their own discarded skins from molting, along with fine waxy threads, they construct little domelike shells, or scales, under which they carry on as unobtrusively as possible, often blending in with the plant. Some are no bigger than a pinhead. By the time you notice them, the infestation may already be out of hand, and they are difficult to eradicate.

Scale insects can be classified as either armored or soft, depending on their hideouts. They come in a great variety of colors, from black, brown, yellow, or white to transparent, gray, green, and even pink. A scale insect sucks out plant juices with mouthparts like a fine filament, often injecting toxic substances or viruses. It lays its eggs (hundreds of them) under its protective coating. When the eggs hatch, the young crawl away and find their own sucking spots. When armored scales find a spot, their legs actually fall off, and they're set for life. The plant under siege loses vigor and begins to wilt or show growth distortion.

▶ CONTROL

Insecticides work only if the spray happens to catch the insects at the odd moment when they are still crawling around. When scale insects are hidden under their shells, they are for the most part impervious to pesticides.

Gardeners once used to sponge off scale with tobacco tea. Instead, use a soapy solution or an oil emulsion for this task. Take a plastic scouring pad or a soft toothbrush and go at the scale. If there are only a few, a fingernail will do the trick. So will swabbing them carefully with rubbing alcohol or turpentine.

Horticultural oils (not dormant oil), sprayed in the late winter before new growth, will suffocate scale, as will glue spray (see *Tactics of Tiny Game Hunting in the Garden*). Insecticidal soap and soapy water work by dissolving their waxy covering.

Natural Enemies When it comes to scale, you need predators! Lacewings and ladybugs are excellent, but you will have to keep the ants away. Like aphids and mealybugs, soft scale insects produce honeydew, so ants often tend them and guard them against predators. Ants may actually lead you to a scale infestation you may not have noticed. As noted earlier, ants can be kept away by wrapping and banding the tree trunk or plant stem with a sticky substance or by placing boric acid bait near their trails (see *Ants*).

Other predators include parasitic wasps, aphid lions, predaceous mites, and syrphid flies. Regularly spraying plants with water will rid them of dust that may inhibit many potential parasites and predators. Remember, too, that beneficials need nectar and pollen, which means your garden needs plenty of blossoms.

SPIDER MITES

We have good reason to hate these mites. Distant relatives of spiders, they cause an amazing amount of damage. And like their other relative, the tick, they can be quite frustrating because they're so hard to see. A magnifying glass (10 or 15 power hand lens) comes in handy when searching for these pests, although their presence eventually becomes quite obvious. Some feed on plant stems and the undersides of leaves with their piercing/sucking mouthparts, causing stippling or yellowing of the leaves, which then drop off.

If your plant looks discouraged, look for spider mites. Gossamer strands or webbing between the leaves gives a clue to the mites' presence. Or hold a piece of white paper under a leaf and tap it. If you see tiny moving dots on the paper, you have mites. Red spider mites (or two-spotted spider mites), the most common garden spider mite, may look like specks of red pepper.

Mites do not thrive in high humidity or under frequent watering. The hotter the weather and the dustier the plant, the more they flourish and the more eggs a female will lay. Quick regeneration is the root of the problem, with the worst damage occurring during the hot summer months.

Although pesticides have destroyed many of their natural enemies, the mites themselves have become quite resistant to pesticides. In fact, some pesticides even cause them to reproduce faster!

▶ CONTROL

Since mites thrive in a dusty and dry environment, spray frequently with strong jets of water, morning and evening. Be sure to aim jets of water at the undersides of the leaves.

Mites are one more reason to mulch; when a plant is water stressed, they seem to do even more damage.

Soap sprays will kill the adult mites but have to be reapplied as the eggs continue to hatch. Use a soap spray once every four or five days for three weeks. Mixing two cups of wheat flour and a quarter of a cup of buttermilk with two gallons of water makes another effective spray for infested plants. Glue spray (see *Tactics of Tiny Game Hunting in the Garden*) will also smother these pests.

Sprays containing citrus peel extracts are effective against mites.

A dormant oil spray can be a good defense when used in the fall or spring. During the growing season, spray with a lighter oil.

When the temperature is between 70° and 90°F, you can dust the plants with sulfur. This is a very old and fairly reliable technique, but, as always, wear a mask when applying the dust.

Diatomaceous earth can also be dusted around the soil and onto the plants. Use a face mask and goggles.

Essential oils that are said to be useful as repellents—at a dilution of 1:50 with water—include coriander oil, oil of lemon grass, lavender oil, and geranium oil. Mites are also repelled by members of the onion family, including chives and garlic.

Natural Enemies Natural predators assume an important role. Tiny black lady beetles, known as spider mite destroyers, lacewing larvae, ladybugs, and predatory mites (we refer to them as mighty mites) can all be ordered from suppliers. Predator mites are almost as invisible as the mites themselves, but they move a lot faster and don't spin webs. All these predators are highly vulnerable to pesticides, so using poisons only leads to greater problems with the harmful mites.

THRIPS

Thrips are so tiny, they are almost invisible. About the width of a fine sewing needle, and endowed with feathery wings, they damage plants by scraping at the tissue and then sucking sap out of the wound. They get into tight places where sprays can't get to them. Often flowers and leaves fail to open and look twisted. Flower thrips are especially attracted to white flowers, such as white roses. Other kinds attack onions, beans, and many other vegetables.

Sometimes the damage they cause looks like that done by mites, except that thrips do not make little webs. Instead, they leave tiny dark specks of excrement and whitish streaked areas on the leaves. The plant may also become susceptible to disease, but thrips usually scar rather than kill plants.

Thrips make a tiny slit in the plant and deposit their eggs inside it.

The eggs hatch and the nymphs feed on the plant for a week or two. Some nymphs drop off the plant and spend time in the soil before climbing back up the stem.

▶ CONTROL

An old remedy for thrips was to spray with tobacco water. We recommend first spraying with water. If they are still bothersome, use an insecticidal soap spray, oil spray, or homemade garlic-hot pepper spray, or a dusting with diatomaceous earth. Ladybugs, lacewings, predatory mites, nematodes, minute pirate bugs, and hover flies will attack thrips, which is why harboring such beneficials is so important.

Thrips are attracted to yellow and blue, so sticky traps of these colors can be used to trap the adults. Or use colored containers of soapy water. Some growers paint the plant stems with sticky substances to keep the young thrips from traveling up the plant. As with aphids, aluminum strips or mulches around the plants will confuse thrips and keep them from landing.

Remove all infested flowers and buds. Controlling weeds is also important when thrips are a problem, because they thrive in them. They tend to be attracted to plants that are water-stressed, so be sure to provide plenty of moisture. Put a good mulch around plant stems, the more impermeable the better.

"TRUE" BUGS

Squash bugs, harlequin bugs, and tarnished plant bugs belong to the fairly small group of insects that have the honor of being designated "true" bugs. (Hence we spell them as two words.) Like other members of the true bug family, they have shield-shaped bodies and sport patterns of triangular shapes on their backs. Many of these bugs are stinkers: when disturbed, they release foul-smelling chemicals.

Squash Bugs Squash bugs are fairly large (three-eighths to one-half inch long), blackish gray bugs, covered with fine black hairs. They dine on the leaves and stems of squash, cantaloupes, cucumbers, melons, and pumpkins, causing them to wilt, turn black, and die. They will also damage the fruit. Look for masses of their orange-yellow or bronze eggs in the early spring on the undersides of leaves, then destroy them. When young, the bugs are green with red appendages, but they later lose their color.

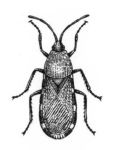

Squash bug

These insects are prime candidates for hand-picking.

You can also set out boards at night around the plants. When they go into hiding after a hard night's sap sucking, they like to hide under flat surfaces. In the morning, go out and squash them.

Squash bugs are repelled by nasturtium plants and also by onions, marigolds, and tansy. Some people place onion skins into newly planted cucumber hills. The food that attracts squash bugs most—summer and winter squash plants—has a bitter odor. Try spraying the leaves with a solution of water and artificial vanilla flavoring to disguise your plant from the marauders. Be sure to get the undersides of the leaves.

Clean up after harvest and rotate your crops each year.

Tarnished Plant Bugs   Also known as lygus bugs, tarnished plant bugs are about one-quarter of an inch long and range in color from light brown to black. The greenish nymphs look like aphids. These bugs suck on hundreds of plants, leaving black spots where they pierce the plant. As befits their name, tarnished plant bugs deform both fruit and flowers. They spend the winter in garden trash (especially weeds).

Shasta daisies in full flower are sometimes used as trap crops.

Handpicking is the best tactic for these bugs. Garden vacuums are effective too.

Harlequin Bugs   As their name suggests, harlequin bugs are colorful black bugs with red, orange, or yellow markings. Common in the South, they go after members of the cabbage family, including broccoli, turnips, and kale, leaving yellow and white blotches on the leaves. They are one of the major pests of cabbage. Look for their striking white-and-black-ringed eggs under leaves.

Harlequin bug

As with other bugs, the best weapons you possess are your hands—for handpicking. But wear gloves, because these insects smell foul. Rather than crushing them, drop them into a can of soapy water. Planting a trap crop of mustard greens, which they love, will lure them away from your other plants and make them easier to find and pick off.

If you don't like the idea of handpicking any of these bugs, zap them with a squirt of soap spray. Sabadilla and pyrethrum can also be used in dust or spray form if you get really desperate.

WHITEFLIES

There is something very discouraging about a plant infested with whiteflies. If you shake it, these tiny, mothlike creatures fly up from the undersides of the leaves in great numbers. When they settle back down, they select an even fresher and more tender leaf than before.

Only about one-sixteenth of an inch long, covered with a powdery wax, and sometimes called "flying dandruff," whiteflies reproduce fast (generally in a month or less), can build up in great numbers, and are known for developing quick immunities to pesticides. Each whitefly lays twenty to twenty-five practically invisible eggs in a circle around herself. These hatch into scalelike larvae or nymphs, which move around for a few days before picking a spot and settling in.

A new whitefly pest recently reached Southern California, the **giant whitefly** (though it is minuscule by our standards and is known elsewhere as the **spiraling whitefly**). It infests more than a hundred species of plants, including many of the exotic varieties that California gardeners love, such as hibiscus, banana, canna lilies, cherimoya, and citrus. The female giant whitefly lays a spiral of eggs on the underside of a leaf. As the nymphs develop, they spin out hairs, until the leaf appears to have a white beard. These hairs prevent significant penetration of any sprays directed

Whitefly

toward them. A parasitoid, *Incarsia* sp., may eventually prove effective, but for now few controls exist against this new pest.

An abundant whitefly infestation can cause a plant to wilt, fade, droop, and die. The honeydew they secrete nourishes a sooty mold, which grows and also damages plants.

▶ CONTROL

Yellow sticky traps are quite effective with whiteflies, which are drawn to this color. Place traps on a stick or hang them slightly above the plant; the whiteflies' tendency to fly upward and to land on yellow will do them in.

You can buy sticky traps or make your own from pieces of yellow plastic, stiff paper, or cans, coated with a sticky substance. In addition to commercial sticky substances such as Stikem Special and Tanglefoot, people have used vegetable oil from a spray can, mineral oil, molasses, and petroleum jelly.

One gardener we know uses a two-by-three-foot sheet of stiff, sticky yellow paper nailed to a stake. She plants it in the ground behind the plant, then lightly sprays the plant with water from the opposite side, forcing the whiteflies off the plant and onto the trap.

Sprays can reduce whitefly populations, but they have to be applied fairly frequently—every four or five days for several weeks. Effective sprays include homemade soap spray, insecticidal soap spray, horticultural oil, and alcohol-soap spray. Use pyrethrum only as a last resort. Don't neglect the undersides of leaves.

There is a good chance that phosphorus- or magnesium-deficient plants play host to these pests. Try to adjust the soil chemistry to include these nutrients.

Plant marigolds and nasturtiums.

You can also suck up these pests with a portable vacuum cleaner. Shake the plant to disturb the white-flies. To make the job even easier, wrap the end of the vacuum cleaner tube with bright yellow electrical tape. The whiteflies will fly toward the yellow end

Vacuuming whiteflies

and you can suck them right up. As with handpicking, this method works well on cool early mornings, when the insects are sluggish. Put the vacuum cleaner bag in the freezer to kill the bugs. Do this once a day for several weeks.

Natural Enemies   Ladybird beetles and lacewings eat whitefly larvae, but the best control for this pest is *Encarsia formosa*, a minute parasitic wasp, also known as the whitefly parasite, which lays its eggs in the whitefly nymphs. In greenhouses, this wasp can control the population of whiteflies to the point where damage is negligible.

TUNNELERS

● ● ● ● ● ● ●

BORERS

Borers can be either caterpillars, which plague annuals, or the larval stage of beetles (grubs), which mostly go after trees. They are called borers because this is how they do their worst damage—boring into plant stems or stalks or tree trunks and then eating their way inside. They may go unnoticed for so long that they utterly destroy plants and trees. Diseases in trees often get their start through borer holes.

SQUASH VINE BORERS

The larvae of these borers are a humdrum white with brown head, but the clear-winged adult moths look like colorful, beautiful wasps and excite admiration with their zippy flight patterns. They go after squash, gourds, pumpkins, and sometimes cucumbers and melons.

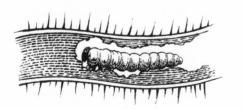

Squash vine borer

▶ **CONTROL**

Use fabric row covers to prevent the moths from laying eggs on plants.

When a plant starts to look wilted from a particular spot on the stem upward, check for the borer's hole, which you can usually see, along with the yellow "sawdust" that gives it away. When you find it, slice the stem upward from the hole to find the fat, well-fed borer and remove it with tweezers or a small crochet hook. Or inject a little shot of Bt into the hole. Cover the damaged stem well by piling up damp dirt around it.

Plant early or late to foil the borers' schedule, or plant resistant varieties.

Plant radishes around the susceptible plants or sprinkle black pepper or wood ashes around on the soil.

EUROPEAN CORN BORERS

European corn borers are great pests of corn, but they go after over 200 other kinds of plants too. They generally feed on the leaves for a while before entering the stalk. Look for little holes with sawdust around them.

▶ CONTROL

By using a light trap around May, you may be able to kill the moths before they can lay eggs on the leaves. Spraying Bt may also control them before they start to bore into the plant; injecting mineral oil in the tips of corn ears will deter them later. Lacewings, ladybugs, and braconid wasps all prey on this pest.

Clearing target plants from the garden right after harvesting will eliminate all borers. Tilling the soil well in the fall helps too.

PEACHTREE BORERS

The peachtree borer, a close relative of the squash vine borer, is found throughout North America in several kinds of fruit trees besides peach. It does its damage around the bottom ten inches of the tree trunk (starting initially at the soil line or just below it). Trees are rarely infested with just one solitary borer.

▶ CONTROL

Borers seem to prefer plants that are weak and undernourished and trees that are stressed from lack of water or those with wounded bark. Watch that lawn mower around the trees!

If you see the tell-tale gum and sawdust mixture, break off the bark and try to locate the borers. Scrape them out or go after them with a piece of stiff wire or the pointed end of a knife. You can also inject parasitic nematodes into the holes. Dig around in the soil and look for the large dark brown cocoons of borers and destroy them.

To prevent borers from getting a start in a tree, surround the trunk in the spring with a good wide barrier of diatomaceous earth, digging it into the soil and replenishing it after rain. You can also wrap the tree at its base with a barrier covered with a sticky substance. Mix wood ashes and water into a thick paste and paint this on tree trunks to control borers.

Gardeners used to hang bars of soap on the trunks of trees. When it rained, the soap would run down the tree and the borers would be repelled by the taste. Squirting a line of liquid hand soap around the tree and letting it run down the bark would accomplish this same purpose.

Pheromone-baited traps are available for many kinds of moths.

Wood-pecking birds (woodpeckers and flickers) are important allies, because they often search for borers. Other predators of borers include ants, spiders, moles, skunks, and mice.

CODLING MOTHS AND APPLE MAGGOTS

CODLING MOTHS

The codling moth is one of the creatures responsible for all those ate-half-a-worm jokes. The worm is so unfunny, however, that apples are among the most heavily sprayed of all commercially grown crops. This is why a lot of people have come to the conclusion that an apple with a wormhole may be preferable to one without. You can always cut around the worm. But can you eat around the poison?

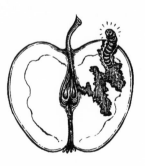

Codling moth worm

The little gray-to-brown codling moth is not one of nature's great beauties. And the worm is even worse—a plump, pinkish white body with a brown head. In the spring, the moth lays her eggs on the branches of walnut and fruit trees, mostly apple, but also pear and quince. When they hatch, the caterpillars tunnel into the middle of the fruit, where they live and eat in the core, leaving the preferred part of the apple for us— if only we weren't quite so squeamish. Later they tunnel out to pupate down at the base of the tree. The only sign of their presence on the apple is a little puncture on the skin with some brown excrement. As moths, they lay more eggs, and the cycle starts all over again. The tree is under siege all summer.

▶ CONTROL

Codling moths spend the winter as cocoons under tree bark, down in the lowest three feet of the tree. To get at them in the spring, scrape off the rough part of the bark and kill them.

If you fail to get the cocoons, try to get the moths by hanging traps in the trees. These traps consist of containers filled with a sweet substance that attracts the moths, which fly right into them. You can use paper cups, glass jars, or plastic milk jugs with an opening cut in the side. (Their handles make it easier to tie them to the tree.) The bait can be a mixture of molasses and water in a 1:8 solution, or a mixture of two parts vinegar to one part molasses. People use a wide variety of formulas with success; for instance, put a banana peel, a cup of sugar, and a cup of vinegar into a gallon bottle, fill it with water, and hang it from the tree. Another sweet bait can be made from a gallon of water, three cups of molasses, a tablespoon of yeast, and half a tablespoon of oil of sassafras. Empty the traps every few days. If you are getting honey bees in the traps, put a one-eighth- to one-quarter-inch screening over the opening.

Pheromone traps can also be purchased from suppliers. These traps attract the male moths and can be quite effective in the home orchard (or tree), although it usually takes two or more years to get a good result. Two pheromone traps should be placed in each tree several weeks before the buds open.

Codling moths can have two or three generations in a summer. Since the caterpillars will make one trip down the tree to complete their cycle in midsummer, in early summer wrap the tree trunk with corrugated cardboard (bumpy side inward), burlap, or a sticky barrier, about two feet from the ground. Pick off this generation of caterpillars as it crawls down the tree and pupates here. Keep the trees wrapped all summer and check them every week or so.

It is wise to pick up and destroy the first infected apples or fruit that falls in the late spring.

Bars of soap were tied to the trunks of trees in the past to keep caterpillars from traveling up and down. Try using liquid soap or vegetable oil cooking spray on the tree trunk to get the same effect.

Woodpeckers are the apple grower's best friend when it comes to controlling codling moths, so place suet in the trees for them. Try to attract ground beetles. You can also order trichogramma wasps, which parasitize codling moths.

APPLE MAGGOTS

Apple maggots, like codling moths, attack fruit in the larval stage. The adult perpetrator is a fly, not a moth, and lays her eggs under the skin of the fruit.

▶ CONTROL

Use the same control as for codling moths. Be sure to remove and destroy dropped fruit. Sticky traps are especially effective. Apple maggots are attracted to yellow and red colors.

Corn earworm

CORN EARWORMS

This caterpillar is also known as the cotton bollworm and the tomato fruitworm. Although it is most famous as a pest on corn, you'll also find it ruining tomatoes, grapes, peas, beans, lettuce, peppers, squash, and okra. It comes in many colors. If you really want to know whether it is a corn earworm, look at it under a magnifying glass. A corn earworm will have hairy warts along its back. The only nice thing about this little worm is that, unlike the corn borer, it enters the corn at the tip, and only one worm inhabits an ear—thanks to its cannibalistic tendencies. So as long as the kids don't see what you're doing, you can always cut the wormy ends off and serve the corn anyway.

▶ **CONTROL**

The classic repellent for corn earworms is a squirt of mineral oil, which smothers the worms, applied with a medicine dropper (half full) inserted into the tip of each ear of corn, three to seven days after the silks have appeared. Some people add hot pepper to the oil. Beneficial nematodes can also be injected into the ears. If you're going to all this trouble, however, you may as well handpick the earworms.

Bt can be used against corn earworms, but it works better on tomatoes, beans, and lettuce than it does on corn. Spray plants every two weeks. Several parasitic wasps, including trichogramma wasps, can be ordered and released. Birds, toads, spiders, and lacewings make excellent predators, while mice and moles feed on pupae in the soil.

Healthy, hearty corn plants are more resistant to these caterpillars, so be sure to give your plants a decent organic, well-fed soil in which to thrive. Rotating the location of the corn every year will give the plants an advantage, because these insects pupate in the soil right under the plant.

PLUM CURCULIOS

Despite their name, these dark-colored, warty weevils do not limit themselves to plums; they scar or ruin peaches, apples, cherries, pears, and apricots too. Because of the enormous snout at the front of their head, they are sometimes called snout beetles.

The adults get into trees and feed on blossoms. When the fruit appears, they insert their eggs into holes made with the tip of their snout and then cut crescent-shaped slits to keep the growing fruit from crushing the eggs. The larva tunnels into the middle of the fruit and then tunnels back out again, gorging all the way. It then drops to the ground and pupates.

Besides scarring and stunting fruit, plum curculios also secrete an enzyme that causes apples to drop prematurely.

▶ *CONTROL*

In the spring, cultivate the soil to kill larvae and pupae.

Spread sheets under the tree and shake it to get the adults to drop from the branches. Repeat this every few weeks.

Pick up and destroy dropped fruit. Or get some chickens to peck around the trees. They'll eat the pests out of the fallen apples.

Plant flowers around fruit trees to attract beneficial wasps; you can order these wasps from suppliers too.

FRIEND OR FOE?

The following insects and animals have often been classified as pests. We think they deserve a little more tolerance—even appreciation—they may well be doing more good than damage in your garden.

CENTIPEDES AND MILLIPEDES

We all know the centipede was named because of its 100 legs, but whoever did the naming wasn't getting close enough to count. A centipede actually sports anywhere from 30 to 346 legs, depending on the species. "Millipede" is even more of a misnomer. A millipede starts out with only three pairs of legs, growing new ones every time it sheds its skin. At the most it can hope for around 400 legs—considerably short of 1,000, although still quite impressive.

Centipedes have certain advantages over millipedes. They can move quite a bit faster and wield a pair of venomous claws, with which they pinch and paralyze their victims. Thus equipped, most centipedes are fine predators. In the garden, they will eat snails, slugs, and many other pests. In the tropics, where centipedes can grow to a foot in length, their victims include mice, birds, and geckos.

Centipede

Millipede

Millipedes generally look like round, hard worms with lots of stubby legs. If disturbed, millipedes have the habit of rolling up into a coil and playing dead, like pillbugs.

Both millipedes and centipedes live nocturnal lives, hiding out in dank, dark places—under rocks, bark, and leaf litter. As a rule, they need lots of moisture, for their bodies are vulnerable to dehydration. Millipedes feed on decaying plant material, are industrious recyclers, and improve the fertility of the soil. They also eat dead snails and insects. In times of drought, however, they will eat live plants for their moisture. Some species suck on plants and feed on roots, whatever the weather happens to be.

▶ **CONTROL**

If millipedes are doing obvious damage to the garden (and you may have to go out at night to see if they are the culprits), you can devise several traps around the yard. Dig a hole in the ground and fill it with compacted decaying vegetation from a neglected corner of the yard. Down at the bottom of this millipede habitat, place a little plastic fruit basket or cottage cheese container with holes cut in it, filled with sliced potatoes or potato peels. Keep the trap damp, and every few days uncover it, pull it out, and dunk the millipedes in soapy water.

The **garden centipede** is not really a centipede, but rather a symphylan (*Scutigerella immaculata*). Very tiny, only a quarter of an inch long, and looking quite like a white centipede, it does a lot of damage to plants by eating their roots, and it gives centipedes a bad name. Symphylans can sometimes be destroyed by flooding the soil. Or make a tobacco tea by soaking a handful of tobacco in a gallon of water and adding a tablespoon of liquid soap to it. Drench the soil around the plant with this liquid. Or drench it with garlic spray (see *Tactics of Tiny Game Hunting in the Garden*). Some nematodes may be effective against them.

EARWIGS

These gruesome-looking scavengers, sometimes called pincher bugs, have an apparatus shaped like forceps on their rear end. Although they can pinch, and some of them can even shoot out a smelly secretion, they are fairly harmless to people. They got their name from the notion that they crawl into people's ears. Perhaps they may have done so more often centuries ago,

Earwig

when many people commonly slept on the ground. One can frequently find earwigs hiding in holes.

Earwigs may also invade houses, where they live like cockroaches. In the garden, for the most part, they do very little harm. Many earwigs feed on decaying plant matter and dead insects and improve the soil and add to its fertility. They also eat aphids, grubs, fleas, and other insects.

Some people insist, however, that earwigs eat their dahlias, zinnias, hollyhocks, and other plants and cause huge problems in the garden. It's probably the same as with dogs and their fleas—some gardens are bothered by earwigs and some aren't. In gardens with plenty of organic mulch, they tend to leave seedlings alone. If you can see for sure that they are causing damage, they can easily be defeated by their own habits.

▶ CONTROL

Trapping these insects, which love to hide in dark, narrow cracks and crevices, is fairly easy. Simply roll up newspapers loosely, dampen them, and place them in a moist, shady location. Rolled-up corrugated cardboard also works well. The earwigs crawl in at night. In the morning, unroll the newspapers and shake the bugs into a bucket of hot or soapy water, or dump them into the compost. Hollow bamboo stakes, rhubarb stalks, or short sections of cut-up garden hose, one to two feet in length, can also be used.

To make the traps more effective, remove as many as possible of the earwigs' usual hiding places, such as stones, boards, and garden debris.

Gardening lore from the 1700s advised hanging "hogs hoofs and lobster tails" on sticks to capture earwigs. Today, English gardeners stuff little flower pots with moss and hang them upside down on sticks. If you don't have any moss, you could use moistened shredded newspaper. Another English practice is to leave dampened rags around in the yard and stamp on them in the morning to kill the earwigs.

Beer traps for snails will capture earwigs, as will small containers with a little vegetable oil and a dollop of bacon grease or fish oil, set around the garden or placed near the foundations of the house, where they like to congregate (see *Slugs and Snails* for more information about beer traps).

Earwigs can also be caught in the act and eliminated as they munch on flowers at night. Simply go out with a flashlight and a spray bottle filled with soapy water and zap them. We recommend this, because it takes care of the earwigs actually doing the damage. Earwigs are often blamed for things they didn't do, proving once again that looks do matter.

OPOSSUMS

Opossums have the misfortune to resemble, at first glance, a rat that's as big as a cat, which doesn't endear them to people. However, these shy, misunderstood nocturnal foragers are quite harmless and will fall over and play dead, or "play possum," if threatened.

North America's only marsupials, they range over a wide territory and are usually simply passing through. Tolerance is the best attitude, especially since their diet consists mostly of snails, mice, rats, and gophers. What could be better?

▶ CONTROL

Since opossums will also help themselves to pet food left outdoors, even sharing it companionably alongside cats, you should move the pet food inside so that the opossums can devote their attention to snails.

Although opossums are rarely carriers of rabies, they are known to carry other diseases, including tuberculosis, relapsing fever, tularemia, salmonella, and more. Handle their droppings with care.

To keep them out of fruit trees (they love avocados), trim any branches that droop close to the ground and band the tree trunk with a two-foot-wide sheet of galvanized metal and some bungy cords. This will keep rats out of the tree too.

SOWBUGS AND PILLBUGS

Are they insects? Are they bugs? Are they incorrigible pests? The answer is no to all three, although many people would answer yes. Sowbugs and pillbugs are terrestrial crustaceans, related to lobsters and crayfish. Both possess seven pairs of legs and segmented bodies; the difference between them is that pillbugs are darker and roll up into tight little balls, whereas the gray sowbugs can't roll up as tightly and have to rely on running away when disturbed. Sometimes called woodlice or "roly-polies," they are actually quite useful, because they recycle decaying vegetation.

They sometimes go after young plants, especially ground cover, eating the roots and stems, or even the skins of ripe melons, cucumbers, squash, and strawberries that happen to touch the ground. (When these vegetables and fruits come in contact with the ground, they can get too much moisture and start to rot, so the bugs move in.) They will also crawl into holes created in fruits and vegetables by pests such as slugs and then get blamed for the damage. If they seem to be a problem, try to keep the garden a little drier. Prop the plants up on tin cans, upside-down berry baskets, or improvised "lifts." Or make little mats for them out of squares of stiff paper.

Sowbugs and pillbugs are frequent tenants of greenhouses, where the dampness provides them with a comfortable habitat. Here they wear out their welcome quickly by gnawing on the plants.

▶ CONTROL

To repel pillbugs and sowbugs, sprinkle the ground around the young seedlings you want to protect with lime, diatomaceous earth, or onion spray (blend three onions with four cups water and strain). Some say remove all dead leaves and, in essence, don't keep any organic mulch around. We would rather have the benefit of the mulch and wrestle with the bugs. Mulch provides a haven for many beneficial insects too.

These creatures are night feeders and find dark, damp places to spend their days. To trap them, turn a dampened clay pot upside down and prop up one edge; they are especially attracted to corncobs, which can be placed inside the pot. In the morning tap the bugs into a bucket and move them to another place in the garden or dump them in soapy water.

Trap for sowbugs and pillbugs

To make a good trap, take a potato, slice it in half, scrape out a little of the inside and place it face down on the ground. Or use half an orange rind. You may also get some slugs. Dampened, rolled-up cardboard or newspapers will also trap pillbugs and sowbugs. Frogs are quite fond of eating them too.

Another trap is made by cutting a two-liter plastic soda bottle in two. Invert the top section as a funnel into the bottom half, and seal them together with tape. Drop the bait into the trap and lay it on its side near the infestation. Sowbugs and pillbugs will walk in through the "tunnel" and drop into the enclosed space to get to the food.

One reader of *Organic Gardening* magazine wrote to say she scattered dried dog food around her plants. The sowbugs liked it so much they left her plants alone.

In dry weather, we turn on a drip irrigation system; when the pillbugs and sowbugs gather around the moisture, we simply scoop them up and toss them into the compost heap. There's plenty of work for them to do there.

YELLOW JACKETS AND WASPS

All yellow jackets are wasps, but not all wasps are yellow jackets. Many people also confuse wasps and honey bees. Yellow jackets get our attention, not only because their bright yellow and black raiment makes them more visible, but because they are highly attracted to our food. Easily angered, they have nothing to lose by stinging us, because they don't have barbed hooks on their stingers, as honey bees do, and can withdraw them and sting over and over again. The venom of yellow jackets and wasps can cause severe allergic reactions in some people.

Yellow jackets like birthday parties, picnics, outdoor weddings, and barbecues. There's hardly an alfresco summer social occasion that they will not visit, provided, of course, that refreshments are served. Sweets, fruit juice, soft drinks, and fresh fruit appeal to them, as do meats and fish.

Yellow jacket

However, yellow jackets are also excellent insect predators. They possess very strong jaws, with which they tear apart insects to take back to their nests to feed the grubs. They also prey on aphids.

Yellow jackets present a potential danger to us; as social wasps, many species build their nests in the ground (often in abandoned animal burrows), in holes in logs, or on shrubbery near the ground. A nest can have more than 5,000 inhabitants, and wasps will protect it ferociously. Anyone who has the misfortune to step on one of these nests and then run for his or her life with an angry swarm of stinging yellow jackets in pursuit is not likely to forget the sheer, unadulterated terror of the experience.

The terms "yellow jacket" and "hornet" refer to different species of the same group of wasps that build their paper nests either underground or suspended from branches (or in other high, sheltered spots), respectively. Another group of wasps, ***Polistes* wasps** (sometimes known as paper wasps), builds nests from chewed-up weathered wood and plants that the wasps mix into a pulp with their saliva. Wasps may have given people the idea of how to make paper. Some species have been used successfully in biological control; their nests have actually been moved and placed close to crops so that they can eliminate pest caterpillars more effectively.

As a group, wasps are more friend than enemy. They are very good at controlling noxious insect pests such as grasshoppers, gypsy moths, tomato hornworms, corn earworms, and cabbageworms. They pollinate crops such as melons and spinach. They even eat the aphid honeydew off of leaves, preventing fungi and forestalling ants.

Many species of wasps, including **mud daubers** and **digger wasps**, live and work alone, seeking out insects to paralyze and lay their eggs on, thus providing their young with a source of fresh meat. They rarely sting, and their venom is not as powerful as that of other wasps. As adults, the wasps themselves feed on nectar and fruit juices while busily hunting down insects and dragging them off to special burrows, where they become fodder for their young. Entomologists often collect the nests of solitary wasps as a shortcut to finding and collecting insect specimens. One spider wasp actually specializes in hunting and capturing black widow spiders.

▶ CONTROL

To prevent a nest from getting established in the yard, watch for wasps and yellow jackets in the early spring, when the queen is just beginning the colony. Try to discourage her by knocking down the foundations of the nest when she begins her work. If she has made up her mind that this is the place, however, she can be killed simply by swatting her. This is much easier than trying to kill several thousand wasps later. Some people hang sticky flypaper near a paper wasp nest to trap these insects.

If the nest is in the ground, you can place a large clear glass bowl upside down over the entrance. (If they can see the sky, they won't attempt a new hole.) There may be more than one hole, so be sure to cover them all. This technique will starve the colony. Some people go out at night and pour gasoline or kerosene into the hole. We do not recommend this. Instead, nematodes can be mixed with water and poured on the soil. Soapsuds in a spray bottle do wonders, but you have to be somewhat fearless (and have a good aim). Pyrethrum sprays also provide instant knockdown.

Any monkeying with the nest must be done at night when these wasps are quiescent, and it must be done in full protective gear, with absolutely no skin left uncovered.

According to *National Gardening* magazine, a naturalist working for the East Bay Regional Park System in Oakland, California, poured honey near the entrance holes to underground yellow jacket nests in a park at closing time. The next morning all the nests had been dug out by skunks or raccoons.

As with flies, keeping nuisance wasps away means keeping garbage cans covered. Do not leave soft drink cans around. If possible, drink from cups with lids and straws. Don't leave ripe fruit lying around under trees, and don't feed pets outside. Be careful when picking up wet towels, because these wasps are highly attracted to moisture.

Do not wear bright colors or perfume around yellow jackets. Stay calm and move slowly; jerky movement can startle them into stinging. Avon Skin-So-Soft bath oil repels them.

Traps   You can buy excellent wasp or yellow jacket traps. The good thing about traps is that they pick off the annoying individuals without destroying the colony. And in view of all the insects they kill and the plants they pollinate, we actually need yellow jackets.

Many traps have very small holes for the wasps to crawl into. It is advisable to first place the bait *outside* the trap, until the yellow jackets have picked up the scent and located it. Wait until they are going back and forth, taking the message to their brethren, then put the bait in the trap.

A simple homemade trap consists of putting Kool-Aid, apple juice, or a sweet food, such as raspberry jam, in the bottom of a jar, fashioning a lid from a piece of paper and a rubber band, and making a small hole in it with a pencil. Wasps enter and can't get out. When the trap is full, drop it in soapy water to kill the wasps.

You can make an old-fashioned trap by hanging a fish over a bucket of soapy water. The yellow jackets always pull off a big piece (not from greed, mind you; they are taking food back to the grubs in the nest). Dropping down before they can fly off, they land in the water. The soap in the water makes them sink. A piece of raw meat works just as well. Hang the meat or spear it with a fork and lean the fork upright against the side of the bucket so that the meat is just above the soapy water.

Yellow jacket trap

217

Or take a plastic gallon milk jug or water bottle and cut a small entrance hole in it. Fill the bottle partway with soapy water. Then tie a piece of meat with thread and hang it inside by wrapping the thread around the top before screwing on the lid.

A trap like this, baited with a pipe cleaner dipped in heptyl butyrate, caught more than 10,000 yellow jackets a day on Santa Cruz Island. It was made more effective by cutting out a two-inch-by-three-inch square on the side of the jug and taping a piece of screen on it, so that they could really smell the bait. Heptyl butyrate is effective but expensive.

Bring along a fly swatter to eliminate early arrivals in a picnic area where wasps have already locked onto the food. Then place a trap twenty to thirty feet upwind. When shooed away, foraging wasps will continue upwind to your trap.

During the beginning of the summer through August, wasps will be looking for protein, such as meats and pet food. Later in the summer, they are more attracted to sugar. Bait the traps accordingly. However, if sweet traps are also attracting bees, switch to meat.

CRITTER CONTROL

DIGGERS
• • • • •

GOPHERS

When you see a raised ridge of earth in your garden or yard, the culprit is likely a mole, not a gopher, and moles are mostly beneficial, in that they eat subterranean insects as they burrow (see *Moles*).

When we say "gopher," we mean the *pocket gopher*, a rodent that eats a wide variety of plants, starting with the roots, including roses, tomatoes, peppers, carrots, gladioli, fruit trees, grape roots, dahlias, delphiniums, hollyhocks, garlic, squash, cucumbers, melons, tulips, and lilies—to name just a few. Our backyard battles with these subterranean scavengers often fluctuate between farce and frustration.

Described as "all mouth and no heart," gophers don't just nibble on a plant, allowing it to send out calls for help in the way of limp or yellow leaves. There's no time for negotiation. One minute the plant is upright and looking fine; then suddenly, with the slightest tremor, it topples over, gone, never to be resuscitated. Even more outrageous is the sight of a plant being pulled into the ground, leaf, stock, and stem. Then you know you have a pocket gopher and not a mole or a ground squirrel.

The only way to keep the gopher from getting the next plant is to get rid of the gopher. This is easier said than done. Busy workers, gophers can dig a 100-foot tunnel in a day. Although they lead solitary lives and will fight with other gophers whom they happen to meet, several gophers can cohabit a plot of land, living entirely alone in separate tunnels. A gopher can have one to three litters a year, with usually five or six young.

Pocket gophers get their name from the fur-lined pockets on their cheeks in which they carry roots and other foods back to their storage chambers. They dig with their teeth, which never wear out because they continue to grow—up to fourteen inches a year. Remarkably, they never get dirt in their mouths.

▶ CONTROL

In their impotence against this wily adversary, people have resorted to poisons that could kill armies. We do not recommend them. Injected with special applicators into the soil, these toxins eventually make their way to the water table. With poisons, too, you never really know if you got the gopher—unless, of course, your dog (or that fabulous eagle) dies from eating the animal. Strychnine, a poison commonly used against gophers, is extremely poisonous to mammals (including people) and fish.

In gopher territory, one of the best systems of defense is a barrier. You can line planting beds with half-inch galvanized wire-mesh fencing, hardware cloth, or aviary wire, buried two feet under the soil. Around the edges, make sure the wire comes all the way up to the surface of the soil and even a few inches above it. Young trees and plants can also be planted into large holes lined with light wire mesh or commercial "gopher baskets." Once mature, the trees will not be as vulnerable to attack.

Do not underestimate the gopher's own predators, which include owls, hawks, skunks, cats, dogs, badgers, coyotes, and snakes. Build a nesting box for barn owls, which can eat several gophers apiece every night. One gardener we know grabs gopher snakes or king snakes when he sees them and stuffs them down gopher holes to do the killing. Local pet stores sometimes have these snakes.

Repellents Gophers reportedly avoid garlic plants. The crown-imperial plant, *Fritillaria imperialis*, has a skunklike smell that gophers supposedly dislike. They are also said to avoid oleander, squill, daffodils, and castor bean plants. If you plant gopher spurge, *Euphorbia lathyris* (also known as mole plant), around the perimeter of the garden, it will keep gophers out.

Another tactic consists of putting pieces of Juicy Fruit gum into the gopher holes. Wear gloves when handling the gum to eliminate your human smell. Other items that can be placed in gopher tunnels are dead gophers, dead fish or fish heads, canned sardines, rotting garbage, used kitty litter, paper towels soaked in rancid oil, commercial ferret scent, pet clippings, urine, and sponges saturated with ammonia. Make sure that all the holes are closed so that the tunnel gets as smelly as possible. We do not recommend broken glass or barbed wire, because these would remain in place and might pose a future hazard.

Some people swear you can use "noise" to discourage gophers, which are acutely sensitive to vibrations. Try placing a plastic pinwheel (or several of them) in the ground near the tunnel. A small windmill, attached to a stake driven deep into the ground, can be augmented with pieces of wood or clothespins attached to the propellers, making it clatter as it turns. You can buy these too. This system requires wind. Don't buy battery-operated electronic vibrators or ultrasonic noise emitters unless they come with a money-back guarantee.

You might try a small battery-operated radio, securely wrapped inside a plastic bag, set on loud static and placed inside the tunnel.

Traps   A good gopher trapper embodies the best of the tiny game hunter: keen observation, great persistence, and creative flexibility. Some areas have professional gopher trappers, who get paid by the body count. They can also teach you how to do the trapping properly.

In order to trap gophers, you will need to locate their tunnels. Both gophers and moles push out dirt mounds from lateral runs off their main tunnels; these are often the most important clues to their presence. A molehill is circular, like a volcano, while a gopher hole consists of a fan-shaped pile of dirt.

Locate the base of the fan-shaped pile of dirt. Sometimes a gopher will plug its hole here after pushing out the dirt onto the mound. It will consist of a small circular depression. Take a probe, for example an extra-long screwdriver, and start jabbing the ground about six to ten inches from this spot. You will feel it break through when it hits the tunnel.

Old-fashioned metal gopher traps (e.g., Victor, Macabee) are probably the most reliable. To be effective, gopher traps must be placed correctly. Considering you are trapping an underground enemy you can't see by covering sensitive mechanisms with dirt, the obstacles are all on your side.

Wash traps in hot soapy water before using them, and wear gloves when handling them, because human odor is a great repellent. Set *two* traps facing in opposite directions inside the tunnel and cover them well, so that no light enters the tunnel. Attach the traps to a rope or chain on a stake, or the gopher may drag them off. Check the traps daily; if you don't catch anything in a day or two, move them.

Flooding   If you need to deep water your trees anyway and can afford the water bill, stick a garden hose down into the tunnel and flood out the gopher. Two hoses at opposite ends of the garden work even better. It may take a while if the tunnels are extensive. Sometimes you can detect movement going along a tunnel. Take a shovel and stick it in the ground to block the gopher's progress. Some people lie in wait and whack the gopher with a shovel when it appears. Others merely pray that it will move next door. Flooding also exposes gophers to predators.

Heavy irrigation tends to chase gophers away, because they find wet soil difficult to dig through.

Fumigation   A gopher can often be smoked out of its tunnel or driven back into a neighbor's yard. One of the easiest ways is to stick lighted "gopher bombs" or highway flares into the tunnel and close it off carefully with dirt so that the gas doesn't escape. Another method is to use flexible metal exhaust pipes, garden hoses, or vacuum cleaner hoses—and lots of duct tape—and fill the tunnels with exhaust from either the tail pipe of a running car or a gas-powered lawn mower.

Gopher Wisdom   With gophers, you must begin the battle as soon as they invade, because once their tunnels are extensive, these will expedite future invasions. If you don't want to kill the gophers, constant harassment, using the above techniques, may eventually discourage them. Keep in mind, however, that their burrowing helps aerate the soil and makes it a better medium for plant growth.

Inquire at your local garden center or agriculture extension office for the names of plants for your area that are resistant to gophers.

MOLES

We're pretty hard on moles, but they actually do a lot more good than harm. Most of their bad reputation is undeserved and comes from an unfortunate association with gophers and mice.

Moles have darker fur than gophers, much smaller eyes (they can hardly see at all), no visible ears, paws like flippers, and a pronounced pinkish, garish snout. Like gophers, they spend most of their life underground, coming up occasionally to shove a little dirt out. A molehill is round and shaped like a volcano, unlike the large (one-foot across) fan-shaped mound of a gopher.

The good that moles do comes mainly from their great appetite for insects. Night and day, they "swim" through the earth, aerating the soil and eating grubs, beetles, slugs, snails, caterpillars, and mice, among other pests. In the past, in England, moles were even deliberately introduced into gardens infested with chafer grubs. Unfortunately, they also eat earthworms, but a healthy population of earthworms will not be eliminated by moles.

On the down side, moles make unsightly ridges in perfect-looking lawns, and their tunnels can injure roots, mainly because mice and shrews sometimes run around in mole tunnels, and they can be harmful to plants. When you discover these ridges, press the earth firmly back down to collapse the tunnels and water well afterward.

▶ CONTROL

We have always simply used flooding to get moles to move on. We stick a garden hose into the main tunnel (usually just a guess), turn it on, and wait until water fills up all the tunnels—which can be extensive. We also remind ourselves that the moles are probably simply passing through, gobbling up slugs and other pests. Fortunately, we don't have a lot invested in the looks of our lawn.

If your lawn has moles, chances are that it also has plenty of Japanese beetle grubs or other harmful pests for the moles to eat. You can thank the moles for pointing this out to you. Get rid of the grubs using an application of milky spore disease (*Bacillus popilliae*) and the moles will leave. It will take some time for the disease to take effect, however. Other grubs in the lawn can be controlled with beneficial nematodes—microscopic roundworms that attack and kill them.

Repellents   Around evidence of mole activity, some gardeners bury soda bottles almost up to their tops in the ground. The sound created by wind passing over the tops of the bottles is very unpleasant to the moles, which have ultrasensitive hearing. Children's pinwheels can also be placed in the ground near tunnels.

Moles can be barred from your garden by digging a trench at least two feet deep all around and filling it with stones and hard, claylike soil, which, especially if you keep it dry, the moles cannot dig through.

Other ways to repel moles include putting peeled garlic cloves down in the tunnel. Folk wisdom of the sixteenth century said garlic would make moles leap right out of the ground. Sprinkling hot pepper into the tunnel is another way to repel them. Some people use pet droppings (which are better buried anyway).

The heads of salted herring are an old remedy for moles, used in the 1800s. Another repellent was elder leaves, which have an odor the moles don't like. A more up-to-date method consists of placing pieces of rolled-up Juicy Fruit gum into the mole tunnel. Wear gloves when unwrapping and placing the gum; if the animal can smell you, it won't touch it.

Castor beans or castor plants are often cited as a mole repellent or poison, but we do not recommend them, because they are very poisonous and too dangerous to have around children. Castor oil is not poisonous, however, and some gardeners pour it (Mole Med, Scoot Mole) on the ground around evidence of moles and claim it works quite well. Make your own by mixing two tablespoons of castor oil in a gallon of water with a tablespoon of liquid soap to get it to disperse. *Euphorbia lathyris*, also called gopher plant, caper spurge, or mole plant, is sometimes planted as a mole repellent.

In warm weather, moles make foraging tunnels quite near the surface, while in the winter they go deep underground, just as earthworms do. In the summer, sometimes, you can actually see their movement as they "swim" through the ground near the surface. They can then easily be dispatched with a shovel or put into a container and removed to another location.

You can also buy "smoke bombs" to place in mole tunnels to smoke them out. Their by-product is actually a fertilizer.

Traps   If you feel you must trap moles, use meat baits, because moles are carnivorous. Knowing the high volume of insects they eat, you wouldn't really want to destroy them. A better method consists of a trap that allows you to capture the mole and move it to another location. Find the tunnel that is active by slightly depressing the earth where you see a ridge. If the mole is using this tunnel, it will soon be repaired. Wearing gloves, carefully open the tunnel and dig a hole into which a large (two- to three-quart) can or glass jar can be placed. The top of the container should be level with the bottom of the runway. Let a little dirt from the top of the tunnel fall on either side of the jar to hide it. Set a board over the top of the hole in the tunnel and cover it well with dirt so that no light gets in. Traveling through the tunnel, the mole will tumble into the container and be unable to get out. You can then relocate it. Don't leave it in the container too long; it can starve very quickly.

Mole trap

FORAGERS

• • • • • •

Humans are territorial animals. We're always deciding whom to allow on our property and whom to keep out. This is certainly true when it comes to animals—some we cherish and others we chase away.

If you don't really know what or who is responsible for chewed-up leaves and disappearing plants, put some white flour or mason's chalk in a sifter and sprinkle it on the ground. The footprints will identify the culprit, so that you can take suitable measures.

The persistence of small garden marauders—woodchucks, rabbits, raccoons, opossums—may force you to build a fence. The best ones are made of loose chicken wire (forty-eight inches high) that flops precariously when the animals start to climb it, forcing them to give up. Spacing the fence posts far apart—eight feet—will cause the fence to sag in a way the animals don't like. The chicken wire must go down into the soil at least twelve inches to keep some of the animals from tunneling underneath.

An electric fence will almost always work, but it smacks of isolationism; and it's expensive. It does, however, require only one or at the most three strands of wire. We recommend using solar electricity and getting professional help when it comes to dispensing shock treatment in a garden skirmish.

Repellents have always been used against animals encroaching on domestic produce. Many rely on smells that bring up bad associations for the animals. Human hair has long been used as an all-around animal repellent (more on this under *Deer*). Another repellent that seems to work for (or against) animals is a border of wood ashes sprinkled around the plants. After it rains, however, the ashes lose their efficacy and must be replaced.

Wormwood can be planted as a border around the garden, because animals don't like it. A border of onions or any member of the garlic family may deter rabbits and other small animals.

Some people take a portable radio, put it in a protective covering like a plastic bag, and tune it to an all-night talk radio station. The sound of human voices keeps animals at bay. Others rig up lights for the same purpose, but we do not recommend this, because shining lights on growing plants at night can interfere with their growth patterns.

One of the more appealing new products is the motion-activated sprinkler (Contech) that provides a harmless but shocking jet of water, causing the four-legged forager to bolt.

DEER

If you have deer encroaching on your property, it is probably because your property is actually encroaching on the deer. Feeding at dawn and dusk, eating ornamentals (they even eat roses), sampling vegetable gardens, and rubbing against tree bark, deer can do a lot of damage to a garden. However, if plants have been cleanly bitten off, it's probably not deer. Deer tear at leaves and stems and leave ragged, torn edges.

Deer rely heavily on their sense of smell (their noses are eight times as large as humans'), so commercial repellents (e.g., Ro-Pel, Bobbex, Hinder, Big Game Repellent) will help curb their appetites for your tender leaves.

Nylon stockings stuffed with human hair collected from a beauty parlor are a classic deer repellent. Soap also receives high ratings. Use nylon stockings filled with Lifebuoy soap chips or bars of strong deodorant soap like Irish Spring or Dial. Hang the hair bags or the soap on each plant or tree you want to protect, two to three feet above the ground.

Manure from members of the cat family (lion, tiger, cheetah, etc.) can be obtained from the zoo and makes a terrific repellent as long as the smell lasts. Spread it on the ground near plants or at the edge of the garden.

A friend who gardens in deer territory has found the following formula to be the most effective of all: mix an egg in a quart of warm water, along with one or two tablespoons of Tabasco sauce. Blend well, strain, and spray. (She uses a portable air sprayer.) It has to be reapplied after heavy rain or new growth.

Spread wire-mesh fencing or chicken wire on the ground. Deer do not like stepping on it, nor do other animals. (People don't either, actually.) Another tactile tactic consists of planting tomato or squash vines and letting them spread out over the ground at the perimeter of the garden. Deer don't like to step on these either. Since you have to wait until the vines mature for this to work, plant them well in advance of the plants you want to protect.

Of course, a dog with a good sense of guardsmanship can be an excellent deer repellent. Human urine has been touted as even better than a dog's.

To protect trunks of trees that are being nibbled or rubbed against, wrap netting, chicken wire, or commercial tree guards around them. These will also protect trees from the nibbling of rabbits and mice.

Aromatic plants such as lavender, sage, onions, and garlic are believed to repel deer because they prevent them from smelling the approach of enemies. Local nurseries and cooperative extension services can provide lists of plants that deer in your area dislike.

Many people believe that with deer, it all comes down to either fencing or sharing. A good rule for fences is to build them before the deer have sampled the banquet you have waiting for them. Fences that are not electric must be at least six feet tall to keep deer out, and if the deer can see through them, even eight feet may not be tall enough. One effective way to fence out deer is to build two fences about five feet apart. Although deer can jump quite high, they are not broad jumpers. The two fences don't have to be any higher than five feet, which makes them much more ornamental. (Some people say the inside fence only has to be three feet high.) Plant a "hedgerow" or potpourri of plants to attract birds and beneficials in between.

If a fence is out of the question, set up a barricade of corn or soybeans, planted just for the deer, and hope they don't get too greedy.

DOGS

We have always wondered about the motives of people who let their dogs invade and befoul other people's yards. If the dogs in the neighborhood are getting into your garbage, sprinkle ammonia around the bases of the cans. And make sure the lids are always on tight.

A repellent spray for dogs can be made by mixing two cups of rubbing alcohol with two teaspoons of lemon grass oil; spray it on the areas where you don't want dogs. Rotten potatoes placed along their route will also keep dogs from lingering for very long. You can purchase commercial repellents, as well as satisfying motion-activated sprinklers that run on batteries.

If your own clunk of a dog refuses to show any respect for your new little seedlings and keeps stepping on them, protect them with upside-down strawberry baskets or cans with both ends cut out.

To keep the dog from digging itself a nice napping spot in the dirt among your plants, take croquet wickets, grape stakes, or wooden stakes (an old broomstick cut into twelve-inch lengths works well), and pound them into the ground at intervals of about one foot.

RABBITS

Rabbits have always loved our gardens, but gardeners have certainly not always loved rabbits. They damage flowers, vegetables, and the bark of fruit trees and ornamentals. Look for their distinctive, round, pea-sized droppings if you suspect rabbits.

When rabbits go after young seedlings, protect them with row covers or aluminum screens bent in half over the plants. Seal off the ends with chicken wire. A three-foot-high chicken-wire fence will also deter them.

Sprinkling bloodmeal on the ground around plants will sometimes repel rabbits. They also dislike the smell of powdered lime and sulfur. Sprinkle hot red pepper, black pepper, or garlic powder on the dampened leaves of plants to make them unpalatable as rabbit food.

The smell of fish may offend rabbits. Mix two tablespoons of fish emulsion in a gallon of water and spray it on the plants. Be warned, however—cats love it. Planting onions throughout the garden may deter rabbits. Short sections of garden hose (imitation snakes) put around your garden to scare off birds may also scare away rabbits.

If rabbits nibble around the tender trunks of saplings, wrap them with fiberglass insulation, plastic pipe that has been slit lengthwise with a saw, or commercial tree wraps. Chicken wire makes another good barrier against rabbits and mice chewing on bark. Some people smear bacon grease or other animal fat on the trunk.

Rabbits are an important link in the food chain. Predators include skunks, raccoons, snakes, coyotes, foxes, hawks, owls, dogs, and cats.

We know a gardener who always plants a patch of lettuce especially for the rabbits, well away from her own lettuce. Sometimes she even steals from the rabbits' patch.

RACCOONS

Raccoons thrive in suburbia. As evidence of their supreme adaptability to our gluttonous, throwaway society, these clever, furry, sociable creatures inevitably go after garbage cans, and they'll eat almost anything we didn't finish. They also eat the fish out of our ponds, the fruit from our trees, and the earthworms from the ground. Raccoons can carry rabies and roundworm, and if you trap one, others may simply come to replace it. They can be difficult to discourage, and their dexterity and persistence is legendary. Still, there are a few things you can do.

First and foremost, never leave out pet food.

Use a bungy cord or heavy rock to secure the lid on the garbage. To keep it from being knocked over, drive a stake into the ground through the handle. Sprinkle the lid with Lysol or Tabasco sauce. Sprinkle hydrated lime or place rags soaked in ammonia around or on the tops of the cans.

Raccoons can even come in pet doors to feed. Lock those doors at night or buy one that can only be opened by a special collar on your pet.

Raccoons love corn, and rows of it can become a battleground. Sprinkling hydrated lime around the vegetables may keep raccoons away. Or take a spray bottle and spritz the corn with water, then sprinkle it with hot red pepper. (It has to be really hot to work.) Another red pepper concoction consists of half a cup of cayenne, one tablespoon of liquid soap, and a pint of water. Mix and let stand overnight, then strain and spray on the ears of corn.

You might have to resort to putting a paper or plastic bag over each ear of corn and securing it with wire string. A reader of *Organic Gardening* magazine wrote that running her hands over each ear of corn apparently gave it a smell that the raccoons did not like. Others have draped dirty and smelly clothing around.

Some gardeners plant pumpkin seeds among the corn plants. The raccoons seem to like eating the corn while standing up, so that they can look around, and the big pumpkin leaves keep them from doing this. They don't seem to like cucumber plants among the corn either. Thin black plastic spread flat around plants on the ground may also deter them.

Go to a pet groomer and get the hair trimmings from the dogs. Put them in mesh bags and set them around to keep the raccoons and other animals away.

Persuade your kids to camp out when the corn is ripening. This will give them idyllic childhood memories.

Put sheet metal barriers around trees to keep raccoons from the fruit. Sprinklers with motion detectors can frighten them off.

The humane society or animal control officer in your area will have live traps that you can borrow and use. Havahart traps and Safe-N-Sound live traps are available from mail order sources.

The best method is exclusion: make sure that chimneys are capped, that attics are animal-proof, and that the undersides of decks and crawl spaces are sealed off. If raccoons are living under the house or deck, and they don't have babies, use ammonia-soaked rags to stink them out. They also dislike bright lights left on all night.

SKUNKS

Not all animals are unwelcome in the garden. If you're lucky enough to play host to a fox, let it alone; it goes after your rodents. Skunks are also great rodent hunters, and they live on insects as well. They like armyworms, grasshoppers, tobacco worms, grubs, cutworms, and potato beetles, among other bugs. New York State even passed a law protecting them, because they were helping the hop growers by eating hop grubs. We feel amiable toward skunks unless they take up residence under the house. Then we feel nervous.

Nocturnal and nomadic, skunks rarely stay in one place for long, except when raising their young. A three-foot-high wire-mesh fence buried six inches in the ground usually keeps skunks off your property. They're more likely to dig under a fence than climb over it.

To avoid attracting skunks, never leave out pet food, and keep compost in sturdy, closed containers.

If a skunk takes up residence under the house or deck, use a fine sprinkling of flour or chalk to track its comings and goings. After it has left to forage for the night, seal up the opening or install a one-way door. (Forget trying this from May to August, when they may have babies in there.) You can also use ammonia-soaked rags to draw the skunk out or keep it out. Or try lights and loud noises to make it uncomfortable. Once it has gone, seal the opening.

Animal control officers will come and trap a skunk for you, but they may also destroy it because of the fear of rabies. If the law allows (it's not legal in California), it would be better to trap your trespasser carefully on your own and release it five to ten miles away from the premises.

The trick with trapping skunks is to use a cage that has been wrapped in canvas or an old blanket, or placed inside of a garbage can on its side. Bait it with cat kibble, sardines, or eggs. Be sure you have a long string on the cage release.

Don't be surprised if you come back to the house to find the skunk's mate and have to repeat the procedure. The best thing to do is try to co-exist with skunks as they pass through the neighborhood, while keeping them from taking up residence under your house.

Skunks will always give fair warning, if they are about to spray, by stamping or pawing their feet. Don't wait for them to turn around. Like acrobats, they stand on their front legs, whip their tails over their heads and aim for the eyes with uncanny accuracy. But take heart if you catch a whiff of nature's ultimate repellent. It was once thought to be good for asthma.

SQUIRRELS

People seem to either love or detest squirrels. Depending on which camp you are in, they are either clever and adorable or clever and abominable. Admittedly, squirrels can be terribly greedy at bird feeders, taking far more than their rightful share, even destroying the feeders themselves. In their defense, however, their practice of burying far more acorns and nuts than they eventually dig up contributes to reforestation.

If you find that squirrels, chipmunks—or any animals—seem to be digging up your plants as soon as you put them in the ground, put screen covers secured with stones over them for a week or two.

If squirrels are eating your bulbs, try coating them liberally with cayenne before planting them. Or lay one-inch hardware cloth or chicken wire on top of the soil after planting. Disguise it with mulch. The plants will come up through the barrier.

If the squirrels are getting into fruit or nut trees, band the trees with metal banding, two feet wide and eight feet off the ground. Tie aluminum pie pans—real aluminum, not foil—to the lower limbs of the trees. Hammer a nail through the pan to make a hole to attach the string. Or make a barricade of plastic milk jugs strung together through the handles. Tie as many jugs as possible around the tree trunk to create a bubble-skirt barrier without any space for the squirrels to get through. It may look silly, but you can take it down after harvesting the fruit. Another barrier can be made by cutting the top half off plastic milk jugs and then stapling or nailing them with the open ends down, right onto the tree trunk and touching each other.

Commercial sticky products may harm squirrels. Try a coating of petroleum jelly to make the climbing surface off-limits. It needs to be reapplied frequently.

Keeping squirrels out of trees and bird feeders may require persistence and ingenuity. When you place your feeders, keep in mind that squirrels are remarkable jumpers, as well as excellent problem solvers. Try buying squirrel-proof bird feeders. Also, put PVC pipe over the pole when you put it up—it's hard to climb on. Or attach a slinky to the feeder and unspool it around the pole.

Another way to keep squirrels out of bird feeders is to hang the feeder from a wire strung between two poles or trees, making sure it is placed farther than the squirrels can jump. Then thread the wire with wooden spools, or film canisters, or plastic soft drink bottles, so that when the squirrels try walking the wire, they'll be spun off to the ground.

If you simply can't stand them, the best defense is to trap them in Havahart traps and move them at least five miles away. Bait the traps for a while without setting them to get the squirrels used to them.

Resources and Mail Order

RESOURCES

Bat Conservation International
P.O. Box 162603
Austin, TX 78716-2603
Bat advocacy, bat houses, and more.

Beyond Pesticides (NCAMP)
701 E Street SE, Suite 200
Washington, DC 20003
(202) 543-5450
www.beyondpesticides.org
Useful information on pesticides and alternatives to their use.

The Bio-Integral Resource Center (BIRC)
P.O. Box 7414
Berkeley, CA 94707
(510) 524-2567
www.birc.org
Excellent source of information on least-toxic pest control. Publications, journal, and quarterly.

The Ecological Farming Association
406 Main Street, #313
Watsonville, CA 95076
(831) 763-2111
www.csa-efc.org
Promotes ecologically sound agriculture.

Environmental Working Group
www.EWG.org
(www.foodnews.org for information about pesticides in food)
Excellent resource for people who are attempting to protect the environment.

Friends of the Earth
1025 Vermont Ave. NW, 3rd floor
Washington, DC 20005
(202) 783-7400
www.FoE.org
Advocacy organization dedicated to protecting the planet. Largest environmental network in the world.

National Pediculosis Association
P.O. Box 610189
Newton, MA 02461
www.HeadLice.org
Health education organization with up-to-date information on lice.

Pesticide Action Network North America (PANNA)
49 Powell St., Suite 500
San Francisco, CA 94102
e-mail panna@panna.org
www.panna.org
Coalition opposing the misuse of pesticides. Supports reliance on safe, ecologically sound alternatives.

Rachel Carson Council
8940 Jones Mill Road
Chevy Chase, MD 20815
(301) 652-1877
e-mail: rccouncil@aol.com
A clearinghouse for pesticide-related information.

U.S. PIRG (Public Interest Research Groups)
e-mail: pirg@pirg.org
www.pirg.org
Coalition of environmental and consumer watchdog agencies.

MAIL ORDER

Arizona Biological Control (ARBICO)
P.O. Box 4247
Tucson, AZ 85738-1247
(800) 827-2847
www.arbico.com
Beneficial insects and organic growing supplies.

Beneficial Insectary
14751 Oak Run Road
Oak Run, CA 96069
(800) 477-3715
www.insectary.com
Beneficial insects, parasites, mites.

BioLogic
P.O. Box 177
Willow Hill, PA 17271
(717) 349-2789
www.biologicco.com
Nematodes.

Bountiful Gardens
18001 Shafer Ranch Road
Willits, CA 95490-9626
(707) 459-6410
www.bountifulgardens.org
Untreated seeds, nontoxic pest controls, educational materials.

Bramen Company, Inc. of Cabot Farm
P.O. Box 70
Salem, MA 01970
(800) 234-7765
Horticultural supplies and tools, earthworm castings, guano, root
maggot collars.

The Bug Store
113 West Argonne
St. Louis, Missouri 63122
(800) 455-2847
www.bugstore.com
Predators, parasites, traps, and up-to-the-minute pest control
supplies.

Earlee, Inc.
P.O. Box 4480
Jeffersonville, IN 47131-4480
(812) 282-9134
Organic products for farm and garden.

Earthly Goods
P.O. Box 4164
Tulsa, OK 74159-1164
(918) 583-1990
Nontoxic pest controls for the garden and home, including pets.

Etex
916 South Casino Center
Las Vegas, NV 89101
(800) 543-5651
www.etex-ltd.com
Electrogun for termites.

Gardener's Supply
128 Intervale Road
Burlington, VT 05401
(800) 955-3370
www.gardeners.com
Earth-friendly gardening solutions, nontoxic pest controls.

Gardens Alive!
5100 Schenley Place
Laurenceburg, IN 47025
(812) 537-8651
www.gardens-alive.com
Safe products for a healthy garden.

Great Lakes IPM
10220 Church Road NE
Vestaburg, MI 48891
(517) 268-5693
Insect traps.

The Green Spot Ltd.
Dept. of Bio-Ingenuity
93 Priest Rd.
Nottingham, NH 03290-6204
(603) 942-8925
www.greenmethods.com
Biological pest controls, information, and guidance.

Harmony Farm Supply and Nursery
3244 Hwy. 116 North
Sebastopol, CA 95472
(707) 823-9125
www.harmonyfarm.com
Irrigation systems, ecological pest controls, garden tools.

Hydro-Gardens, Inc.
P.O. Box 25845
Colorado Springs, CO 80936-5845
(800) 634-6362
www.hydro-gardens.com
Hydroponic supplies and biological controls.

IFM
Integrated Fertility Management
333 Ohme Gardens Road
Wenatchee, WA 98801
(800) 332-3179
Beneficial predators and parasites; products and services for natural growing.

Kunafin
Route 1, Box 39
Quemado, TX 78877
(800) 832-1113
www.kunafin.com
Beneficial insects and fly parasites.

M & R Durango, Inc.
Bio Logical Pest Control
P.O. Box 886
Bayfield, CO 81122
(800) 526-4075
www.goodbug.com
Beneficial insects, predators, and biological controls.

Medina Agricultural Products Co., Inc.
P.O. Box 309, Highway 90 West
Hondo, TX 78861
(830) 426-3011
www.medina.com
Products for better soil.

The Natural Gardening Company
217 San Anselmo Avenue
San Anselmo, CA 94960
(707) 766-9303
www.naturalgardening.com
Garden supplies and natural pest controls.

Natural Pest Control
8864 Little Creek Drive
Orangevale, CA 95662
(916) 726-0855
www.natpestco.com
Suppliers of beneficials to consumers and retailers.

Nature's Control
P.O. Box 35
Medford, OR 97501
(541) 899-8318
Nontoxic pest controls, beneficial insects, and parasites.

Nitron Industries, Inc.
P.O. Box 1447
Fayetteville, AR 72702-1447
(800) 835-0123
www.nitron.com
Organic soil conditioners and fertilizers, garden supplies.

Planet Natural
1612 Gold Ave.
Bozeman, MT 59715
(800) 289-6656
www.planetnatural.com
Earth friendly products including pest controls.

Rincon-Vitova Insectaries, Inc.
P.O. Box 1555
Ventura, CA 93022
(800) 248-2847
www.rinconvitova.com
Beneficial insects, parasites, and predators; predator
(decollate) snails.

Sea Born Lane, Inc.
P.O. Box 204
Charles City, IA 50616
(800) 457-5013
Seaweed fertilizers.

Seabright Laboratories
P.O. Box 8647
Emeryville, CA 94662
(800) 284-7363
www.seabrightlabs.com
Traps and barriers. Makers of Stikem Special.

Solarcone, Inc.
P.O. Box 67
Seward, IL 61077-0067
(800) 807-6527
Manufactures the Green Cone food waste recycler.

Spaulding Laboratories
760 Printz Road
Arroyo Grande, CA 93420
(800) 845-2847
Fly and flea predators.

Worm's Way
7850 North State Road
Bloomington, IN 47404-9477
(800) 274-9676
www.wormsway.com
Hydroponic equipment and pest controls.

Select Bibliography

Andrews, Michael. 1977. *The Life That Lives on Man.* New York: Taplinger.

Ball, Jeff. 1988. *Rodale's Garden Problem Solver.* Emmaus, Pa.: Rodale Press.

Ballantine, Bill. 1967. *Nobody Loves a Cockroach.* Boston: Little, Brown.

Berenbaum, May R. 1989. *Ninety-Nine Gnats, Nits, and Nibblers.* Urbana: University of Illinois Press.

Blassingame, Wyatt. 1975. *The Little Killers: Fleas, Lice, Mosquitoes.* New York: Putnam.

California Center for Wildlife, with Diana Landau and Shelly Stump. 1994. *Living with Wildlife.* San Francisco: Sierra Club Books.

Campbell, Stu. 1998. *Let It Rot: The Gardener's Guide to Composting.* Pownal, Vt.: Storey Books.

Conniff, Richard. 1996. *Spineless Wonders: Strange Tales from the Invertebrate World.* New York: Holt.

Cowan, Frank. 1865. *Curious Facts in the History of Insects.* Philadelphia: Lippincott.

Cullen, Mark, and Lorraine Johnson. 1992. *The Urban/Suburban Composter.* New York: St. Martin's Press.

Davidson, Ralph H., and William F. Lyon. 1987. *Insect Pests of Farm, Garden, and Orchard.* New York: Wiley.

DeBach, Paul. 1974. *Biological Control by Natural Enemies.*
Cambridge: Cambridge University Press.

Dennis, John. 1985. *The Wildlife Gardener.* New York: Knopf.

Dick, William B. 1879. *Dick's Practical Encyclopedia of Receipts and Processes.* New York: Funk & Wagnalls.

Ebeling, Walter. [1975] 1978. *Urban Entomology.* Berkeley: University of California Division of Agricultural Sciences.

Ernst, Ruth Shaw. 1987. *The Naturalist's Garden.* Emmaus, Pa.: Rodale Press.

Evans, Howard Ensign. 1966. *Life on a Little-Known Planet.* New York: Dutton.

Flint, Mary Louise. 1998. *Pests of the Garden and Small Farm.* Berkeley and Los Angeles: University of California Press.

Flint, Mary Louise, and Steve Dreistadt. 1998. *Natural Enemies Handbook.* Berkeley and Los Angeles: University of California Press.

Foelix, Rainer F. 1982. *Biology of Spiders.* Cambridge, Mass.: Harvard University Press.

Foster, Catharine Osgood. 1972. *The Organic Gardener.* New York: Knopf.

Graham, Frank, Jr. 1984. *The Dragon Hunters.* New York: Dutton.

Hartnack, Hugo. 1939. *202 Common Household Pests of North America.* Chicago: Hartnack.

Hillman, Hal. 1978. *Deadly Bugs and Killer Insects.* New York: M. Evans.

Hunter, Beatrice Trum. 1971. *Gardening Without Poisons.* Boston: Houghton Mifflin.

Jeavons, John. 1995. *How to Grow More Vegetables.* Berkeley, Calif.: Ten Speed Press.

Kramer, Jack. 1972. *The Natural Way to Pest-Free Gardening.* New York: Scribner.

Kress, Stephen W. 1985. *The Audubon Society Guide to Attracting Birds.* New York: Scribner.

Lehane, Brendan. 1969. *The Complete Flea.* New York: Viking.

Martin, Deborah L., and Grace Gershung, editors. 1992. *The Rodale Book of Composting.* Emmaus, Pa.: Rodale Press.

National Geographic Society. *Our Insect Friends and Foes and Spiders.* 1935. Washington, D.C.: National Geographic Society.

Nechols, R. R., S. A. Andres, J. W. Beardsley, R. D. Goeden, and C. G. Jackson, editors. 1995. *Biological Control in the Western United States: Accomplishments and Benefits of Regional Research Project W-84, 1964–1989.* Univ. of California Div. of Agriculture and Natural Resources. Publication 3361.

Olkowski, William, Sheila Darr, and Helga Olkowski. 1991. *Common-Sense Pest Control.* Newtown, Conn.: Taunton Press.

Ordish, George. 1976. *The Constant Pest: A Short History of Pests and Their Control.* New York: Scribner.

Philbrick, Helen, and John Philbrick. 1974. *The Bug Book.* Pownal, Vt.: Garden Way.

Repetto, Robert, and Sanjay Baliga. 1996. *Pesticides and the Immune System: The Public Health Risks.* Washington, D.C.: World Resources Institute.

Ritchie, Carson I. A. 1979. *Insects, the Creeping Conquerors.* New York: Elsevier/Nelson Books.

Schultz, Warren, editor. 1994. *Natural Insect Control.* Brooklyn: Brooklyn Botanic Garden.

Stawell, Mrs. Rudolph. 1921. *Fabre's Book of Insects.* New York: Tudor.

Stout, Ruth. 1961. *Gardening Without Work.* Old Greenwich, Conn.: Devin-Adair.

Teale, Edwin Way. 1962. *The Strange Lives of Familiar Insects.* New York: Dodd, Mead.

Tuttle, Merlin. 1988. *America's Neighborhood Bats.* Austin: University of Texas Press.

Wild Neighbors. 1996. Washington, D.C.: Humane Society of the United States.

Winston, Mark L. 1997. *Nature Wars: People vs. Pests.* Cambridge, Mass.: Harvard University Press.

Index

Aedes mosquitoes, 64
Africanized honey bees, 26–27
Alcohol. *See* Rubbing alcohol
Alcohol-soap spray, and control of
     whiteflies, 201
Aluminum, as barrier against army-
     worms, 168
Aluminum foil, and control of aphids,
     191–92
Ambush bugs, 157
American cockroaches, 33
American dog ticks, 100–101
Ammonia
     and control of: ants, 22; gophers, 221;
        raccoons, 230, 231; skunks, 232;
        slugs and snails, 186–87
Ammonium sulfate, and control of slugs
     and snails, 185, 186
Anise oil, and control of Japanese beetles,
     175
Anopheles mosquitoes, 64
Antlions, 159
Ants, 14–22, 54–55
     benefits of, 14–15, 19
     control of, indoors, 15–18
     control of, outdoors, 17, 19–22, 127,
        137, 140, 157, 158, 191
     and control of: bed bugs, 14, 25;

clothes moths, 14; cockroaches, 14;
     conenose bugs, 14; fleas, 14; flies,
     14, 52; mosquitoes, 66; peach tree
     borers, 204; praying mantises, 161;
     silverfish, 14; spiders, 14; termites,
     15, 90, 93, 94
in houseplants, 54–55
and pathogens, 15–16
as protectors of aphids, 19, 20, 191
as protectors of scale insects, 19, 195
Apartments, pest control in, 11
Aphidius wasps, 154, 155
Aphid lions, 151. *See also* Green
     lacewings
Aphids, 54, 149, 190–92
     control of, 124, 125, 126, 128, 129,
        130, 132, 134, 138, 139, 140,
        191–92
     and eliminating ants, 19, 20, 191
     in houseplants, 53–57
     natural enemies of, 151, 155, 157,
        158, 159, 192, 211
Aphid wolves, 151
Apple maggots, 206
Argentine ants, 15
Armyworms, 139, 154, 168. *See also*
     Cutworms
Ashy gray ladybirds, 152

Asian cockroaches, 33, 35
Asian lady beetles, 108–9
Asian tiger mosquitoes, 64
Asparagus, and control of nematodes, 181
Assassin bugs, 157
Avon Skin-So-Soft
    and control of: mosquitoes, 67; ticks, 67, 103; yellow jackets, 217

Bacillus popilliae (milky spore disease), 132
    and control of: Japanese beetles, 132, 176, 224; June beetles, 132, 179
Bacillus thuringiensis (Bt), 131
    and control of: armyworms, 168; cabbage loopers, 163; caterpillars, 131; Colorado potato beetles, 165; corn earworms, 207; cutworms, 168; Eastern tent caterpillars, 169; European corn borers, 203; fall webworms, 169; fungus gnats, 57; gypsy moths, 174; imported cabbageworms, 163; squash vine borers, 203; tomato hornworms, 179
    precautions for, 174
Bacillus thuringiensis israelensis (Bti), 68, 131
    and control of: flies, 51; fungus gnats, 57; mosquitoes, 66; mosquito larvae, 131
Bacillus thuringiensis San Diego, and control of Colorado potato beetles, 131
Bacillus thuringiensis ssp. *tenebrionis*, and control of Colorado potato beetles, 165
Bacon grease, as barrier against rabbits, 229
Bacterial controls, 131–32. See also *Bacillus popilliae* (milky spore disease); *Bacillus thuringiensis* (Bt); *Bacillus thuringiensis israelensis* (Bti); *Bacillus thuringiensis* San Diego; *Bacillus thuringiensis* ssp. *tenebrionis*; *Nosema locustae*
Badgers, as gopher predators, 220
Baits, 126. *See also* Boric acid; Insect growth regulators; Molasses; Traps; Vinegar
    for attracting: ants, 17–18, 194; apple maggots, 205; cockroaches, 36, 37; codling moths, 205; fire ants, 21; flies, 50–51; Japanese beetles, 175; snails, 187–88; termites, 95; yellow jackets, 217–18
Barriers: aluminum, 168, 198; bacon grease, 229; bran, 164, 185; charcoal, 17; cinnamon, 17; cleanser, powdered, 17; copper, 185; diatomaceous earth, 130, 182, 185; eggshells, 168, 182, 185; fences, 226, 228; floating row covers, 127, 163, 166, 177, 193, 202; glue, 17; hair, 185; hickory leaves, 167; mineral oil, 203, 207; molasses grass, 104; oak leaves, 168, 182, 185; oyster shells, 185; petroleum jelly, 17, 233; sawdust, 182, 185; screen cone covers, 166; soot, 168; steel wool, 81; sticky barriers, 127, 191, 194, 195, 204; walnut leaves, 167; wood ashes, 166, 185. *See also* Repellents
Basil
    and control of: flies, 49; mosquitoes, 65; tomato hornworms, 178
Bat Conservation International, 142, 143, 235
Bats, 141–43
    and control of insects, 66, 142
Bay leaves
    and control of: flies, 49; mosquitoes, 67; pantry pests, 72
Bean leaf beetles, 177
Bear ticks, 101

Bed bugs, 22–25
control of, 24–25, 86, 134
Beer traps
and control of: cockroaches, 35;
earwigs, 212; flea beetles, 170;
grasshoppers 172; slugs and snails,
187–88
Bees, 25-28
Africanized ("killer"), 26–27
benefits of, 25-26
control of, 26-27
and insecticidal soaps, 128
natural enemies of, 161
as susceptible to pesticides, 25
Beetles
beneficial, 157–59
kinds of: carpet, 30–31, 69; cigarette,
70; click, 183–84; cucumber, 137,
140, 165–67; deathwatch, 99;
drugstore, 70; flea, 139, 169–70;
flour, 69; furniture, 99; ground,
157–58, 164, 172, 174, 180, 188,
206; Japanese, 132, 140, 175–
76; ladybird (ladybugs), 152–53;
Mexican bean, 129, 176–77; old
house borers, 99; powderpost, 98;
rove, 158, 183, 189; saw-toothed
grain, 70; soldier, 158, 165, 189,
192; tiger, 158; wood-boring, 98–99
and control of: ants, 157, 158; aphids,
157, 158, 192; apple maggots, 206;
cabbage loopers, 164; caterpillars,
158; codling moths, 206; Colorado
potato beetles, 165; cucumber
beetles, 167; cutworms, 157, 168;
Eastern tent caterpillars, 169; fall
webworms, 169; flies, 157; fly eggs
and maggots, 158; grasshoppers,
172; gypsy moths, 157, 174; imported cabbageworms, 164; June
beetles, 179; mosquitoes, 157;
nematodes, 158; root maggots,
183; slugs and snails, 157, 158,

188; spider mites, 158, 197;
termites, 157
traps for, 126
Behavioral disorders, and pesticides, 4
Beneficial insects, 149–61. *See also under
names of specific insects*
Beyond Pesticides (NCAMP), 12, 235
Big-eyed bugs, 157, 193
Bio Integral Resource Center (BIRC),
29, 54, 235
Biological controls, 131–33
Bird mites, 106
Birds, 143–46
benefits of, 146
and control of: aphids, 192; apple
maggots, 206; cockroaches, 36;
codling moths, 206; corn earworms, 207; cutworms, 168;
Eastern tent caterpillars, 169; fall
webworms, 169; fire ants, 21; flies,
52; gophers, 220; grasshoppers,
172; gypsy moths, 174; insects,
143–45; Japanese beetles, 176; June
beetles, 179; mice and rats, 75, 77;
mosquitoes, 66; peach tree borers,
204; rabbits, 229; scorpions, 113;
slugs and snails, 189–90; termites,
90; tomato hornworms, 178;
wireworms, 184
as pests, control of, 138, 145–46
as vulnerable to pesticides, x, 117,
189–90
Black flies, 47
Black lady beetles, 197
Black pepper
and control of: ants, 17; pantry pests,
73; rabbits, 229; squash vine borers,
203
Black walnut leaves
and control of: cutworms, 167; fleas, 45
Black widow spiders, 86–87
Bloodmeal, and control of rabbits, 229
Blue bottle flies, 47

Body lice, 59

Bonemeal, and control of ants, 20

Borage, and control of tomato hornworms, 178

Borax, 130. *See also* Boric acid
and control of fleas, 44

Borers, control of, 130, 154, 202–4

Boric acid, 130
and control of: ants, 18, 20, 130, 191,
195; carpenter ants, 18, 130; caterpillars, 130; cockroaches, 36, 37,
130; crickets, 130; silverfish, 84,
130; termites, 97, 130

Boron compounds, and control of
termites, 97. *See also* Boric acid

Botanical pesticides, 133–35. *See also*
Neem; Nicotine; Pyrethrum;
Rotenone; Ryana; Sabadilla

Boxelder bugs, 109

Braconid wasps, 155, 178

Bran
and control of: Colorado potato
beetles, 164; slugs and snails, 185

Brown-banded cockroaches, 32–33

Brown garden snails, 184, 189

Brown recluse spiders, 86, 87–89

Bt. See *Bacillus thuringiensis*

Bti. See *Bacillus thuringiensis israelensis*

Bt San Diego. See *Bacillus thuringiensis
San Diego*

Buttermilk spray, and control of spider
mites, 56, 196

Cabbage loopers, 162–64
control of, 136, 137, 139, 154, 163–
64, 176

Cabbage root maggots, 181–83

Cabbageworms. *See* Imported cabbageworms

Californians for Pesticide Reform, 94

Camphor, 29
and control of: ants, 17; clothes
moths, 29; flies, 49; rodents, 82

Cancer, and pesticides, 4, 10, 51

Carbaryl (Sevin), 25

Carpenter ants, 15, 18
as distinguished from termites, 18

Carpet beetles, 30–31, 69

Carrot rust flies, 182

Casemaking clothes moths, 28–29

Castor oil
and control of: moles, 224; mosquitoes, 67

Caterpillar hunters, 157

Caterpillars
control of, 129, 130, 131, 136, 137,
139, 158
kinds of: apple maggots, 204–6; armyworms, 139, 154, 168; cabbage
loopers, 136, 137, 139, 154, 162–
64, 176; codling moths, 135, 204–
6; corn earworms, 206–7; cutworms, 127, 138, 147, 154, 157,
167–68; Eastern tent caterpillars,
168–69; fall webworms, 168–69;
imported cabbageworms, 136, 137,
140, 162–64, 177; tomato hornworms, 137, 178–79; wireworms,
138, 154, 183–84
natural enemies of, 145, 147, 154,
155, 157, 158, 159, 161

Cat fleas, 39

Catnip
and control of: cockroaches, 34; cucumber beetles, 165; flea beetles,
170

Cats
and fleas, 42–43
as predators of: birds, 145, 146;
gophers, 220; lizards, 146; rabbits,
229; rats, 77
repellents against, 55, 145
and ticks, 102

Cayenne. *See* Hot pepper

Cedar, 29
and control of: clothes moths, 29;
fleas, 45; mosquitoes, 67
as spray, 140

Centipedes, 110
and control of: clothes moths, 110;
cockroaches, 110; flies, 110; silver-
fish, 110; slugs and snails, 188, 209
Chagas disease, 24
Chalk powder, and control of cucumber
beetles, 166
Charcoal, as barrier against ants, 17
Chickens
and control of: cockroaches, 35;
grasshoppers, 172; plum curculios,
208; slugs and snails, 188
Chiggers, 99, 104–5
Chinaberry leaves, 140
and control of flies, 49
Chipmunks, 174
and control of gypsy moths, 174
Chlordane, 10, 29, 94
Chrysanthemum, as repellent, 123.
See also Pyrethrum
Cigarette beetles, 70
Cinnamon
and control of: ants, 17; pantry pests, 73
Citronella
and control of: fleas, 45; mosquitoes,
65, 67, 68; ticks, 103
Citrus-based cleaners, and control of bird
mites, 106
Citrus oil/orange oil/citron
and control of: ants, 17, 22; clothes
moths, 29; fire ants, 22; fleas, 17,
42–43, 45; termites, 97; ticks, 42
Citrus peels/citrus peel spray
and control of: ants, 16–17; armyworms, 139; cotton bollworms,
139; mosquitoes, 68; spider mites,
197; tomato hornworms, 178
Cleanser, powdered, and control of ants,
17
Click beetles, 183
Clothes moths, 28–30
Cloves
oil of, and control of: ants, 17;
mosquitoes, 67

whole, and control of: clothes moths,
29; flies, 49
Cluster flies, 110
Cockroaches, 31–38
control of, 34–38, 132, 134
on houseplants, 54
natural enemies of, 35–36, 146, 147
resistance to pesticides, 34
Codling moths, 135, 204–6
Coffee, and control of root maggots, 182
Cold treatments
and control of: pantry pests, 71;
termites, 96
Colorado potato beetles, 164–65
control of, 131, 164–65, 177
Companion planting, 123, 177
Compost, 119–20
and control of nematodes, 181
Compost tea, 122
Conenose bugs, 24
Conniff, Richard, 75
Container traps
and control of: codling moths, 205;
flea beetles, 170; moles, 225; rats,
80; silverfish, 84; slugs and snails,
188; yellow jackets, 218
Convergent lady beetles, 152
Convergent ladybirds, 152
Copper, as barrier against slugs and
snails, 186
Coriander/coriander oil, 73, 123, 140
and control of: aphids, 140; clothes
moths, 29; pantry pests, 73; spider
mites, 197
Corn earworms, 206–7
Cotton bollworms, 139
Cover crops, 123
and control of nematodes, 181
Coyotes, 220, 229
Crab lice, 59–60
Cranshaw, Whitney, 187
Crickets, 110–11
Crown imperial plant, and control of
gophers, 220

Cucumber, and control of cockroaches, 34
Cucumber beetles, 165–67
    control of, 137, 140, 165–67
Culex mosquitoes, 64
Cutworms, 167–68
    control of, 127, 138, 147, 154, 157, 167–68

Damp-wood termites, 92
Damsel bugs, 157
Damselflies, 47, 159–60
    and control of: aphids, 159; leafhoppers, 193; mosquito larvae, 160
Darwin, Charles, 120, 149
Darwin, Erasmus, 149
DDT
    and cancer, 10
    and extermination of: bats 142; gypsy moths, 173; ladybugs, 152
    historic uses of, 29, 124
    persistence of, in environment, 10
    resistance of insects to, 24, 51, 65
Deathwatch beetles, 99
DeBach, Paul, 131
Decollate snails, and control of brown garden snails, 189
Deer
    control of, 226, 227–28
    and ticks, 101, 104
Deer ticks, 101
DEET (N,N-diethyl-meta-toluamide), 67, 103
Delusory parasitosis, 62
Democritus, 23
Diatomaceous earth
    and control of: ants, 17, 20, 191; aphids, 130; bed bugs, 24; borers, 130; boxelder bugs, 109; cabbage pests, 164; carpenter ants, 18; caterpillars, 130; cluster flies, 110; cockroaches, 36, 54; crickets, 111;

cucumber beetles, 166; cutworms, 168; earwigs, 111; fleas, 43, 44; flies, 130; leafhoppers, 130, 193; pantry pests, 71; peach tree borers, 204; root maggots, 182; scorpions, 113; silverfish, 84; slugs and snails, 130, 185; sowbugs and pillbugs, 213; spider mites, 130, 197; thrips, 130, 198
    as harmful to bees, 27, 28
    as harmless to birds, 129–30
Digger wasps, 216
Dill
    and control of: pantry pests, 73; tomato hormworms, 178
    to attract tachinid flies, 167
Diseases transmitted by pests: allergies, 32; asthma, 32; Chagas disease, 24; cholera, 46; Colorado tick fever, 101; dengue fever, 63, 64; diarrhea, 46; dysentery, 46, 74; encephalitis, 63, 64; hantavirus, 75; hepatitis, 46; hookworm, 46, 74; Lassa fever, 74; Lyme disease, 101–2; malaria, 63; meningitis, 74; pinworms, 46; plague, 39–40, 74, 75; rabies, 230, 232; rat bite fever, 74; relapsing fever, 59, 101, 212; Rocky Mountain spotted fever, 100, 101; roundworm, 230; salmonella, 46, 74, 212; tapeworm, 40, 46, 74; tick paralysis, 101; trench fever, 59; tuberculosis, 212; tularemia, 40, 100, 101, 212; typhus, 40, 46, 59, 74; yellow fever, 63, 64
D-limonene, 42. *See also* Citrus oil / orange oil / citron; Limonene
Dog fleas, 39
Dogs, 228–29
    and beer traps, 188
    control of, 228–29
    and fleas, 42–43

as predators of: deer, 228; gophers, 220; rabbits, 229; rats, 77
and ticks, 102
Doodle bugs, 159
Dormant oil. *See* Oils, horticultural
Dragonflies, 47, 159–60
and control of: fire ants, 21; mosquitoes, 66, 160; termites, 90
Drugstore beetles, 70
Dry-wood termites, 91–92
Ducks and geese, and control of slugs and snails, 188
Dung flies, 47
Dust mites, 105–7
Dusts, 129–31. *See also names of specific dusts*
precautions for use of, 129

Earthworms, 120–21
and snail poison, 189
Earwigs, 211–12
as beneficial, 211
control of, indoors, 111
control of, outdoors, 128, 211–12
as predators of: aphids, 192, 211; fleas, 211; grubs, 211
Eastern tent caterpillars, 168–69
Ebeling, Walter, 34, 95
Eggshells
as barrier against: cutworms, 168; root maggots, 182; slugs and snails, 185
Elderberry, 140, 170
Elder leaves, and control of moles, 224
Electricity/electrocution traps, 126
and control of: cockroaches, 35; flies, 51; mosquitoes, 66; rodents, 79; termites, 96
Electronic sound devices, 80, 221
Encarsia formosa (parasitic wasp), 155, 202
Encephalitis, 63, 64
Environmental Protection Agency (EPA), 4, 9, 10, 12

Environmental Working Group, 9, 236
Enzyme cleaners, 128
Ernst, Ruth Shaw, 147
Essential oils. *See* Oils, essential
Eucalyptus, 140
and control of: clothes moths, 29; fleas, 45; flies, 49; lice, on koalas, 58; mosquitoes, 67; silverfish, 84; ticks, 103
Euphorbia lathyris (gopher spurge, mole plant), 221, 225
European corn borers, 159, 203–4
Evans, Howard Ensign, 2
Exterminators, 13, 44, 85

Fall webworms, 168–69
Fences, 226, 228
Fenugreek, and control of pantry pests, 72
Fertilizers
fish emulsion, 128, 181, 229
high-nitrogen, as attractive to insects, 119, 191, 193–94
organic, 122–23
Feverfew, 140
Filth flies, 47
Fire ants, 20–22, 134
Firebrats, 83
Fireflies, 47, 160
and control of: cutworms, 160; slugs and snails, 160
Fish emulsion fertilizer, 128
and control of: nematodes, 181; rabbits, 229
Fish moths. *See* Silverfish
Flea beetles, 139, 169–70
Fleas, 39–46, 86
control of, indoors, 41–46, 134
control of, outdoors, 44–45, 211
diseases transmitted by, 39, 40
healthy pets and, 45–46
nontoxic extermination of, 44
Flesh flies, 47

Flies, 46–53, 110, 156, 158–59
  beneficial, 131, 156, 158–59.
    See also Hover flies; Tachinid
    flies
  control of, 48–53, 110, 126, 134,
    140, 157, 158
  and control of: aphids, 159, 192;
    armyworms, 168; cabbage loopers,
    164; caterpillars, 159; cucumber
    beetles, 167; cutworms, 168;
    European corn borers, 159; flies,
    51–52, 156; grasshoppers, 159;
    gypsy moths, 159, 174; imported
    cabbageworms, 164; leafhoppers,
    159; mealybugs, 194; scale insects,
    159, 195; snails and slugs, 188;
    thrips, 159, 198; true bugs,
    159
  diseases transmitted by, 46
  resistance to pesticides, 51
Flies, parasitic, 131, 156. *See also*
  Tachinid flies
Floating row covers, 127
  as barrier against: cabbage pests, 163;
    cucumber beetles, 166; leafhoppers,
    193; Mexican bean beetles, 177;
    squash vine borers, 202
Flour beetles, 69
Flour moths, 28, 68–69
Flower flies. *See* Hover flies
Forbes, Charles, 95
Formosan subterranean termites, 91
Foxes, 75, 229, 231
Frogs, 147–48, 161
  and control of: flies, 52; insects, 147;
    mosquitoes, 66; slugs and snails,
    188; sowbugs and pillbugs, 214;
    termites, 90
Fruit flies, 48, 50–51
Fumigation
  and control of: gophers, 222; moles,
    225; termites, 94–95
Fungus, 131, 132
  and control of: aphids, 132; cock-

roaches, 37, 132; crickets, 132;
    fire ants, 21; grasshoppers, 132;
    mosquitoes, 66; mosquito larvae,
    132; nematodes, 181; termites, 95;
    whiteflies, 132
Fungus gnats, on houseplants, 54, 55, 57
Furniture beetles, 99

Gambusia (mosquito-eating fish), 66
Garden centipede, 210
Gardening strategies for pest resistance,
    117–23
  companion planting, 123
  compost, 119–20
  cover crops, 123
  earthworms, 120–21
  good soil, 118–19
  mulch, 121–22
  organic fertilizers, 122–23
Garlic, 123
  and control of: aphids, 138, 191;
    cutworms, 167; deer, 228; flea
    beetles, 170; fleas, 46; gophers,
    220, 224; Mexican bean beetles,
    177; moles, 224; mosquitoes, 66,
    67, 138; onion flies, 138; rabbits,
    226, 229; rodents, 138; spider
    mites, 197; symphylans, 210;
    ticks, 103
Garlic-pepper spray, 138–39
  and control of: aphids, 191; thrips,
    198
Garlic spray, 136, 137–38, 210
  and control of: cabbage loopers,
    163; Colorado potato beetles,
    164; flea beetles, 170; imported
    cabbageworms, 163; Mexican
    bean beetles, 177; millipedes,
    172
Geckos, 146
  and control of: cockroaches, 146;
    mosquitoes, 146
Geranium, 123
  and control of leafhoppers, 193

Geranium oil, 140
  and control of: mosquitoes, 67; spider
    mites, 197
  dilution of, 197
German cockroaches, 32
Giant whiteflies, 200
Ginger, and control of slugs and snails,
  185
Glowworms (firefly larvae), 160
Glue/glue spray
  and control of: ants, 17; scale insects,
    139, 195; spider mites, 139, 196
Gophers, 219–23
  benefits of, 223
  control of, 212, 220–22
Gopher spurge (*Euphorbia lathyris*), 221
Grasshoppers, 161, 170–72
  control of, 171–72
Grease ants, 15
Green bottle flies, 47
Green lacewings, 149, 150–51, 167
  care of mail-order lacewings, 150, 151
  and control of: aphids, 151, 192;
    boxelder bugs, 109; Colorado
    potato beetles, 165; corn earworms,
    207; cucumber beetles, 167; Euro-
    pean corn borers, 203; leafhoppers,
    193; mealybugs, 151, 194; scale
    insects, 151, 195; spider mites, 151,
    197; squash vine borers, 203; thrips,
    151, 198; tomato hornworms, 179;
    whiteflies, 202
Ground beetles, 157–58, 164, 172, 174,
  180, 188, 206
Growth regulators. *See* Insect growth
  regulators
Gypsy moths, 157–58, 172–74

Hair clippings
  as barrier against slugs and snails, 186
  as repellent for: deer, 227; raccoons,
    231
Handpicking, 125, 202
  and control of: armyworms, 168; Colo-

rado potato beetles, 164; cucumber
beetles, 166; cutworms, 168; grass-
hoppers, 171; gypsy moths, 173–
74; harlequin bugs, 200; Japanese
beetles, 175; mealybugs, 194;
Mexican bean beetles, 177; slugs
and snails, 186; squash bugs, 199;
tarnished plant bugs, 199; tomato
hornworms, 178
Hantavirus, 75
Harlequin bugs, 199–200
Hartnack, Hugo, 24
Head lice. *See* Lice
Heat treatments
  and control of: fleas, 41; pantry pests,
    71–72; termites, 96–97
Hedgehogs, 36
Heptyl butyrate, 218
Hickory leaves, as barrier against
  cutworms, 167
Honey bees. *See* Bees
Horse flies, 47
Horticultural oils. *See* Oils, horticultural
Hosing. *See* Water/hosing
Hot pepper (cayenne, ground red pepper,
  Tabasco)
  and control of: ants, 17; corn ear-
    worms, 207; cucumber beetles, 166;
    deer, 227; moles, 224; rabbits, 229;
    raccoons, 230; rodents, 82, 137;
    squirrels, 233; tomato hornworms,
    178
Hot pepper-onion-garlic spray, 138–
  39
  and control of: Colorado potato
    beetles, 164; grasshoppers, 172
Hot pepper spray, 136, 137
  and control of: ants, 137; cabbage
    worms, 137; caterpillars, 137;
    cucumber beetles, 137; grasshop-
    pers, 172; tomato hornworms, 137,
    178
House dust mites, 105–7
House flies, 46–53

Houseplant pests, 53–57
Hover flies (syrphid flies, flower flies),
    48, 118, 159
    and control of: aphids, 191; mealy-
        bugs, 194; scale insects, 195; thrips,
        198
Human bot flies, 48
Human fleas, 39
Hunter, Beatrice Trum, 140
Huxley, Thomas, 190
Hydramethylon, 37
Hydrated lime. *See* Lime

Ichneumon flies, 155–56
Imported cabbageworms, 162–64
    control of, 136, 137, 140, 163–64,
        177
Incarsia sp., 201
Indian meal moths, 68–69
Insect growth regulators, 132
    and control of: ants, 21; cockroaches,
        37; fire ants, 21; fleas, 42, 132;
        pantry pests, 68; termites, 95
Insecticidal soaps. *See* Soaps and soap
    sprays
Insecticides. *See* Pesticides
Insects. *See also names of specific insects*
    benefits of, 3–4, 118–19
    beneficial, 149–61
    characteristics of, 2–3
    as competitors with humans, 3
    as resistant to pesticides, 24, 41, 51,
        65, 117
    superstitions about, 3
Integrated pest management (I.P.M.),
    13
Itch mites, 106–7

Japanese beetles, 175–76
    control of, 132, 140, 175–76
Juicy Fruit gum
    and control of: gophers, 221; moles,
        224
June beetles, 179

control of, 132, 176, 179
    and control of flies, 49
Junebugs. *See* June beetles

Kelp/seaweed
    and control of: nematodes, 181; slugs
        and snails, 185–86
    as fertilizer and mulch, 122, 128, 169,
        181
"Killer" bees, 26–27

Lacewings. *See* Green lacewings
Ladybird beetles. *See* Ladybugs
Ladybugs, 152–53
    care of mail-order species, 150,
        152–53
    and control of: aphids, 57, 124, 192;
        boxelder bugs, 109; Colorado
        potato beetles, 165; cucumber
        beetles, 167; European corn borers,
        203; leafhoppers, 152; mealybugs,
        57, 194; Mexican bean beetles,
        177; scale insects, 152, 195; spider
        mites, 197; squash vine borers,
        203; thrips, 152, 198; tomato
        hornworms, 179; whiteflies, 202
    and insecticidal soap sprays, 128
Lavender, 140
    and control of: ants, 17; clothes
        moths, 29; deer, 228; ticks, 104
Lavender oil
    and control of spider mites, 197
    dilution of, 197
Leafhoppers, 134, 192–93
Leafminers, 128
Learning disabilities, and pesticides, 4
Lemon grass oil, 140
    and control of: dogs, 228; spider
        mites, 197
    dilution of, 197
Lemon peels, and control of pantry
    pests, 73
Lemon verbena, and control of clothes
    moths, 29

Lice, 57–62
  control of, 60–62
  diseases caused by, 59
  kinds of: body lice, 59, 134; crab lice,
    60; head lice, 60–61
Lightening bugs. *See* Fireflies
Light traps
  and control of: European corn borers,
    203; moths, 112; tomato horn-
    worm moths, 178–79
Lime (calcium carbonate), 131
  and control of: cucumber beetles, 166;
    cutworms, 168; pillbugs and
    sowbugs, 213; rabbits, 229;
    raccoons, 230; root maggots, 182;
    slugs and snails, 185
Limonene. *See also* Citrus oil/orange
    oil/citron; D-limonene
  and control of: aphids, 191; cotton
    bollworms, 139; fall armyworms,
    139
Linalool, and control of aphids, 191. *See
    also* Citrus oil/orange oil/citron
Lindane, 24, 60, 61
Live traps
  and control of: raccoons, 231; rodents,
    79–80; skunks, 232; squirrels, 233
Lizards, 146
  and control of: fire ants, 21; mosqui-
    toes, 66; praying mantises, 161;
    scorpions, 113; slugs and snails,
    188; termites, 90
  natural enemies of, 146, 161
Locusts. *See* Grasshoppers
Lone star ticks, 100
Long-tailed mealybugs, 193
Lygus bugs, 199
Lyme disease, 101–2
Lysol, and control of raccoons, 230

Mail-order predators, 150–56
  care of, 150
Malaria, 63
Malathion, 191

Manure, and control of deer, 227
Marigold, 123
  and control of: cucumber beetles, 165;
    flies, 49; Mexican bean beetles, 177;
    nematodes, 180; squash bugs, 199;
    tomato hornworms, 178; whiteflies,
    201; wireworms, 184
May beetles. *See* June beetles
Mealworms, 69
Mealybug destroyers, 153
  and control of: mealybugs, 57, 153,
    194; scale insects, 153
Mealybugs, 193–94, 56–57
  control of, in houseplants, 53, 54,
    56–57
  control of, outdoors, 129, 151, 153,
    194
Medflies, 190
Mediterranean meal moths, 68–69
Methoprene. *See* Insect growth regulators
Methyl bromide, 68, 94, 180
Mexican bean beetles, 134, 176–77
Mice, 74–82, 212
  control of, 76–82, 138
  and control of: gypsy moths, 174;
    peach tree borers, 204; scorpions,
    113
  diseases transmitted by, 75
Midges, 47
Milky spore disease. See *Bacillus popilliae*
Millipedes, 209–10
Mineral oil
  and control of: corn earworms,
    207; European corn borers, 203;
    whiteflies, 201
Mint, 123, 140
  and control of: ants, 17, 19; aphids,
    140; flea beetles, 170; flies, 49;
    pantry pests, 73; rodents, 82
Minute pirate bugs, 157, 198
  and control of thrips, 198
Mish-mash spray, 136
  and control of: cabbage pests, 136,
    163; caterpillars, 136

Mites, outdoors
  beneficial, 156, 195, 197, 198
  repellents against, 138, 139
  spider, 128, 129, 139
Mites, indoors, 99, 105–7
  in houseplants, 54–56
  kinds of: bird mites, 106; house dust
    mites, 105; scabies (itch mites),
    105–6; spider, 54, 55, 56
  repellents against, 138, 139
Molasses, for baiting traps, 50, 126, 172,
  205
Molasses grass, and control of ticks, 104
Mole plant (*Euphorbia lathyris*), 221
Moles, 219, 223–25
  benefits of, 223
  control of, 223–25
  and control of: beetles, 223; caterpil-
    lars, 223; cutworms, 168; earth-
    worms, 223; gypsy moths, 174;
    Japanese beetle grubs, 176, 223;
    June beetles, 179; mice, 223; peach
    tree borers, 204; slugs and snails,
    188, 223
Mosquitoes, 62–68, 86
  control of, indoors, 64–65
  control of, outdoors, 65–68, 146,
    147, 157
  diseases transmitted by, 63, 64
  repellents against, 67–68, 138
Mosquito hawks. *See* Dragonflies
Mothballs, toxicity of, 29
Moths
  clothes, 28–30
  codling, 135, 204–6
  gypsy, 157, 172–74
  night-flying, 111–12
Motion-activated sprinklers
  and control of foragers, 227, 229,
    231
Mud daubers, 216
Mulch, 121–22
  and control of: Colorado potato
    beetles, 164; cucumber beetles,

165; cutworms, 168; earwigs, 211;
  grasshoppers, 171; nematodes, 181;
  slugs and snails, 185–86; spider
  mites, 196; thrips, 198
Myrrh, and control of mosquitoes, 68

Nail-polish remover (acetone)
  and control of mealybugs, 56, 194
  and removal of ticks, 104
Nasturtiums, 123
  and control of: aphids, 191; cucumber
    beetles, 165; Mexican bean beetles,
    177; squash bugs, 199; whiteflies,
    201
National Coalition Against the Misuse
  of Pesticides (NCAMP), 12, 235
National Pediculosis Association, 60, 61,
  62, 236
Neem, 133–34
  and control of: armyworms, 134;
    boxelder bugs, 109; cockroaches,
    134; corn earworms, 134; crickets,
    111; cucumber beetles, 166; flea
    beetles, 170; fungus gnats, 57;
    grasshoppers, 134; gypsy moths,
    174; mealybugs, 194; Mexican bean
    beetles, 134, 177; mosquitoes, 66,
    67, 134; termites, 134
Nematodes, 131, 154, 179–81
  beneficial (parasitic), 154
  and control of: armyworms, 154, 168;
    borers, 154; cabbage loopers, 154;
    cockroaches, 37; Colorado potato
    beetles, 154; corn earworms, 207;
    cucumber beetles, 167; cutworms,
    154, 168; flea beetles, 170; fleas,
    45; Japanese beetle grubs, 154, 176,
    224; June beetles, 154, 179; peach
    tree borers, 204; root maggots, 154,
    183; symphylans, 210; termites, 95,
    154; wireworms, 154, 184; yellow
    jackets, 216
  harmful, control of, 154, 158, 179–81
  and healthy soil, 154

Neurological development in children,
  and pesticides, x
Nicotine, 135
  and control of houseplant pests, 56, 57
  and control of outdoor pests, 133,
    135, 210
N,N-diethyl-meta-toluamide (DEET),
  67, 103
Norway rat, 74–75
Nosema locustae, and control of grasshoppers, 172

Oak leaves
  as barrier against: cutworms, 168; root
    maggots, 182; slugs and snails, 185
Odorous house ant, 15
Oils, essential, 140
  dilution of, 197
  kinds of: anise, 175; cedar, 29; citrus
    or orange, 17, 22, 42–43, 45, 97;
    clove, 17, 67; coriander, 140, 197;
    eucalyptus, 29, 67, 103; fennel,
    175; geranium, 67, 140, 197;
    lavender, 140, 197; lemon grass,
    140, 197, 228; limonene, 139;
    mint, 140; rose, 175; sage, 140;
    sassafras, 205
Oils, horticultural, 129
  and control of: aphids, 129, 130, 191;
    beetles, 129; caterpillars, 129;
    Eastern tent caterpillars, 169; fall
    webworms, 169; houseplant pests,
    55; mealybugs, 129, 194; scale
    insects, 129, 195; spider mites, 129,
    197; thrips, 55, 198; whiteflies, 55,
    129, 201
  dormant oil, 191, 195, 197
  recipe for, 129
Old house borers, 99
Onion/onion juice, 213
  and control of: cutworms, 167, 168;
    deer, 228; flea beetles, 170; pillbugs
    and sowbugs, 213; rabbits, 226;
    spider mites, 197; squash bugs, 199

Onion root maggots, 181–83
Opossums, 212
  and control of: gophers, 212; mice
    and rats, 212; slugs and snails, 188,
    212
Orange oil. *See* Citrus oil/orange
  oil/citron
Organic fertilizers, 122–23, 194
Oriental cockroaches, 32
Oriental rat fleas, 39
Oyster shells, as barrier against slugs and
  snails, 185

Pantry pests, 68–73
  attracted by dead rodents, 73
  control of, 68, 70–73
Parasites of flies, 156
Parasites and parasitoids, 131, 133. *See
  also* Flies, parasitic; Wasps, parasitic
Parasitic flies. *See* Flies, parasitic
Parasitic nematodes, 154
Parasitic wasps. *See* Wasps, parasitic
Parkinson's disease, x
Parsley, and control of mosquitoes, 67
Pavement ants, 15
Peach tree borers, 203–4
Pediobius wasps, 177
Pennyroyal
  and control of: ants, 140; clothes
    moths, 29; fleas, 45; flies, 49;
    mosquitoes, 65, 67; ticks, 103
Pentatomid bug, 24
Pepper. *See* Black pepper; Hot pepper
Peppermint
  and control of: ants, 19; fleas, 45;
    mosquitoes, 67; rodents, 82;
    silverfish, 84
Peppermint soap
  and control of: silverfish, 84; ticks,
    103
Pepper spray. *See* Hot pepper spray
Permethrin, and control of ticks, 103–4
Pesticide Action Network (PANNA),
  236

Pesticides
diseases caused by, x, 4
fallacy of safety of, 4
found in food and water, 4, 9–10
giving up and disposing of, 11–13
increasing use of, ix, 4, 9, 13
insect resistance to, 24, 41, 51, 65,
117
labeling of, x, 2, 12
as public health threat, ix, x, 4–5, 12
and threat to birds, x, 117, 189
toxicity of, x, 4–5, 10
Pet droppings, and control of moles, 224
Petroleum jelly
as barrier to: ants, 17; squirrels, 233
and removing ticks, 104
on sticky traps, 126
Pets, and fleas. *See* Fleas
Petunia, as repellent, 123, 193
Pharaoh ants, 15
Pheromones/pheromone traps, 126, 132
and control of: codling moths, 205;
gypsy moths, 174; Japanese beetles,
175; pantry pests, 68, 72; peach
tree borers, 204
Pillbugs, 213–14
Pine oil, and control of fleas, 45
Pine tar
and control of: mosquitoes, 67;
rodents, 82
Piperonyl butoxide (PBO), 133
Pirate bugs, 157
Pliny the Elder, 99
Plum curculios, 207–8
Pocket gophers. *See* Gophers
Poisons. *See also* Pesticides
and control of: gophers, 220; rats
and mice, 76–77; slugs and snails,
189–90
Polistes (paper) wasps, 215
Powdered cleanser, as barrier against ants,
17
Powderpost beetles, 98
Praying mantises, 161

as predators of beneficial and harmful
insects, 161
Predators, beneficial, 133, 141–61
Predatory mites, 156, 197
and control of: scale insects, 195;
spider mites, 156, 197
Psyllids, 128
Pubic lice, 59–60
Pyrethrin, 134
and control: of carpenter ants, 18;
pantry pests, 71
Pyrethroids, 134
Pyrethrum, 134–35
allergic reactions to, 135
and control of: aphids, 134; bed bugs,
24; beetles, 134; body lice, 134;
carpenter ants, 18; cockroaches,
134; Colorado potato beetles, 165;
cucumber beetles, 166; fire ants, 22;
fleas, 43, 134; flies, 134; harlequin
bugs, 200; leafhoppers, 134; lice,
61; mealybugs, 194; Mexican bean
beetles, 177; pantry pests, 71;
termites, 134; thrips, 134; ticks,
103–4; whiteflies, 134, 201; yellow
jackets, 216
precautions for use of, 61, 134
as toxic to bees and ladybugs, 28, 134

Quassia spray, 136, 139
and control of: aphids, 139; caterpillars, 139; mealybugs, 194
Quicklime. *See* Lime

Rabbits, 228, 229–31
Rabies, 230, 232
Raccoons, 230–31
control of, 230–31
and control of: earthworms, 230; fish,
230; rabbits, 229
diseases transmitted by, 230
Radishes
and control of: cucumber beetles, 165;
squash vine borers, 203

Rats, 74–82
    control of, 76–82, 137, 138, 212
    and control of: mice, 76; slugs and
        snails, 82, 188
    diseases transmitted by, 74, 75
    value to science, 82
Red imported fire ants, 20–22
Red pepper. *See* Hot pepper
Red spider mites, 196
Repellents, 135–140. *See also* Barriers;
    Oils, essential; Repellent sprays
    kinds of: ammonia, 22, 186–87, 221,
        230, 231, 232; ammonium sulfate,
        185, 186; asparagus, 181; Avon
        Skin-So-Soft, 67, 103, 217; basil,
        49, 65, 178; bay leaves, 49, 67, 72,
        140; black pepper, 17, 73, 203, 229;
        black walnut leaves, 45, 167; blood-
        meal, 229; borage, 178; bran, 164,
        185; camphor, 17, 29, 49, 82; castor
        oil, 67, 224; catnip, 34, 165, 170;
        cedar, 29, 45, 67, 140; chalk, 166;
        chinaberry, 49, 140; cinnamon, 17,
        73; citronella, 45, 65, 67, 68, 103;
        citrus-based cleaners, 106; cleanser,
        powdered, 17; cloves, 29, 49, 67;
        coffee, 182; coriander, 29, 73, 123,
        140; crown imperial plant, 220; cu-
        cumber, 34; dill, 73, 178; elderberry,
        140, 170; elder leaves, 224; eucalyp-
        tus, 45, 49, 58, 67, 84, 140; *Euphor-
        bia lathyris*, 221, 225; fenugreek, 72;
        feverfew, 140; garlic, 46, 103, 123,
        138, 167, 177, 191, 197, 220, 224,
        226, 228, 229; geranium, 67, 123,
        193; ginger, 185; gopher spurge,
        221; hair clippings, 226, 227; horse-
        radish, 136; hot pepper, 17, 82,
        136, 137, 166, 207, 224, 227, 229,
        230, 233; Juicy Fruit gum, 221, 224;
        lavender, 17, 29, 104, 140; lemon
        grass, 140; lemon peel, 73; lemon
        verbena, 29; lime (hydrated), 131,
        166, 168, 182, 185, 213, 229, 230–

31; Lysol, 230; manure, 227; mari-
        gold, 49, 123, 165, 177, 178, 180,
        184, 199, 201; mineral oil, 203,
        207; mint, 17, 19, 49, 82, 123, 140,
        170; myrrh, 68; nasturtium, 123,
        165, 177, 191, 199, 201; onion,
        140, 167, 168, 197, 199, 226, 227;
        parsley, 67; pennyroyal, 29, 45, 49,
        65, 67, 103, 140; peppermint, 19,
        45, 67, 82, 84; permethrin, 103–4;
        pet droppings, 224; petunia, 123,
        193; pine, 45; pine tar, 67, 82;
        quassia, 136, 139, 194; radishes,
        165, 203; rhubarb, 140; rose gera-
        nium, 140; rue, 49, 123; sage, 68,
        104, 123, 228; santolina, 84; sas-
        safras, 67, 140; seaweed, 169; sour
        milk, 163; spearmint, 73, 136;
        sulfur, 229; sweet clover, 49; tansy,
        19, 29, 49, 65, 123, 140, 199; tea,
        182; thyme, 123; turmeric, 17, 72–
        73; vanilla, 67, 136, 166, 199; vine-
        gar, 16, 67; wood ashes, 163, 166,
        168, 182, 203, 204, 226; worm-
        wood, 29, 123, 140, 170, 226
Repellent sprays. *See also* Soaps and soap
    sprays
    kinds of: alcohol-soap spray, 201;
        buttermilk spray, 56, 196; citrus
        peel spray, 16–17, 139, 178, 197;
        deer repellent spray, 227; garlic-
        pepper spray, 138, 191, 198; garlic
        spray, 136, 137–38, 163, 170, 177,
        210; glue spray, 139, 195, 196; hot
        pepper-onion-garlic spray, 138–39,
        164, 172; hot pepper spray, 136,
        137, 172, 178; limonene spray,
        191; linalool spray, 191; mish-mash
        spray, 136, 163; onion juice spray,
        170, 213; peppermint soap spray,
        84, 103; quassia spray, 136, 139,
        194; rhubarb spray, 140; seawater,
        163; tomato leaf spray, 137;
        wormwood spray, 140

Rhubarb spray, 140
Robber flies, 159
Rocky Mountain wood ticks, 101
Rodents. *See* Mice; Rats
Roof rats (*Rattus rattus*), 75, 78, 82
Root-knot nematodes, 180
Root maggots, 154, 181–83
Rosemary, and control of mosquitoes, 68
Rotenone, 135
    and control of: beetles, 135; borers, 135; cabbage pests, 163; caterpillars, 135; Colorado potato beetles, 165; cucumber beetles, 167; Mexican bean beetles, 177; weevils, 135
    as toxic to beneficial insects, 135
Rotten potatoes, and control of dogs, 228
Rove beetles, 158, 183, 189
Row covers. *See* Floating row covers
Rubbing alcohol
    and control of: aphids, 191; flies, 48; mealybugs, 56, 194; scale insects, 195
    and removing ticks, 104
Rue, 123
    and control of flies, 49
Ryana, 135

Sabadilla, 134
    and control of: cabbage pests, 163; grasshoppers, 172; harlequin bugs, 200
    precautions for use of, 134
Sage, 123
    and control of: deer, 228; mosquitoes, 68; silverfish, 84; ticks, 104
Salmonella, 46, 74, 212
Salt
    and control of: fleas, 44; snails, 185, 186; termites, 97
Santolina, and control of silverfish, 84
Sassafras
    and control of: aphids, 140; mosquitoes, 67
Sassafras oil, as bait, 205

Sawdust
    as barrier against: root maggots, 182; slugs and snails, 185
Sawflies, 128
Saw-toothed grain beetles, 70
Scabies (itch mites), 106–7
Scale insects, 54, 194–95
    control of, in houseplants, 53–57
    control of, outdoors, 128, 129, 139, 151, 153, 195
    protected by ants, 195
Scorpions, 112–13
    and control of: bed bugs, 113; carpet beetles, 113; clothes moths, 113; cockroaches, 35–36; spiders, 113
Screen cone covers, as barriers against cucumber beetles, 166
Screwworms (blow flies), 47
Seawater spray, 163
Seaweed/kelp
    and control of: nematodes, 181; slugs and snails, 185–86
    as fertilizer and mulch, 122, 128, 169, 181
Sharpshooters. *See* Leafhoppers
Shrews
    and control of: gypsy moths, 174; slugs and snails, 188
Silica aerogel, 130
    and control of: ants, 17; bed bugs, 24; carpenter ants, 18; cockroaches, 36; fleas, 44; pantry pests, 71; scorpions, 113; silverfish, 84; termites, 97
Silverfish
    control of, 83–84
    and control of: ants, 83; termites, 83
Skunks, 231–32
    benefits of, 231
    control of, 231–32
    and control of: armyworms, 231; Colorado potato beetles, 231; cutworms, 231; gophers, 220; grasshoppers, 172, 231; grubs, 231; gypsy moths,

174; Japanese beetles, 176; June beetles, 179; mice and rats, 75, 77, 231; peach tree borers, 204; rabbits, 229; slugs and snails, 188
Slugs. *See* Snails and slugs
Smokeybrown cockroaches, 33
Snails and slugs, 184–90
  control of, 138, 185–90
  natural enemies of, 82, 147, 157, 158, 188–89, 212
  plants attractive to, 185
  plants repellent to, 190
Snakes, 147
  and control of: earthworms, 147; flies, 52; frogs, 147; gophers, 147, 220; grasshoppers, 172; mice and rats, 75, 77, 147; rabbits, 229; rodents, 77; scorpions, 113; slugs and snails, 147, 188; termites, 90
Snap traps
  and control of: gophers, 222; rodents, 78–79
Snout beetles, 207–8
Soaps and soap sprays, 127–28, 135.
  See also Repellent sprays
  and beneficial insects, 128
  and control of: ants, 16–17; aphids, 128, 191; bees, 27; bird mites, 106; borers, 204; boxelder bugs, 109; cluster flies, 110; codling moths, 206; Colorado potato beetles, 65; deer, 227; earwigs, 128, 212; fire ants, 22; flea beetles, 170; fleas, 42, 45; flies, 58, 128; harlequin bugs, 200; houseplant pests, 55–56; leaf-hoppers, 193; leafminers, 128; mealybugs, 194; peach tree borers, 204; psyllids, 128; sawflies, 128; scale insects, 128, 195; spider mites, 128, 196, 198; spiders, 88; thrips, 128, 198; ticks, 102, 103; wasps, 127; whiteflies, 128, 201; yellow jackets, 216
  enzyme cleaners, 128

Soapy water
  and control of: aphids, 191; chiggers, 105; fleas, 42, 43; scabies, 106–7; thrips, 198
  and handpicking pests, 125, 172
  and houseplant dips, 55–56
Solarization, and control of nematodes, 180
Soldier beetles, 158, 165, 189, 192
Soldier bugs, 157
  and control of Colorado potato beetles, 165
Soot, as barrier against cutworms, 168
Sour milk, and control of cabbage pests, 163
Southern fire ants, 20–22
Sowbugs, 213–14
Spearmint, and control of pantry pests, 73
Spider mite destroyers, 197
Spider mites, 54, 196–97
  control of, in house plants, 54, 56
  control of, outdoors, 125, 128, 129, 138, 139, 196–97
  natural enemies of, 151, 152, 157, 158, 159
Spiders, 84–89, 124
  benefits of, 84–85
  black widows, 86, 87
  brown recluse, 86, 87–88
  control of, 88–89
  and control of: bed bugs, 25, 85; bees, 84; clothes moths, 30; cockroaches, 85; corn earworms, 207; fire ants, 21; flies, 52, 85; grasshoppers, 85, 172; gypsy moths, 85; leafhoppers, 193; mosquitoes, 66; pantry pests, 72; peach tree borers, 204; termites, 90
  tarantulas, 86
Spined soldier bugs, 157
  and control of Mexican bean beetles, 177
Spiraling whiteflies, 200

Spotted cucumber beetles. *See* Cucumber beetles
Sprays/spraying. *See* Repellent sprays; Soaps and soap sprays
Squash bugs, 140, 198–99
Squash vine borers, 202–3
Squirrels, 232–33
  benefits of, 174, 232
  control of, 232–33
  and control of gypsy moths, 174
Stable flies, 47
Steel wool, as barrier against rodents, 81
Sticky barriers, 127
  and control of: ants, 19–20, 194, 195; peach tree borers, 204
Sticky traps, 126, 201
  and control of: aphids, 191; cockroaches, 35; flea beetles, 170; flies, 51; fungus gnats, 57; leafhoppers, 193; rodents, 79; thrips, 57, 198; wasps, 216; whiteflies, 57, 201
Stout, Ruth, 121, 163, 168
Striped cucumber beetles. *See* Cucumber beetles
Strychnine, 220
Subterranean termites, 91
Sugar, and control of nematodes, 181
Sulfur, 130–31
  and control of: bed bugs, 23–24; chiggers, 105, 130; lice, 58; mites, 130; rabbits, 229; scabies, 107; spider mites, 197
Sulfuryl fluoride (Vikane), 94
Sweet clover, and control of flies, 49
Symphylans, 210
Syrphid flies (hover flies, flower flies), 48, 118, 159
  and control of: aphids, 192; mealybugs, 194; scale insects, 195; thrips, 198

Tabasco. *See* Hot pepper
Tachinid flies, 48, 159, 164, 167, 168, 174

Tansy, 123, 140
  and control of: ants, 19–20, 140; clothes moths, 29; flies, 49, 140; Japanese beetles, 140; mosquitoes, 65; squash bugs, 140, 199; striped cucumber beetles, 140
Tapestry moth, 29
Tarantulas, 86
Tarnished plant bugs, 198–99
Tea, and control of root maggots, 182
Tent caterpillars, 168–69
Termites, 89–98
  benefits of, 89
  control of, 92–98
  as distinguished from carpenter ants, 18, 89–90
  natural enemies of, 90, 93, 94, 147, 157, 159
Thief ants, 15
Thrips, 54–57, 197–98
  control of, in houseplants, 54–57
  control of, outdoors, 125, 128, 134, 151, 198
Thyme, 123
Ticks, 99–104
  control of, 67, 102–4, 134
  diseases transmitted by, 99, 101–2
  removing, 104
Tiger beetles, 158
Toads, 133, 147–48
  and control of: caterpillars, 147; cockroaches, 36; Colorado potato beetles, 165; corn earworms, 207; cucumber beetles, 167; cutworms, 147, 168; fire ants, 21; flies, 52; grasshoppers, 172; insects, 133; June beetles, 179; mosquitoes, 147; scorpions, 113; slugs and snails, 147, 188; termites, 147
Tobacco. *See* Nicotine
Tomato hornworms, 137, 178–79
Tomato leaf spray, 137
Traps, 126
  kinds of: beer, 35, 170, 172, 187–88,

212; electrocution, 35, 51, 66, 79, 126; light, 112, 178, 203; live animal, 79–80, 231, 232, 233; pheromone, 68, 72, 126, 132, 174, 175, 204, 205; snap, 77–79, 222; soapy water, 43, 126, 191, 198; sticky, 35, 51, 57, 79, 126, 170, 191, 193, 198, 201, 206, 216

Trichogramma wasps, 155, 179, 206

"True" bugs
beneficial, 157
and control of: Colorado potato beetles, 165; leafhoppers, 193; thrips, 198
harmful, 198–200

Tsetse flies, 48, 49

Turmeric
and control of: ants, 17; pantry pests, 72–73

Turtles
and control of: mosquitoes, 66; slugs and snails, 188

Two-spotted lady beetles, 152

Two-stabbed lady beetles, 152

U.S. Geological Survey, 4

Vacuuming, 11
and control of: Asian lady beetles, 109; bird mites, 106; boxelder bugs, 109; carpet beetles, 31; centipedes, 110; clothes moths, 30; cluster flies, 110; cockroaches, 37; earwigs, 111; fleas, 41, 44; house dust mites, 105; houseplant pests, 57; Japanese beetles, 175; lice, 62; pantry pests, 71; silverfish, 84; tarnished plant bugs, 199; ticks, 102; whiteflies, 57, 201–2

Vanilla
and control of: cucumber beetles, 67, 136, 166; mosquitoes, 67; squash bugs, 136, 199

Vedalia beetles, 152

Vermiculture, 121

Vinegar
and control of: ants, 16, 22; codling moths, 205; fruit flies, 50–51; mosquitoes, 67; snails and slugs, 186

Violin spiders. See Brown recluse spiders

Viruses, as biological control, 132

Warfarin, 76

Wasps
benefits of, 215–16
kinds of: digger, 216; mud dauber, 216; parasitic (see Wasps, parasitic); *Polistes*, 215; yellow jacket (see Yellow jackets)

Wasps, parasitic, 131, 133, 154–56
care of mail-order species, 150
and control of: aphids, 155, 192; armyworms, 168; beetles, 154, 155; cabbage loopers, 164; caterpillers, 154, 155, 156; cockroaches, 36; codling moths, 206; Colorado potato beetles, 165; corn earworms, 207; cutworms, 168; Eastern tent caterpillars, 169; European corn borers, 203; fall webworms, 169; flies, 52, 154, 156; gypsy moths, 174; imported cabbage worms, 164; June beetles, 179; leafhoppers, 193; mealybugs, 194; Mexican bean beetles, 177; plum curculios, 208; root maggots, 183; scale insects, 195; squash vine borers, 203; tomato hornworms, 179; whiteflies, 155, 202; wood-boring beetles, 156
and insecticidal soaps, 128
species of, 154–56

Water/hosing, 125
and control of: aphids, 19, 125, 191; deer, 227; gophers, 222; houseplant pests, 53–54; leafhoppers, 193; mealybugs, 194; spider mites, 125, 196; thrips, 125, 198

Webbing clothes moths, 28
Webworms, 168–69
Weevils, 69
Western black-legged ticks, 101
Whiteflies, 54, 200–202
    control of, on houseplants, 54–57
    control of, outdoors, 125, 134, 138,
        201–2
Whitefly parasites, 202
Wilson, E. O., 3
Wireworms, 183–84
    control of, 138, 154, 184
Wood ashes
    and control of: cabbage pests, 163;
        cucumber beetles, 166; cutworms,
        168; peach tree borers, 204; root
        maggots, 182; slugs and snails, 185;
        squash vine borers, 203
Wood-boring beetles, 98–99
    control of, 93–98

Woolly aphids, 190
World Resources Institute, x
Worm castings, 121, 122
Wormwood, 123
    and control of: cabbage worms, 140;
        clothes moths, 29; flea beetles, 140,
        170
    as spray, 140

Yamamoto, Robert, 132
Yellow "bug lights," 65, 88
Yellow jackets, 214–18
    benefits of, 215–16
    control of, 216–18
    and control of: aphids, 215; cabbage
        loopers, 164; corn earworms, 215;
        grasshoppers, 215; gypsy moths,
        215; imported cabbageworms, 164,
        215; tomato hornworms, 215
    stings, 215

Compositor:	Integrated Composition Systems
Text:	11/14 Adobe Garamond
Display:	Frutiger Bold
Printer and binder:	Rose Printing